Developing
and Branding
the Fashion
Merchandising
Portfolio

Developing and Branding the Fashion Merchandising Portfolio

Janace Bubonia-Clarke

Texas Christian University

Phyllis Borcherding

University of Cincinnati

Fairchild Publications, Inc.
New York

Executive Editor: Olga T. Kontzias

Acquisitions Editor: Joseph Miranda

Assistant Acquisitions Editor: Jaclyn Bergeron

Senior Development Editor: Jennifer Crane

Development Editor: Michelle Levy

Production Manager: Ginger Hillman

Production Editors: Beth Cohen and Jessica Rozler

Assistant Editor: Justine Brennan

Copy Editor: Vivian Gomez

Interior Design and Layout: Mary Neal Meador

Cover illustrations by Emily Hensler

Library of Congress Catalog Card Number: 2006934570

ISBN: 978-1-56367-427-3

GST R 133004424

Printed in Canada

TP14

This book is dedicated to our families and friends, who have encouraged and supported us, and to our students, who have inspired us and touched our lives. May our desire, motivation, and passion for what we do never die.

Believe in yourself. Follow your dreams.

Contents

Extended Contents

Preface

Developing and Branding the Fashion Merchandising Portfolio was written to provide students with a user-friendly, visually inspiring approach to creating and updating portfolios specific to the merchandising, marketing, and product development segments of the industry. Merchandising portfolios should communicate the skills of the individual in a professional manner. This book is divided into ten chapters that focus on content development, organization, execution, and effective use of a portfolio. The authors have included many visual examples of work, created by students and industry professionals, meant to inspire individuals and demonstrate a professional approach to portfolio development. This book provides guidelines for building a portfolio and creative, inspirational ideas for personalizing the presentation through brand identity. The comprehensive approach to *Developing and Branding the Fashion Merchandising Portfolio* helps individuals to target the jobs that maximize their skills, conduct effective job searches, develop resumes, network with professionals, write cover letters, prepare for interviews, and present portfolios during interviews.

The text contains activities, checklists, and evaluation tools specific to each stage of portfolio development and an appendix containing worksheets to help you create and select appropriate portfolio content and layout for project work, professional achievements, and research. Tools for writing resumes and cover letters, evaluating your own interview techniques, and maintaining and updating the portfolio are also included. Important terminology within the text is featured in the glossary at the end of the book to provide easy access to definitions.

Chapter 1 provides a brief overview of the book. We discuss changes that have affected hiring practices within the industry and define the role of portfolios in today's marketplace. We break down the merchandising industry into segments and list jobs within each category to assist individuals in focusing their interests. Activities in this chapter enable individuals to determine the types of positions they seek, provide insight into how to effectively research jobs, and give guidance with compilation of potential employer lists. Individuals who complete these activities are able to focus on the portfolio development process as well as on specific positions within the industry.

In Chapter 2, the model for merchandising portfolios is introduced. Assessment of skills and evidence that document these skills are also discussed. Activities allow students to apply the research skills needed for specific career positions, compile skills that match specific career positions, and gather work that demonstrates those skills.

Chapter 3 discusses portfolio encasements and styles, content focus, and types of presentation. Activities assist individuals in determining portfolio types (traditional, custom, or digital), portfolio concentration (general versus focused), and portfolio focus toward a specific area (such as buying and merchandising, apparel and accessory product development, textile product development, store management, and fashion marketing—including visual merchandising, promotion, brand development, and advertising).

Chapter 4 focuses on organizing contents based on the portfolio's concentration and integrating evidence of skills possessed. This chapter also explores branding and how to incorporate brand image into a portfolio. Activities encourage individuals to create a brand identity for the portfolio, select items for inclusion that demonstrate skills, and develop and present an individual marketing piece (IMP). A checklist for evaluating portfolios is also included.

Chapter 5 provides direction for presentation formats and page layout based on design elements and principles, as well as guidance for developing and maintaining the brand identity. Activities help determine the impact of various layouts

and determine which layouts are more appropriate for different types of merchandising positions and which most accurately represent the individual. An additional activity includes developing a brand image for the portfolio. You will prepare sample introductory and divider pages. Examples of layout and content for pages are highlighted.

Chapter 6 is targeted toward the creation of digital portfolios, Web sites, and CD-ROMs. The activities in this chapter assist individuals to determine the best use of technology for their portfolios in relation to industry segment and company research. In addition, individuals are engaged in creating page layouts using the computer.

Chapter 7 focuses on communicating brand image and essence through the presentation of the merchandising portfolio. Since each portfolio should reflect each student's personality, it is important for students to figure out how to best represent themselves. The importance of consistency and continuity of brand image and personalizing the portfolio is emphasized. A checklist for evaluating portfolio presentation is included.

Chapter 8 discusses resume formats and provides general guidelines for development, and it includes resume do's and don'ts. Activities

help individuals to select the best resume formats for their experience and job search. Resume development and formatting ideas are accompanied by visual examples from successful candidates. An exercise in updating resumes is also included.

Chapter 9 provides information pertaining to cover letter development, networking, and interviewing. Here you will improve your ability to identify the specific skills companies seek and tailor your presentation toward achieving rapport with potential employers. Activities focus on interviewing skills as well as specific exercises for creating cover letters and conducting mock interviews utilizing the portfolio. A mock interview evaluation sheet is included to assist individuals in determining more effective ways of incorporating their portfolios into their interviews.

Lastly, Chapter 10 discusses maintaining and updating portfolios. Activities engage individuals in reviewing the presentation and organization of contents, integrating new work, and redesigning and updating the brand image of the portfolio.

The authors sincerely hope this book will inspire, motivate, and launch students to develop strong, effective portfolios that will provide them with the tools and confidence to follow their dreams.

Acknowledgments

We would like to thank everyone who has made this book a reality. To the Fairchild Publications staff, including: executive editor Olga T. Kontzias; acquisitions editor Joseph Miranda; senior development editor Jennifer Crane; development editors Michelle Levy and Jason Moring; production manager Ginger Hillman; production editor Beth Cohen; assistant editor Justine Brennan; copy editor Vivian Gomez; interior designer Mary Neal Meador; and last, but certainly not least, art director and cover designer: Adam B. Bohannon.

Thank you to the following reviewers, selected by Fairchild Books, for your valuable comments: Peter M. Bartlett, University of Cincinnati; Michele Granger, Missouri State University; Joseph H. Hancock, Drexel University; Jennifer Roberts, Missouri State University; Carolyn A. Thomas, IADT-Vegas; and Connie Ulasewicz, San Francisco State University.

Thank you to the faculty and staff in the Department of Design, Merchandising and Textiles at Texas Christian University and the Department of Fashion Design and Product Development at the University of Cincinnati for your support and encouragement during the preparation of this book.

Students and industry professionals who have provided us with profiles, quotes, portfolio material samples, resumes, and cover letters, thank you for your dedication and willingness to provide information and work to inspire others.

Thank you to our families, who believed in us and encouraged us to pursue this exciting and rewarding endeavor. Your unwavering support and love are greatly appreciated.

Developing
and Branding
the Fashion
Merchandising
Portfolio

Chapter 1

Introduction to the Merchandising Portfolio

The fashion industry is one of the largest employment sectors in the world, providing job opportunities for many. In 2000, the International Labor Organization (ILO) reported that there were 30 million people employed in just the manufacturing of clothing and textile products during the 1990s. By 2005, this sector had grown to 40 million people. Globally, the clothing and textile sector accounts for $350 billion a year (ILO 2005). According to Dora Radwick of The NPD Group, a leading consumer and retail information company, "total U.S. apparel sales reached $181 billion in 2005, a 4 percent increase over 2004" (2006). There are more than 5.24 million people employed in the U.S. industry: 4.3 million in retail sales and nearly 1 million in the development and manufacturing of textile products, retail buying, and wholesale segments (Bureau of Labor Statistics, U.S. Department of Labor 2006–2007). Job opportunities range from research and development of textile products, product design and development, buying, sourcing, and manufacturing to merchandising, marketing, branding, and promotion of retail products and services. Job seekers find the fashion industry exciting, fast paced, and ever changing. The marketplace is often highly competitive, requiring individuals to find ways to market themselves better. Within the fashion industry, careers in merchandising encompass both creative and analytical job opportunities. Merchandising jobs range from buying, planning, and allocations to the marketing and promotion of products and services, and now extend into areas of design, such as product development, textile design, and trend forecasting. A dynamic and individually branded portfolio of work and experience adds to the marketability of an individual seeking employment in the fashion industry by showcasing tangible proof of ability and by providing a visual element that allows an employer to make an association between individuals and their work.

First, individuals must be employable. **Employability** is the capacity that potential employees add to the existing value of a company, namely through their ability to achieve and facilitate results in a given job. For example, to be a good job candidate, one must have acquired the skills required by the job. Candidates can obtain such capabilities and **proficiencies** either at school or by way of hands-on application of skills, seminars/workshops, and on-the-job training from internships and/or previous jobs. For applicants to be marketable, they must be able to effectively communicate the skills they possess and demonstrate the types of results they can deliver. For example, if you designed a package that helped boost sales of a product, your portfolio and resume must communicate and show evidence of this accomplishment. In the portfolio, you could provide before and after photos of the packaging to visually demonstrate the effectiveness and appeal that led to the increase in sales and profit for the company. Your resume should state the specific increase in sales (e.g., you could write that you designed a new packaging that attributed to a 20 percent increase in sales). Employers want to know that the person they hire can efficiently and successfully perform the tasks necessary for the job. As employers redefine positions within their companies, workers need to provide employers with evidence of their growth as the needs of the job expand, as well as their understanding of the tasks of their peers. This asset has become even more important in the last two decades since many companies have adopted team approaches to bringing products into the marketplace. Product teams often include designers, merchandisers, marketers, and production personnel. It is essential that potential employees have an understanding of the importance of teamwork and demonstrate their abilities to work with others. For example, if you have in any way motivated others to perform or been recognized by a group of your peers for your leadership, make sure to indicate this on your resume and during the job interview, talk about how your motivational tools or leadership impacted the company's sales or morale. Job candidates should strive to illustrate their understanding of the job functions of others on their "team" and to show work that

substantiates this. This work needs to be presented with your own branded image that makes the presentation uniquely yours—easily distinguished from any other candidate's work. A **brand** is the perception others have of you. An identifiable image that reflects your personality, work ethic, level of professionalism, creativity, individuality, quality of work you produce, and how you carry yourself. Your brand is communicated through your brand image or brand identity. **Brand identity** is an image created through the use of colors, logo, graphic elements, text, and layout that allows a potential employer to connect an individual to his or her work and make a memorable impression; it ultimately leads either to hiring or promotion.

The Changing Environment: Gaining a Competitive Edge

During the twentieth century, employers in the fashion merchandising segment of the industry usually relied on personal interviews and recommendations from references to determine the fitness of candidates for positions within companies. Some firms also administered standardized personality tests to determine the morals, principles, and work ethic of individuals. Rarely were fashion merchandising applicants asked to show evidence of creativity and productivity or demonstrate their capabilities during the application and interview process. However, the fashion design segment of the industry has always required applicants to provide a portfolio demonstrating evidence of skills in addition to the standard cover letter, resume, and application materials. Employers have in good faith relied

on information provided by applicants and trusted the information supplied was truthful and an accurate depiction of skills, competencies, and capabilities.

During the 1980s, retail businesses expanded, providing many job opportunities for people in the fashion industry. The addition and growth of new specialty store chains such as Abercrombie and Fitch, Ann Taylor, Banana Republic, Bath and Body Works, Victoria's Secret, Gap Kids, and American Eagle Outfitters diversified the marketplace and provided customers with products developed for niche markets. In the 1990s, fashion companies began a redefining process. The number of staff was reduced, while the workload of current employees expanded. This was due not only to the tough economic times in the early part of the decade, when both companies and individuals were recovering from the devastating impact of the stock market crash in 1987, but also to the sophisticated technology added to the workplace. Point-of-sale (POS) registers in stores conveying up-to-the-minute selling information, Quick Response reorder programs, and CAD/CAM software in the development process allowed companies to employ fewer people and increase their productivity and job scope.

The impact of technology was also positive for the job market. Through the new venue of the Internet, many companies expanded their products and services beyond brick-and-mortar stores and printed catalogs. The World Wide Web provided opportunities for international expansion that for some companies would otherwise not have been a viable option. Companies began hiring individuals to implement services online.

The twenty-first century brought corporate scandals and the tragedy of September 11, 2001, which devastated the U.S. economy. Firms in all industries downsized, which forced employers to increase the responsibilities of existing employees. This has led to more comprehensive job scopes for positions within the industry. Since then, the number of jobs has increased due to the growth of the fashion apparel market.

The twenty-first century offers a highly competitive marketplace and increased responsibility for individual job positions. Therefore, people entering or moving within the industry have been challenged to market themselves differently from the way they have done so in the past. Portfolios are one way for merchandising, marketing, or product development candidates to gain a competitive edge because it allows them to provide visual evidence of their capabilities and skills. The portfolios allow candidates to stand out much more than the rote written words on resumes and even interview conversations.

The Fashion Merchandising Industry

The field of merchandising is extremely diverse and an integral part of the fashion industry on many levels. In the book *Inside the Fashion Business* (2003), Kitty Dickerson describes the fashion industry in terms of a pipeline, which runs from the fiber manufacturers and suppliers through yarn and fabric manufacturers to converters, to apparel and accessory manufacturers, and finally to retailers. Merchandising is relevant

in all of these arenas. **Merchandising** is the process of planning, developing, selecting, marketing, and presenting cohesive, consumer-targeted goods for profit in a competitive market with regard to timing, assortment, styling trends, and price point.

Industry Segments

Each segment of the industry researches trends and develops product lines based upon trends. The size and scope of the line is then determined and balanced according to customer needs and industry timing. Products are costed, sourced, produced, and marketed to relevant markets. All segments of the industry offer distinct opportunities for employment in the merchandising area.

Textile Product Development

Textile product development is the first step in the manufacture of apparel products. Fibers are either grown or chemically developed, and marketed to yarn and fabric companies. Producers and trade associations, such as DuPont and Cotton Incorporated, promote fibers and fabrics. Marketing efforts for this segment of the industry involve product research and development, consumer research, and brand development (see Box 1.1). Many textile companies offer the same fiber, such as Nylon 6.6, under different brand names, such as DuPont's Antron and Supplex, and market these fibers to different segments of the industry—carpeting and apparel respectively. Textile marketers

Box 1.1 CAD/Textile Industry Profile

Paula Meyers graduated college with a degree in fashion merchandising and began her industry career working for the Associated Merchandising Corporation in New York City. AMC is a retail resident buying office, and Paula's primary responsibility was to develop the seasonal color and fabric trend forecast information and develop the trend books for AMC clients. She visited all of the trend office presentations and developed inspirational boards for inclusion in the trend books sent to AMC's clients. After two years with AMC, she left and took a position with Cotton Incorporated to be a fabric trend analyst. She had the wonderful opportunity of traveling to all of the top fabric shows in the United States and Europe. She wrote trend analysis reports and projected top color stories and fabric trends for the company. She stayed with Cotton Incorporated for five years, moving up to a management position. She then went to work for a major fabric company, where she was responsible for merchandising entire lines of fabric offerings. She would select the various fabric lines from fabrics developed by the designers in the company. She would plan three to four lines per year. Today, she has her own freelance consulting business and develops fabric lines for companies all around the globe.

research fiber, color, print trends, and consumer needs, and they develop fabric lines by season. Sales representatives present the sample fabric lines at major trade fairs and showrooms throughout the world. Fabric companies are involved in marketing and sales through advertising and promotion to their industry customers, as well as to the ultimate consumer. Jobs within the Textile Product Development segment of the industry include fabric research and development; trend research: fiber, yarn, and fabric buying; product management; product merchandising; visual merchandising; product sourcing; sales; marketing; and product design and production.

Apparel and Accessory Manufacturers

Fashion manufacturers, also known as wholesalers, develop products for sale to retailers under their own brands. They also develop specification products for retailers who wish to engage in private branding for their stores. They research color, fabric, and styling trends, and if they are a branded company they will conduct consumer research. Based on completed research, designers sketch initial garments and collaborate with merchandisers on fabrics, colors, and assortments for the product line. Buyers purchase the fabric and findings and often buy prints developed by converters exclusively for that company. In addition, the company may employ their own CAD designers who develop unique fabrics for the company (see Box 1.2). The merchandiser works with technical designers and production experts to develop and produce garments. Branded manufacturers will show sample lines of their products to potential retail buyers. Sales representatives take the orders and follow up with the retail buyers to track sales after the merchandise has been received. Branded manufacturers also promote their brands to both retailers and directly to consumers through means of advertising, trunk shows, point-of-sale promotion tools, Web sites, and videos. Private-label manufacturers work very closely with their retail clients to ensure that product design and development are consistent with the brand and profit margin requirements.

Jobs within the Apparel and Accessory Manufacturers segment include trend forecasting, creative design, technical design, fabric development and styling, piece good buying, merchandising, product management, production, marketing, and sales.

Retail Product Development

Retail stores have long realized the value of having their own exclusive, branded merchandise, either utilizing the store's name, such as The Gap, Limited Too, Ann Taylor, or Abercrombie and Fitch, or their exclusive brands, such as INC for Federated, BP for Nordstrom, Mix It for JCPenney, or Mossimo for Target. As private label branding has grown in the past

---

Box 1.2 CAD/Design Industry Profile

Melissa Carrelli graduated in 1998 with a degree in fashion design and began her industry career as a freelance CAD designer for Mercantile Stores, Inc., where she used U4ia software and PrimaVision to create embroidery layouts, graphics, prints, and woven fabric designs. A year and a half later, Melissa accepted a full-time CAD position with Sears, Roebuck, and Co., where she worked closely with the design team for young men's and men's private label brands. In 2000, she joined Limited Too stores as a CAD designer developing prints, woven fabrics, knits, graphics, and embroideries for sweaters and denim products. After two years, she was promoted to assistant designer in sweaters, where she became involved with line building, creating design flats, maintaining deadlines, and product development. After one year in this position, she was promoted to associate designer and again to designer just one year later. She is currently the designer for three different areas of Too, Inc.—shirts, skirts, and sweaters. As a designer, she heads up the design team, sets trend direction, and originates and follows all production for each style. She travels both domestically and internationally to collect trend research and finalize production lines. She has been involved in all aspects of the CAD process and product design, from fabric and print design to flat sketching, as well as product development and staff management.

Source: Courtesy of Melissa Carrelli

few decades, retail companies have added product development teams to create unique products that are produced by contracted manufacturers and sold exclusively in the franchised stores. The extent of the retail firm's involvement varies by company but, whether done so internally or externally, products are designed, merchandised, sourced, and marketed directly to the consumer.

The process involved in retail **product development** holds many opportunities for both design and merchandising professionals (see Box 1.3). Figure 1.1 shows the model for design-driven product development, which includes all the steps involved with bringing a fashion product to the marketplace. The model includes the typical activities of design, merchandising, and marketing that take place in retail product development. Problem definition, the first step, is defining what needs to be accomplished. This is often simply developing a seasonal line plan for a company that usually involves a new product line every eight to ten weeks. Both merchandising and financial plans are included. The research stage includes fashion trend forecasting, market analysis, and competitive store research. Fashion trend research includes color forecasting, fabric and trim trends, and product styling. Depending on the size of a company, this is done by one or more merchandising professionals. Overall environmental trend research is also included, such as socioeconomic, cultural, and technological trends. Consumer target market trends and profiles are developed, as well as lifestyle trend analysis. Marketing and merchandising professionals are involved with this

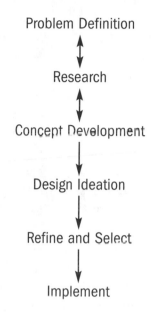

Design-Driven Product Development Model

Problem Definition

↕

Research

↕

Concept Development

↓

Design Ideation

↓

Refine and Select

↓

Implement

Figure 1.1 Model for design-driven product development.

Box 1.3 Product Development Industry Profile

Jennifer Daggy was the winner of the student Target/CFDA Design Initiative award in 2002 and began her career as a CFDA associate designer for Target Corporation upon graduation with a degree in fashion product development in 2003. For one year, she trained in a number of different departments before moving to Los Angeles and becoming the assistant designer for Mossimo Girls— a private label company that currently designs and develops goods for Target stores under the Mossimo label. Jennifer has been promoted twice and currently oversees both girls' and Mossimo Red active sportswear, knits, and woven bottoms. She travels to Minneapolis once a week to work with the buying and technical teams at Target's corporate office. Jennifer loves the opportunity of working with both the manufacturer and the retailer to develop trendy products for Target that keep design on the cutting edge. She has been involved with design, merchandising, allocation, product specifications, and sourcing for fabrics and production.

Source: Courtesy of Jennifer Daggy

step in the process. The research is then analyzed in the concept development stage by the entire merchandising team, and *mood boards* or conceptual images are developed to help guide development of a product line. Concept drives color palettes, fabric choices, and styling for design and merchandising. Design ideation allows design and merchandising professionals to develop various scenarios for line elements. This is referred to as the design portion of product development. Styles are designed, color palettes are identified, and fabrics are developed in house or sourced from fabric manufacturers. CAD artists may be involved in developing textile prints, weaves, and knit designs for a line. In the refinement and selection stage, final adjustments and decisions are made and the product line content is decided. After the product line has been refined and selected, the line is merchandised for sizing and color so it can be finalized. The implementation stage includes production of the product line and the final presentation and sale to the consumer. Jobs within the Retail Product Development segment of the industry include trend research, product design, product merchandising, product marketing, visual merchandising, and brand management.

Retail Buying and Sales Management
Retailers are the ultimate link to the consumer. Retailers may be brick-and-mortar stores, mail order or Internet companies, or a combination of these. The function of retailers in the industry is to determine the needs of their target consumer and procure goods for them, while maintaining quality, price, and image for

their stores. Retailers may buy goods from branded manufacturers by visiting showrooms and purchasing goods or by developing merchandise themselves with the assistance of either branded manufacturers or private label companies. Retailers work with either internal or external product developers to ensure the integrity of their product offerings. The companies then merchandise the lines in stores, catalogs, and/or on the Web. Store managers and their teams work with visual merchandisers to present the products to consumers, and the sales team offers customer service to facilitate the purchase of the goods. Jobs within the Retail Buying and Sales Management segment of the industry include retail buying, distribution planning, allocation, retail merchandising, retail sales management, visual merchandising, and marketing (see Box 1.4).

Visual Merchandising
Visual merchandising is the manner in which the retail or wholesale company conveys its image to prospective customers. In retail stores, visual merchandising involves the store layout, arrangement of fixtures within departments, interior and window displays, lighting, and signage. Wholesale manufacturers utilize visual merchandising to showcase merchandise in their showrooms and at trade shows. Jobs within the Visual Merchandising segment of the industry include creative display, visual styling, merchandising, store planning, set building, and visual merchandise management (see Box 1.5).

Fashion Promotion, Brand Development, and Marketing
Fashion promotion, whether wholesale or retail, is planned to sell products, establish or reinforce brand

Nicole Mertz began gaining industry experience in visual merchandising when she interned at Neiman Marcus in the company's flagship store. Nicole also gained valuable hands-on knowledge volunteering for a few years as a visual stylist for a large charity auction and fashion show event. Upon graduating with a degree in fashion promotion in 2002, Nicole was hired to work as a visual stylist for a Nordstrom store. That same year, she was promoted to visual manager and moved to oversee an entire store. A year later, Nicole was offered the visual manager position at a larger format Nordstrom store that was getting ready to open. After working for several years with Nordstrom, she was hired by Anthropologie to work as a visual manager. In all these positions, she was involved in planning, budgeting, and managing all aspects of in-store and window displays, lighting, signage, merchandising fixtures, and floor sets. After almost two years with Anthropologie, she was invited to interview for a position as a designer with Beazer Homes, where she currently works today. This exciting new challenge has allowed Nicole to grow professionally while applying her knowledge and experience as a visual merchandiser to the design and merchandising of interior home spaces. She is responsible for making decisions based on architectural design, target market, and geographic areas of Beazer model homes across the nation. Nicole is involved in the planning, budgeting, purchasing, and merchandising of all aspects of the model homes, from creating color stories and selecting wallpapers down to the placement of details such as candleholders. This position allows Nicole to travel and be involved personally in the installation and merchandising of these model homes.

Source: Courtesy of Nicole Mertz

image, and excite consumers. Promotion involves three components: advertising, publicity and public relations, and special events. This is accomplished by planning a season's worth of events to showcase the company's product line and may include runway or showroom events, print or digital advertising, outdoor media and place-based media (e.g., billboards, taxicabs, wrappers on buses and cars, blimps, sports arenas, shopping malls, and anything else that reaches customers who are on the move), videos, and trunk shows. Special events are planned and may involve the company designer, celebrity spokesperson, or sales personnel. Companies sponsor special events and community functions to connect with customers and to promote corporate citizenship. Planning can be long or short term depending on the medium. This segment of the industry is very fast paced and exciting and involves dynamic personnel. Brand development and marketing focus on nurturing, developing, and maintaining a consistent brand image for a company. Brand managers have a strong understanding of the brand's philosophy and mission, the core target market, and how to deliver a consistent product or service at the determined quality level and price the consumer has come to expect. Marketing forms the image of a company or brand by establishing market position in relation to the target market and the competition. Evaluation of changes in the target market and marketplace, as well as social, cultural, political, and economic influences impacting consumer purchasing, are central to this segment. Market penetration, development, and diversification assist in the expansion of the target market, sale of products or services, and creation of new products or services to attract new customers through marketing and promotional efforts. Jobs within the Fashion Promotion, Brand Development, and Marketing segment of the industry include trend forecasting, advertising (art direction, layout, copywriting, and media buying), styling, public relations, marketing and planning, and brand management (see Box 1.6).

The Role of Portfolios

A **portfolio** is a compilation of a body of work that visually documents examples of skills that individuals possess and the assets they offer

Ashley Beale graduated in 2005 with a fashion merchandising degree. She was always interested in apparel and accessories and began designing handbags as a hobby. In May 2000, Ashley and her handbag designs were featured in *CosmoGirl* and *Fashion! Dallas*. While in school, Ashley completed an internship with Michael Faircloth, where she gained experience in marketing, special events, and public relations. During her senior year Ashley was offered a part-time position as a marketing and communications assistant with Stanley Korshak, an independently owned luxury retailer in Dallas, Texas. In this position, she scheduled and coordinated designer trunk shows and personal appearances, assisted in the facilitation of special events and in-store fashion shows, and maintained correspondence with store clientele. Upon graduation, Ashley took a full-time position within the company as an assistant buyer for women's couture. While in this position, she heard there were changes being made to the marketing department and that there would be a position opening up. Ashley really enjoyed her buying position but her heart and passion were in marketing. After talking with the human resources department and conveying her interest, she was soon hired as the marketing and communications coordinator. Ashley currently works on the development of all graphics and copy for direct mailers, writes and submits press releases accompanied by press photos, and coordinates trunk and fashion shows, while building and maintaining client relationships.

a company. Students and professionals alike have utilized portfolios to provide potential colleges/universities and employers with tangible evidence of their skills and capabilities. Merchandising students and professionals have developed work from school and/or industry, yet have not widely utilized portfolios in the past to showcase their work. Now there is a growing interest on the merchandising part of the industry to see this evidence, driving the need for merchandising portfolios. The **merchandising portfolio** is highly text-driven with a **balance** of visual images and elements that create excitement and interest in the presentation. Text-driven content can include computer-generated pieces such as market analyses, product specification and costing sheets, merchandising and allocation plans, and promotion materials. Visually driven content can include concept and storyboards; original designs of fabric, apparel, or other product lines; spatial plans and store layouts that can be communicated through illustrations, technical drawings, and CAD-generated pieces; and photographs of visual merchandising displays. Merchandising portfolios may contain some content similar to design portfolios; however, the **fashion design portfolio** is primarily visually driven and can include original designs of fabric, apparel, or other product lines that can be communicated through fashion illustrations, technical drawings, sketches, and CAD-generated pieces.

Employers are looking for better ways to assess the skills of potential applicants as well as ways to predict how potential new hires will perform. In addition, employers are increasingly looking for applicants with multiple skills, who can adapt to more inclusive job descriptions. Portfolios provide immediate visual evidence of what a person is capable of and can communicate hands-on experience more explicitly than a resume can on its own. In addition, portfolios can increase a candidate's marketability through documentation of evidence of results they can deliver. As the importance of merchandising portfolios progresses, it is essential to determine the best **format** for visually communicating the knowledge and skills individuals have acquired and become proficient in, to better serve their job search.

Activities

1. Identify and compile a list of five to ten jobs within the fashion merchandising industry for which you might apply.

2. Research these positions and document the job responsibilities and skills required for each.

3. Create a list of 20 companies that employ individuals within these positions.

4. Make a list of a few items that you might include in your portfolio that will showcase some of the skills required for positions you researched. For example, you might include text-driven elements such as a market or vendor analysis, a merchandising plan, or a press release. Visually driven content could include a photograph of a visual display you created, a concept board, or a textile print you have developed.

Chapter 2

Merchandising Portfolio Model

The authors have spent several years researching and developing the merchandising portfolio model (Bubonia-Clarke and Borcherding, 2002). See Figure 2.1. We've helped students and graduates to create successful portfolios using the merchandising portfolio model, and they were successful in attaining internships and industry positions. The model was developed specifically for the merchandising, marketing, and product development segments of the fashion industry; however, people in the fashion design segment can also use it effectively.

Our research began with a survey of professionals in the fashion industry and their companies' hiring processes for positions within merchandising and design, and the elements that executives like to see in portfolios. These professionals were asked to comment on various aspects of portfolio **content**, layout, length, and presentation, as well as preferred **resume formats** and **interview** protocol. The merchandising portfolio model was developed based on information gathered from industry feedback. Merchandising students then developed portfolios based on this model. Feedback was obtained from both students and industry professionals concerning the effectiveness of these merchandising portfolios. Some comments obtained from professionals included: "Content is very well organized;" "Great portfolio, it really conveys your talents and skill level;" and "I am impressed with your portfolio and the way you have used it to demonstrate your abilities." The merchandising portfolio model is clearly and concisely outlined to help

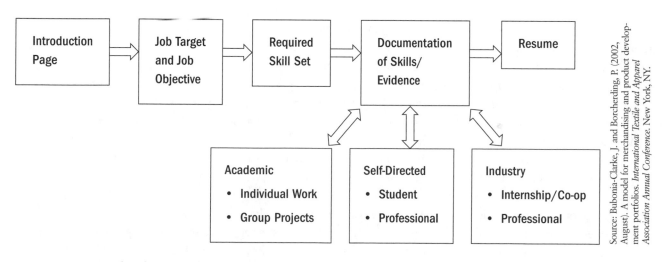

Figure 2.1 Merchandising portfolio model.

Source: Bubonia-Clarke, J. and Borcherding, P. (2002, August). A model for merchandising and product development portfolios. *International Textile and Apparel Association Annual Conference.* New York, NY.

individuals develop strong professional tools to increase their marketability and advance within the companies at which they are ultimately hired.

Creating the Merchandising Portfolio

Portfolios need to convey a strong, orchestrated image to employers that identifies the candidate. The term *portfolio* is commonly used to refer to collections of work that document experience but do not necessarily follow a logical format and layout that best represents a candidate's skill and competency for a job, an internship, or a co-op position. In fact, a frequent problem with many merchandising portfolios today is that they lack organization and fail to emphasize skills and competencies. It is not enough for a potential candidate to prepare a portfolio that records and demonstrates experience if it is not presented in a professional format that best represents what that individual can offer a potential employer. A portfolio needs to be more than just a collection of work. It needs to have a purpose and a format that is easily followed by others.

Every aspect of a portfolio must be carefully planned and executed with the utmost professionalism. Most important, the finished portfolio must provide an accurate depiction of the individual's skills and represent their **style** and personality. That said, individuals must never overlook the importance of updating. Portfolios should always carry work that is as current as possible, and sometimes this requires the development of new work. Those individuals who include industry work must remember that it

is imperative to exclude proprietary information; they must also request *and obtain* permission to use industry work in their portfolios.

Working with a standard format when developing a merchandising portfolio is crucial to its success because it contains information for which prospective employers are searching in a format and layout that is appealing. Rest assured, using a standardized format does not mean that your portfolio will look exactly the same as everyone else's portfolios. In fact, you can and should customize the format to the positions for which you wish to apply. The purpose of a merchandising portfolio model is to provide a standard that students, faculty, and professionals can rely on to create an organized compilation of their work and thus demonstrate the skills they have developed.

This compilation of work and skills must then be presented in a manner that best suits the candidate's style—their brand image. Today's candidates need to market themselves, much like a company markets its brands. In a 2004 interview with Chris Warren, David D'Alessandro, CEO of John Hancock Financial Services, said, "[A] personal brand, just as with corporations, is your reputation: the reputation of your product, [the] reputation of yourself . . . aka, brand" (56). He added, "A brand that needs to be developed and marketed can create opportunities that equally skilled and talented people might never see." Furthermore, David D'Alessandro summarized, "Make sure you stay a contender. It's never too late to change your brand. Be conscious every day of what kind of

brand you're building, and don't let setbacks deter you" (56). *Career Warfare* (McGraw-Hill 2005) by David D'Alessandro is a must-read for anyone who wants to learn more about personal branding.

An individual's brand image must be clear and transmitted in an acceptable format to its target audience—potential employers. Your brand image needs to be consistent, from the **cover letter**, resume, and merchandising portfolio to the manner in which you present yourself during an interview. "Your brand is constantly being compared with your peers'. Don't be afraid to offer something different" (D'Alessandro & Owens 2004, 199).

Portfolio Introduction Page

The **introduction page** is typically the first page of the merchandising portfolio that an employer will see, so it should be well thought out and carefully planned. This page summarizes who you are. This page should contain a visual image tied to your industry specialty and your name to communicate your personal brand identity. Brand identity is an image created through the use of color, logo, graphic elements, text, and layout that connects individuals to their work and makes a memorable impression on prospective employers. In Marty Neumeier's *The Brand Gap* (New Riders Press, 2003), he discusses design and its traditional view: ". . . it has four possible goals: to identify, to inform, to entertain, or to persuade. But with branding there's a fifth: to differentiate" (35). Original artwork, a collage of images, or a simple graphical component are examples that can enhance the first page. For some people, this is the most challenging page of the merchandising portfolio to develop. It should reflect style and personality—in essence, the individual's brand—while providing visual insight into the person (see Figures 2.2 and 2.3). The selection of font, color, and texture are important, as they will provide continuity to the portfolio when applied to the **divider pages**.

Division of Components/Sections

Divider pages help organize the portfolio, as chapter opener pages organize a book. Each dividing page should provide information about the skills and competencies within the section to which you wish to draw the viewer's attention. Each dividing page communicates the skills highlighted in that section and reinforces the individual's brand. Keep it simple

akarasun seanglai

Figure 2.2 An introduction page containing an original graphic design by Akarasun Seanglai.

Figure 2.3 Brittany Weiss encloses her name within an original graphic element.

Figure 2.4 A divider page by Brittany Weiss that uses the graphic from her introduction page and allows space for her to insert text that identifies each portfolio section.

and state skills and competencies clearly and concisely. The viewer should be able to quickly glance at the information presented on the dividing pages without having to stop to do much reading. Some people choose to use bullets or a list style presentation when laying out this information.

Since the introduction page sets the image and layout for the dividing pages that follow it, use the same font, color, texture, and brand elements as well as page layout to provide continuity and consistency. This adds to the professionalism of the presentation (see Figure 2.4).

Job Target and Statement of Job Objective

The **job target** is simply the title of the job for which a person is applying. Examples of job targets include assistant buyer, assistant brand developer, visual stylist, director of sourcing and global licensing, media buyer, and CAD technician. Table 2.1 provides a more comprehensive list of possible job targets within each segment of the fashion industry.

The **job objective** is what you want the job to offer you; it is also your aim, goal, motive for applying, and personal dream. The objective statement includes the activities you would like to see in your ideal job, functions of the job, responsibilities, and opportunities. A job objective should never be so broad or vague that it is unclear what type of position an applicant seeks. Examples of job objectives include the following:

1. Buying and merchandising for a retail store with an opportunity to define customer needs, increase turnover, procure merchandise, and generate revenue.
2. Fashion marketing with the opportunity to develop and grow brand identity and image, while coordinating marketing efforts for a branded manufacturer or retail company.
3. Visual stylist for a retail store with the opportunity to be creative in implementing visual cues, to increase sales through effective merchandising techniques that indirectly sell merchandise.
4. Product development for a manufacturer or retailer with the opportunity to analyze product and market research, interpret trends, and create products that represent the brands for the specified target market.

Continued on page 17

Table 2.1 Job Targets

Industry Segment

Textile Product Development

Job Targets

CAD Artist	Color Trends Manager	Managing Textile Designer
CAD Designer	Colorist	Materials Buyer
CAD Manager	Forecast Analyst	Senior Knits Specialist
CAD Technician	Freelance Textile	Textile Design Assistant
Color Analyst	Designer/Developer	Trend Specialist
Color Design Consultant	Knits Specialist	VP, Design/Development

Industry Segment

Apparel & Accessories Manufacturing

Job Targets

Apparel/Accessories Test Engineer	Forecast Analyst	Materials Assistant
Color Analyst	Global Planning Manager	Merchandise, Costing, and Production Analyst
Color Design Consultant	Import Production Coordinator	Production Manager
Color Trends Manager	Import Traffic Coordinator	Purchasing Manager, Textiles
Colorist	International Sourcing Coordinator	Quality Assurance Specialist
Customs Compliance Assistant	Knit Production Manager	Quality Control
Director, Customs	Licensing Manager	Sourcing Manager
Director of Sourcing and Global Licensing	Logistics Inventory Analyst	Supply Chain Analyst
Fabric Sourcing	Manager, Domestic and International Transportation	Trend Analyst
Fashion Research	Manager of Operations	

Industry Segment

Retail Product Development

Job Targets

Apparel Development Manager	Forecast Analyst	Planning Supervisor
CAD Designer	Freelance Product Development	Product Designer
CAD Manager	Global Planning Manager	Product Development Coordinator, Buyer
Color Analyst	Import Manager	Product Development Manager
Color Design Consultant	International Sourcing Coordinator	Product Stylist
Color Trends Manager	Licensing Manager	Purchasing Manager, Textiles
Colorist	Materials Assistant	Sourcing/Production Manager
Director of Product Development and Sourcing	Merchandise, Costing, and Production Analyst	Trend Analyst
Fabric Sourcing	Merchandiser	VP, Licensing
Fashion Research Assistant		

Table 2.1 Job Targets (*cont.*)

Industry Segment
  Retail Buying and Sales Management
Job Targets

Buyer	Global Planning Manager	Product Coordinator, Buyer
Design and Product Market	Inventory Analyst	Product Manager
Analyst	Merchandiser	Replenishment Analyst
Director, Merchandise Planning	Merchandiser/Product	Retail Analyst
Distribution/Allocation	Developer	Retail Buying Allocator
Manager	Merchandising Field Manager	Retail Inventory Control
Divisional Merchandise Manager	Planner	Coordinator

Industry Segment
  Sales Management
Job Targets

Account Executive	Director of Sales	Regional Manager
Account Manager	District Manager	Retail Analyst
Category Manager	Division Head	Retail Merchandiser
Chargeback Collection	Merchandise Coordinator	Sales Operations Analyst
Supervisor	National Sales Manager	Sales Representative
Compliance Coordinator	Private Label Sales	Store Manager
Customer Service Representative	Purchase Order Expediter	Wholesale Sales Manager

Industry Segment
  Visual Merchandising
Job Targets

Corporate Visual Merchandising	Fashion Promotion, Brand	Public Relations
Manager	Development and Marketing	Special Events Director
Creative Director	Fashion Promotion Copywriter	Stylist
Director of Promotions	Fashion Show Coordinator	Visual Merchandising Store
Director, Promotional	Freelance Merchandiser	Manager
Merchandise	Manager, Windows Styling	Visual Merchandising
Director of Visual	Marketing Manager	Writer/Editor
Merchandising	Media Buyer	Visual Product Planner
Editor	Media Planner	Visual Stylist
Fashion Director	Merchandise Coordinator	Window Dresser

Table 2.1 Job Targets (cont.)

Industry Segment
Brand Development

Job Targets

Brand Developer	Costing and Production Analyst	Product Director
Brand Manager	Creative Director	Production Manager
Brand Marketing Director	Fabric Sourcing	Trend Analyst
Color Analyst	Merchandise Coordinator	VP, Brand Management
Colorist	Planner	VP, Brand Marketing

Industry Segment
Sales Management

Job Targets

Apparel Account Executive	Brand Marketing Director	Market Researcher
Assistant Product Marketing Manager	Customer Marketing Manager	Retail Marketing Coordinator
Assistant Specialty Marketing Coordinator	Market Analyst	VP, Brand Marketing
	Marketing Manager	

Continued from page 14

5. Promotion for a branded manufacturer with the opportunity to analyze the effectiveness of past promotional strategies, research market trends, and act as a coordinating element with marketing to increase awareness and sales.

A job objective should be realistic and represent the position duties, as well as what the applicant seeks. When preparing a job objective, the focus is on the type of position sought for the next step in a career path. Individuals should absolutely have long-term career goals; however, they should avoid the trap of preparing a job objective statement that looks too far into the future. Applicants should update their job objectives each time they seek new positions or promotions so that the job objectives reflect their next successive steps.

Whether a resume utilizes a job target and/or objective statement, it is important that it provide focus and direction when used in a portfolio. The job target and objective can be incorporated into the same page (see Figure 2.5).

Skill Set Required for Job Target and Job Objective

A **skill set** is made up of a person's knowledge and ability to perform the necessary tasks required by a job and therefore be successful in that targeted job. In the skill set page, individuals have the opportunity to show their potential employers that they have researched the available position and obtained information regarding the types of skills desired and required for the specific job. Furthermore, potential employers have the ability to match the skill set necessary for the job they need to fill to the skill set showcased in the portfolio. The skill set page leads into the actual documentation section, where examples illustrate the skills and tasks required by the position.

Skill refers to knowledge learned through hands-on experience, which provides an individual with competency or expertise in a given area. It is important for the portfolio to communicate what a person can *do* to enhance marketability and gain a competitive edge. What skills does the person possess for the position the company seeks to fill? First, the individual should research the position and obtain information regarding

Job Target

Assistant Buyer

Job Objective

Opportunity with national retail chain in retail buying and merchandising with responsibilities of planning, procurement, and profit.

Figure 2.5 *A job target and job objective page with simple graphics to coordinate with the candidate's resume. The addition of the job objective on the page broadens the scope of the job search to possibly include a position at a company that might have these objectives with a different job title.*

Job Target

Assistant Product Manager

Skill Set for Position

Strong sense of color and styling; ability to conceptualize color schemes, windows, patterns, packaging

Proficiency with software a plus

Fabric knowledge, pattern development, and merchandising

Conceptual direction for line development

Figure 2.6 *This example shows the same page layout, combining job target with a skill set for a position.*

the types of skills desired or required for the job. The person then matches his or her skills with the skills the employer desires. You can use the Skills Inventory Worksheets included in this text's appendix to organize and compile your competencies and capabilities.

Proficiencies and competencies are outlined on the **skills page** and are reiterated on the corresponding divider pages to organize the evidence of capability in the portfolio. The skills page can be incorporated with the job target and job objective or can occupy a page of its own (see Figures 2.6 and 2.7). It is not recommended to incorporate the introduction, statement of job objective and job target, and skills all on one page. Chapter 3 discusses at greater depth the presentation formats and layouts recommended to assist in the documentation and assemblage of work.

Documentation of Skills/Evidence
The documentation of skills/evidence section is the largest component and is considered the main body of the

portfolio. Evidence of skills should be reflected through examples of work. A visual statement and verification of skills and ability provide the employer with evidence of your hands-on capability. Proof of results is the most important information the employer gathers from reviewing your portfolio. Therefore, the work you include should provide clear evidence of the skills you wish to emphasize. Careful selection of work is vital to the effective use and presentation of the merchandising portfolio. Select quality over quantity. Strong examples of work should be incorporated into the portfolio presentation to emphasize strengths, while weaker examples should be excluded to minimize weaknesses. Figure 2.8 show color forecasting and swatches of a fabric concept. Examples of work can be divided into different categories depending on your status (e.g., student seeking an internship or a co-op, student seeking employment, industry professional seeking employment or

Products...

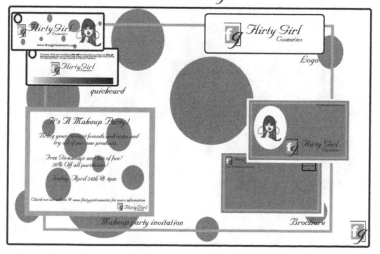

Marketing...

Figure 2.7 These sequential skill set pages showcase Heather Brock's ability to identify and describe a target market and specific customer profile for a new product line of cosmetics called Flirty Girl, merchandise the cosmetics appropriate for this customer, and show various marketing ideas aimed at connecting the customer with the product. These skill set pages showcase presentation skills as well as competency skills, such as marketing and merchandising for the beauty industry. The text, layout, branding logo, and content work together as a total presentation.

Color Forecasting

Women's Wear
Spring 2004

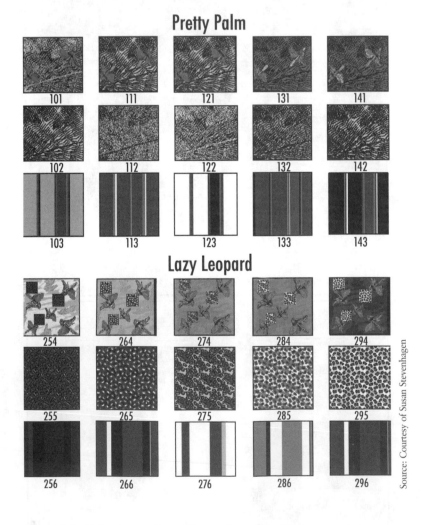

Pretty Palm

101	111	121	131	141
102	112	122	132	142
103	113	123	133	143

Lazy Leopard

254	264	274	284	294
255	265	275	285	295
256	266	276	286	296

Source: Courtesy of Susan Stevenhagen

Figure 2.8 Color forecasting and swatches of the fabric concept.

movement within a company). Main categories that you can use to divide the evidence section include industry, internship or co-op, academic project work, and self-directed work. Work samples should be further subdivided by skill set.

Academic

As students work through academic programs at colleges and universities, they acquire knowledge through lectures and demonstrations. More important, students learn the application of these skills through hands-on exercises and project work.

Project Work Typically, students who seek internships or co-op positions or work after graduation do not have much industry experience, if any, to include in their portfolios. Students should therefore incorporate individual or group class project work to demonstrate the skills and capabilities they possess. Doing so allows them to demonstrate the application of skills in which they are proficient, which they cannot include in their resumes because they have not had the opportunity to apply their knowledge in industry settings. The contents of the documentation of skills and evidence section for a student who is seeking an internship or a co-op may solely contain class project work. Examples of work might include a buying project, target market research, a photograph of a line storyboard, a promotion project, and more.

Industry

An individual may have acquired industry work experience through an internship or a co-op experience, freelance work, or full- or part-time employment. The merchandising portfolio model separates internship and co-op work from professional employment because the level of supervision, involvement, and responsibility is often quite different.

Internship/Co-op. For students who have completed internship or co-op work, it is important to include evidence of results accomplished during the experience because it shows to potential employers that they possess the skills needed to complete a particular task and have actually applied them in industry settings. Evidence of work completed during internships or co-op positions will often carry more weight than class project work alone. Examples of work might include a press release accompanied by newspaper clips of any press coverage, a comparative shopping report, photographs of visual displays created, and more.

Professional. Professional work included in the portfolio may come from freelance work or full-time employment in the industry. Individuals who are unable to include work samples because the work is the property of a company may supplement the portfolio with **self-directed work**. The individual creates self-directed work for the sole purpose of showcasing creativity, expertise, or skill. This type of work can be very important because it can be tailored to appeal to a particular company. Chapter 4 discusses more in-depth how to demonstrate your skills in an organized manner and provides examples of what might be included in a successful portfolio.

Self-directed

Self-directed work, as described above, can be very effective in a portfolio, whether presented by students or professionals. Merchandising professionals may not have permission to share company work or concepts. Self-directed work allows them to develop projects on their own that showcase the skills they utilize at their jobs (see Box 2.1). For example, a professional visual merchandiser may wish to show styling skills of mannequin groupings, museum cases, or floor sets through volunteer or freelance work that can be photographed for use in the portfolio. (This is why it is important to maintain written and visual records and archives of accomplishments.) Line merchandisers can demonstrate their garment costing and specification skills by independ-

ently developing documents in Microsoft Excel.

Some students may lack the opportunity to apply certain skills in assigned class project work. Therefore, they may choose to develop self-directed work, much like some professionals, to provide evidence of their knowledge and skills in a particular area. For example, a student may have contributed to one aspect of a group project, but wishes to demonstrate competency in all areas of the project. Another example might include a target market profile assignment. The class project may have been for a team of students to develop a customer profile, similar to the one shown in Figure 2.7. A student might then choose to independently develop a target market analysis to supplement the customer profile, based on the findings. This illustrates

---

Box 2.1 Self-Directed Work

"Your portfolio is your opportunity to artistically express your creative vision and abilities. It should be exciting and fluid and represent your talents and creativity. It should also be updated [periodically] to reflect changes as you mature in your professional career.

Corporate executives are challenged to find the best talent in the industry. Corporate environments require merchandisers who can translate talent and skill to specific brand identities. Preparing a small project when interviewing can demonstrate initiative and, more important, whether you 'get it.' Corporations demand that you have an eye for detail, a natural proclivity for fashion trends, and strong team-building skills.

Let your portfolio be a true reflection of the artist behind it. Keep it focused, clean, and [updated] and you're sure to impress!"

Jennifer Koh
American Eagle Outfitters

Source: Jennifer Koh, human resources manager for American Eagle Outfitters

both creativity and initiative on the part of the student.

It is common for industry professionals to create self-directed work for their portfolios. Particularly for those working in industry segments such as product development, where merchandise is being designed, it is important to respect the secrecy of a company's new products that are not yet on the market. Any firm that develops products will respect the decision to exclude evidence of work that is proprietary or not yet public. Therefore, self-directed work can make up a significant portion of the portfolio. Although developing this type of work is time-consuming, it is well worth the effort. Self-direction allows individuals to target the work they are developing for a specific firm or area of specialization, thereby providing potential employers with evidence of skills that represent the target company.

Resume

The last page of the merchandising portfolio is the resume. A **resume** is a written document that summarizes education and work experience; highlights capabilities, accomplishments, and results; and features additional information regarding software knowledge, industry memberships or affiliations, volunteerism, language proficiency, and additional support for an applicant's fitness for a particular position. Resumes should reflect the professionalism of the applicants and their brand identities while detailing their capability to do the job for which they are applying. The resume acts as a conclusion and provides closure to the portfolio by summarizing capabilities and work experience. The

same graphic elements and brand identity used in the portfolio are integrated into the resume layout to create a strong, cohesive presentation and build brand recognition and awareness. Chapter 8 discusses more in-depth the development of resumes and various formats that can be used and provides useful tools for resume development.

Getting Started

Strong portfolios can significantly increase applicants' marketability by providing tangible evidence of the skills they possess. After all, it is essential for applicants to focus on what they can offer employers rather than what they will personally gain. Creating a merchandising portfolio can often seem to be a daunting task. Although initially overwhelming, this process is exciting and energizing because it marks a step toward a new career or stage of growth in life. It is important to be true to yourself so that the finished portfolio is not only a visual example of your capabilities and evidence of work but also reflects your personality and brand image. You should begin by identifying the segment of the merchandising industry in which you are interested in working.

Skills Assessment

Skill assessment is an important step in the process of portfolio and resume development. Employers want to know what you have to offer, and the merchandising portfolio is a great way to provide visual documentation of your competencies, capabilities, and proficiencies. Skills Inventory Worksheet 2.1: Skills You Possess, available in the appen-

dix of this text, helps you to compile and organize competencies and capabilities you have acquired. It is important to be honest in documenting the skills you possess. The portfolio should convey your strengths and minimize your weaknesses. Capability or proficiency should never be overstated or embellished, as this may mislead a potential employer and lead to disappointments down the line. You should update your skills inventory often so you can include newly acquired expertise.

Researching Skills

Once you have listed the skills you currently possess, begin researching the skills employers seek for specific job positions. Web sites such as Stylejobs.com, Stylecareers.com, and 24seventalent.com, among others (see Table 2.2), as well as career sections of company Web sites, outline the skills and experience needed for particular positions within the fashion merchandising industry. These sites may not provide a neatly compiled list of skills; you may need to evaluate the job description and based on this, determine the skills for which the employer is looking. Skills Inventory Worksheet 2.2: Skills Needed for a Specific Job Objective or Job Target, available in the appendix of this text, helps you to document the skills employers seek. Once you complete both Skills Inventory Worksheets 2.1 and 2.2, go to the Skills Inventory Worksheet 2.3: Matching Skills Possessed with Skills Needed for Specific Position (also available in the appendix) to compile, organize, and prioritize the information demonstrated by the collection of work examples.

Table 2.2 Web Sites for Job Listings in the Fashion Industry

Web Address	What they offer
24seventalent.com	Job listings for fashion, sports, home, beauty, and entertainment industries.
About.com	Jobs and Careers section has useful articles on career planning as well as current job openings in a broad range of fields.
Apparelsearch.com	Online guide to the apparel industry boasts a wealth of information for numerous fields of interest. Employment Guide for the fashion and clothing industry offers extensive job listings at reputable corporations.
Careerbuilder.com	General career site enables you to search jobs by keyword, location, and industry. Section devoted to Fashion/Apparel/Textiles posts up-to-date job listings.
Clothingindustryjobs.com	A focused job search site that allows you to browse by job target. An interesting feature of this site is that each job listing shows how many people have clicked to view it, which may indicate how popular or competitive a position is.
Fashioncareercenter.com	Apparel and retail jobs and resumes posted online. Free, unlimited access to jobs and resumes. This site offers Portfolio Services for a fee—portfolio hosting on the Internet or the creation of a self-booting CD.
Hotjobs.com	One of the most popular general job search sites, sponsored by Yahoo! Search by keyword, location, or job category. It includes helpful career tools and informative articles.
Monster.com	Another popular, general job search site allows you to find jobs, post your resume, and read career advice. A free account allows you to create a Search Agent that will alert you via e-mail when jobs matching your criteria open up.
Stylecareers.com	Browse job listings by job category, job function, and region. This fashion-only job listing site also enables you to post your resume. Associate site, Styleportfolios.com, allows you to create a one-page portfolio online.

Evidence of Skills

Providing tangible evidence of skills is the most important aspect of the merchandising portfolio. Once you have documented the skills you possess and matched them with the skills needed for the position you seek, you must gather evidence of results. Your results section might include work from class projects, internship or co-op experiences, industry positions held, or newly created self-directed work developed specifically for the portfolio.

Gathering and Categorizing Work

At this stage, do not worry about which examples are strong and which are weak; just find work that proves your ability to perform specific tasks and apply knowledge for the specific job opening. Be sure your samples of work represent the segment of the industry in which you wish to be employed. By doing so, you provide the employer with evidence of the skills you have acquired that apply directly to the position for which you are applying. The translation of evidence should be straightforward and your fitness for the position easy for the employer to verify. The Skills Inventory Worksheet 2.3 should help you to focus on compiling all examples of work that include the matched skills from this assessment.

Activities

1. Research and gather information on the jobs you listed in the first Activities question in Chapter 1. You can begin by searching Internet job sites or company Web sites for job targets and descriptions. Document the actual job titles, record the job descriptions, compile a list of skills needed for the position, and list the companies with current positions available.

2. The following worksheets have been developed to assist in documenting and pairing the skills necessary for a particular job position or industry segment. It is therefore important to accurately depict the skills you currently possess. Once you complete Worksheets 2.1, 2.2, and 2.3, you should know exactly what skills to emphasize in the portfolio, which will help you to select work samples.

3. Chapter 4 shows you how to select and organize items of work that demonstrate the skills listed above. Begin collecting work now that expresses the skills documented on Worksheet 2.3. Try to place all of the items in one area so they will be protected and easy to find later.

Chapter 3

Portfolios

Portfolios provide individuals with the opportunity to visually communicate their skills, **competencies,** interests, and **understanding** of the fashion industry by showcasing original work that demonstrates results. The fashion industry is concerned with **deliverables**—tangible results of work—in business situations. When employers interview potential employees, they have expectations and try to gauge candidates' abilities to fulfill those expectations. The methods candidates choose to showcase their skills and experience can effectively demonstrate personality or character traits through visual representation of their best research, planning, organization, and presentation abilities. These elements communicate process (how candidates evolve ideas), style (unique brand identity), concept, inspiration, and execution of tangible materials. Preparing a creative presentation is key to successful portfolio development, whether a candidate is interested in a creative position or an analytical one. Your portfolio can be presented in many different ways, and you must make choices through portfolio type, layout, and format.

Portfolio Types

The portfolio actually consists of two separate parts: the outward **encasement** or form of the portfolio, which can be traditional, custom, or digital, and the contents of the portfolio, which can be either general or focused. This chapter discusses both portfolio types. After reading about each presentation style, consider which one suits your work style and job target best.

Traditional Portfolios

A traditional portfolio is encased in a purchased, professional presentation case that has a metal binder and sheet protectors to hold contents. The style of the case will vary according to the materials used, size, type of closure, and configuration for carrying. Each page is individually fastened into the portfolio, allowing for variance in the number of pages used and ease of insertion, organization, and maintenance of contents.

An affordable choice is a portfolio case that contains protector sheets that are heat-sealed into the binding and cannot be removed. Since the sheets are fixed in place, work must be removed from all of the protector sheets to reorganize the order of contents. Anyone who seeks employment in the fashion merchandising industry can adapt a traditional portfolio to his or her specific needs. See Figure 3.1 for examples of traditional portfolios.

Custom Portfolios

Custom portfolios are the most creative and individualized paper portfolios. This style offers a wide variety of presentation possibilities. The most professional custom portfolios are individually created and bound into a book. Custom portfolio books can be easily assembled by

Figure 3.1 Examples of
traditional portfolio
encasements that may
be purchased at art
stores nationwide.

printing or color-copying your work, laminating the pages, and either spiral- or adhesive-binding the contents. Custom portfolios are more challenging to develop but have a wider range of size options and offer more creativity and personalization than traditional formats. This portfolio format is recommended if multiple portfolios are developed for various segments of the fashion industry. This is also the best option when the portfolio is to be directed toward one specific company. This style is typically utilized by individuals seeking employment or currently employed in creative segments of the industry and by those who have a limited body of work.

Another type of custom portfolio case is the kind that is purchased from a vendor. Portfolio cases can be custom designed and manufactured for a personal presentation. Companies such as Brewer-Cantelmo (www.brewer-cantelmo.com) in New York will custom design a portfolio case and content sheets based on your specifications. This ensures a professional presentation while allowing for individuality and reflection of personal style. With this option, the encasement always remains the same—the pages inside are altered for presentations and updated over time. See Figure 3.2 for examples of custom portfolio covers.

Figure 3.2 Nancy Friedman created her own cover and back page for her custom portfolio. Erin Isaacs designed her custom portfolio with a text project cover image and spiral binding.

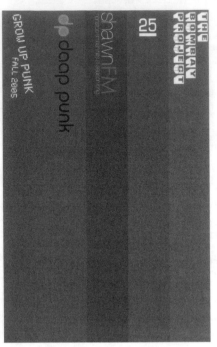

Figure 3.3 Shawn Ormsby designed his digital portfolio and packaged it into a PDF format book that contains multiple pages of work. He can color-print and mail or e-mail his portfolio to potential employers; he can send the portfolio in its entirety or send select pages as a smaller, more focused portfolio. Similarly, it is easy to change a digital portfolio from a general one to a focused one, depending on the jobs for which you are applying.

Digital Portfolios

Digital portfolios are virtual presentations of work that can be presented by way of CDs, e-portfolios, personal Web sites, or postings on career sites. Information that is saved to a CD can be mailed to an employer, accompanied by a resume and cover letter, or it can be offered to an employer during an interview. The **e-portfolio** consists of a **PDF** file that contains content and images that can be set up to open individually or be viewed as a continuous group.

The **Web-based portfolio** is the most complex **virtual presentation** used today. A personal Web site is established and maintained to showcase portfolio contents. Some employment and fashion industry Web sites now offer options for posting portfolios. When creating digital portfolios, software must be carefully selected to make sure the employer can easily access the information. It is not uncommon for individuals to compile a paper portfolio, in addition to a digital version, that is comprehensive or summarizes their work and is used as an individual marketing piece that is mailed to an employer or left at the end of an interview. Figure 3.3 shows an eye-catching sample from a digital portfolio.

Comparison of Portfolio Types

As you can see, there are a variety of portfolio types that offer excellent encasement choices for creating your merchandising portfolio. It is important to consider the advantages and disadvantages for each type before making your final selection. You might choose to create a traditional or custom portfolio that is enhanced by the addition of a digital version or vice versa. The goal of any portfolio is to showcase work through the best possible venue while providing the target audience with viewing access.

Virtual portfolios create broader access for employers. Web-based portfolios can be accessed by anyone connected to the Internet. Those who seek new employment opportunities outside a company and do not want their current employers to know should not consider using this type of digital portfolio. A better digital choice would be the e-portfolio because the candidates e-mail images of their work as attachments to specific prospective employers. This means of sending the digital portfolio is effective because it's faster than regular mail but just as private, since the portfolio is not posted on a Web site that everyone can access. Images can be opened and viewed during a phone or personal interview. As with the CD, individuals can print out contents and assemble them into a traditional portfolio. The CD and e-portfolio are focused in distribution. Remember that distribution is focused, not limited. An e-portfolio can quickly and easily be forwarded to someone else.

Advantages and Disadvantages to Portfolio Types

All of the portfolio types have advantages and disadvantages. Before determining the format that best suits your style and **job search**, weigh the strengths and weaknesses of each.

Advantages of Traditional Portfolios

- Cases are readily available for purchase in a variety of styles and sizes.

- Easy for you to organize and update because you can remove work and quickly reposition or replace it.

- Easily customized to the requirements of different job positions or companies.

- Versatile and reusable case.

- Widely accepted format.

- Can be cost-effective.

Disadvantages of Traditional Portfolios

- May be heavy or cumbersome, since you need to carry it around.

- May be difficult for you to present easily in smaller spaces.

- Eliminates or restricts your ability to interview at other companies if a prospective employer requests that you leave the portfolio behind for further review.

- Size is limited to available standard dimensions.

- Case may not reflect your personal style.

- Can be initially expensive.

Advantages of Custom Portfolios

- Opportunity to reflect personal style.

- Since you can create multiple books, you can leave them behind after interviews, if the interviewer requests it, without prohibiting additional interviews.

- You can customize the layout for each interview.

- Demonstrates individuality, creativity, and originality.

- You can prepare multiple books that address job targets in various industry segments.

Disadvantages of Custom Portfolios

- You may need to reformat portfolio contents and rework images for each interview.

- Creating multiple books takes time and resources.

- You must consider and execute each layout carefully.

- To achieve a professional look, you need to use presentation software.

- Although you need to be creative, remember to keep it simple, so that it is not perceived as unprofessional.

Advantages of Digital Portfolios

- Easy to adapt and format contents.

- Demonstrates creativity, use of technology, and technical expertise.

- Allows for immediate delivery.

- Enables you to incorporate animation, sounds, and special effects into the presentation.

- Cost-effective.

- Wide exposure.

Disadvantages of Digital Portfolios

- Can be time-consuming to create and maintain.

- Interviewer may not have compatible software to view the images or may not have time or be receptive to using virtual means for assessing a candidate.

- You may need to bring your laptop to the interview to ensure they view files as you intended rather than dealing with software compatibility issues.

- You run the risk of having your files sent or forwarded to people for whom you did not intend to send the files.

- When you post a portfolio on a career Web site, you also direct employers to other candidates' posted portfolios.

- Web sites must be maintained and protected.
- File corruption is possible.

Now that you have reviewed the advantages and disadvantages of the various portfolio types, you must consider the material you will include and the manner in which you organize it. There are two categories of portfolio contents: general and focused.

General Portfolio

General portfolios allow individuals to showcase a wide array of skills and competencies, especially when their job search is broad. General portfolios present work that spans a variety of areas rather than targeting one type of position. Presenting these types of portfolios is ideal in times of economic recession or industry slowdowns, since showing that you are versatile increases your chances for employment. Students who seek internships or co-ops or candidates who seek entry-level positions usually use this type of portfolio since they often search in a variety of areas. General portfolios allow individuals to highlight a wide spectrum of skills in an organized and logical format.

Organization and Layout

As this text has emphasized, the main aim of portfolios is to showcase competencies and demonstrate results and accomplishments, but they also need to have a brand identity and deliver a consistent brand image. By definition,

general portfolios contain a diverse body of work that highlights a broad range of skills for a variety of positions. And while the work must be diverse for the portfolio to be general, it must still be consistent and have continuity from page to page and in terms of layout, text, and graphics. Color, style and texture of layout paper, text selection and color, and graphics are used to establish brand identity. It is important to have one consistent element throughout all of the pages. Graphics are an excellent means of unifying a presentation. Graphics can consist of original icons you create or can be simply a line, shape, or shadow. Once you choose graphics, be consistent in how you use them throughout the portfolio, resume, cover letter, and individual marketing piece.

The **individual marketing piece** or **IMP** is a personalized and condensed element in which individuals introduce themselves as brands. It is crucial to brand yourself in today's market so you can promote *you,* as the brand, to prospective employers. The actual physical marketing piece can be a small version of your portfolio or a condensed version of your resume. Whatever form it takes, it should definitely communicate the very best asset you bring to a potential employer, whether it is the experience you have gained at the companies at which you have worked, the various areas of the industry that you have explored, or your presentation skills. Your name, field, brand graphic, signature, or picture can be on the IMP. It might take the form of a small bound book, or *look book* as they are called in the

fashion industry. It could take the form of a postcard, business card, or promotional pamphlet.

You should organize your work so it demonstrates your thought processes and industry knowledge. You should show concepts, target market research, and analysis; fabric and color presentations; buying and merchandising plans; and any marketing pieces you have created. The manner in which you organize your work should follow the process used by the industry to bring products to market and should build, or grow, into a cohesive whole.

Examples of General Portfolios

The general portfolio contains, by definition, a wide variety of work that addresses the different areas of the industry. This work often comes from school or work-related projects and may require you to develop additional pieces to add to the portfolio's flow or to fill any gaps in the work. Portfolio flow will be discussed in depth in the next chapter.

The general portfolio shown in Figure 3.4 uses lines and dots as the graphical element that unifies the work. Figure 3.5 provides another example from a general portfolio, where a logo that represents the individual's initials is used as the unifying element. This graphic monogram conveys her branded identity and unifies the diversified portfolio. A brand and consistent layout unify the general portfolio in Figure 3.6. Note that the layout of work is consistent, page to page, which allows for a brand name to be used and not conflict with the work. A simple shadow under the name of each piece of work connects all elements in the general portfolio shown in Figure 3.7.

Focused Portfolio

A **focused portfolio** showcases a targeted body of work. People who conduct well-defined and narrow job searches tend to use this type of portfolio. The two most important messages that you need to convey in a focused portfolio are your complete understanding of the needs of a specific field or position and that you possess the necessary skills to perform the job. Students who completed internship or co-op experiences and know the specific area of the industry in which they wish to be employed tend to use the focused portfolio. Individuals who currently work in the industry and wish to continue along a particular career path also use this portfolio type.

Organization and Layout

A focused portfolio showcases work directed toward one of five industry segments: textile product development, apparel and accessory product development (retail or wholesale), buying and merchandising, store management, and fashion marketing (includes visual merchandising, promotion, brand development, and advertising).

The focused content you present in a focused portfolio highlights a very specific set of skills that speak to one particular segment of the industry, possibly even just one position. You should therefore ensure that your focused portfolio communicates the preparedness of your skills and knowledge for a desired position. You

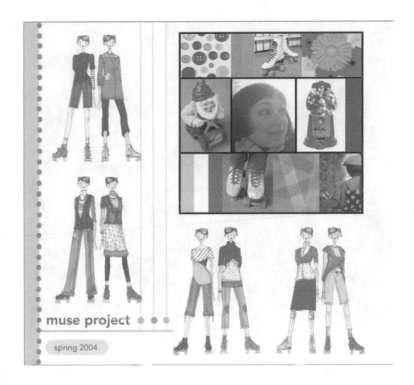

Source: Courtesy of Lisa Bruemmer

Figure 3.4 Lisa Bruemmer's two-page layout of portfolio pages uses lines and dots as the visual element that connects the work in the portfolio.

Source: Courtesy of Katie Keller

Figure 3.5 Katie Keller uses her monogram as her signature icon for each page of her portfolio. This graphic element unifies the portfolio and connects her brand identity to her work.

Source: Courtesy of Heidi Cooper Ludwig

Figure 3.6 Heidi Cooper Ludwig chose "Encore" brides for a project, and these two pages show her target market and images of possible second-marriage venues. She continues the grid layout throughout the portfolio to provide consistency.

Figure 3.7 Mary Wolf uses a shadow line graphic that connects all the pages of her general portfolio. She successfully shows work for the women's apparel, children's, and accessories markets.

Mary M. Wolf
fashion design

Louis Vuitton children's wear

raw silk one-piece jumper
handpainted patch
leather embroidery

Mary M. Wolf

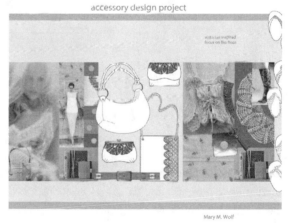

accessory design project

Mary M. Wolf

Source: Designed, created, and illustrated by Mary M. Wolf

need to include work that demonstrates your knowledge of processes; however, you also must include work that conveys your skills. Skills work is based on specific tasks within a position. For example, if the focus is a career in buying, show your understanding of profit and loss statements, open-to-buy forms and terminology, pricing, cost/retail relationships, and negotiation skills. In addition, show evidence of your ability to research a specific target market, identify competition, and spot trends. These skills are important to buying positions, so demonstrating competency in these areas is essential. Organization and attention to detail are highly desired skills that can be communicated through the organization of a focused portfolio.

When selecting content for your portfolio, be prepared to create a successful presentation by reading specific job descriptions carefully. Review each qualification and determine how you can demonstrate this in your portfolio.

The focused portfolio still needs to show a diverse body of work even within a narrow job focus. Keep in mind that the sense of diversity is not the same as it is in a general portfolio; you demonstrate diversity in a focused portfolio by including work that shows your ability to perform tasks within a given position, your ability to use different media to complete work, and/or your ability to expand industry focus (e.g., menswear, womenswear, or accessories). For example, a merchandiser might

Projected Sales

Dept.	Class	Item	Retail	March Units/Store	March Total Units	March Total $	April Units/Store	April Total Units	April Total $	May Units/Store	May Total Units	May Total $	June Units/Store	June Total Units	June Total $	March thru June Total Units	March thru June Total $
100	10	White short-sleeve tee	$ 20.00	36	14,400	$ 288,000	38	15,200	$ 304,000	35	14,000	$ 280,000	38	15,200	$ 304,000	58,800	$ 1,176,000
100	10	Black short-sleeve tee	$ 20.00	28	11,200	$ 224,000	24	9,600	$ 192,000	20	8,000	$ 160,000	14	5,600	$ 112,000	34,400	$ 688,000
100	10	Pink short-sleeve tee	$ 20.00	22	8,800	$ 176,000	24	9,600	$ 192,000	26	10,400	$ 208,000	30	12,000	$ 240,000	40,800	$ 816,000
100	10	White camisole	$ 18.00	24	9,600	$ 172,800	28	11,200	$ 201,600	32	12,800	$ 230,400	36	14,400	$ 259,200	48,000	$ 864,000
100	10	Black camisole	$ 18.00	17	6,800	$ 122,400	21	8,400	$ 151,200	24	9,600	$ 172,800	30	12,000	$ 216,000	36,800	$ 662,400
100	20	White button-down shirt	$ 25.00	18	7,200	$ 180,000	16	6,400	$ 160,000	14	5,600	$ 140,000	13	5,200	$ 130,000	24,400	$ 610,000
100	20	Pink button-down shirt	$ 25.00	14	5,600	$ 140,000	12	4,800	$ 120,000	13	5,200	$ 130,000	15	6,000	$ 150,000	21,600	$ 540,000
100	20	Blue blouse	$ 30.00	17	6,800	$ 204,000	14	5,600	$ 168,000	15	6,000	$ 180,000	12	4,800	$ 144,000	23,200	$ 696,000
100	20	Ivory blouse	$ 30.00	17	6,800	$ 204,000	15	6,000	$ 180,000	11	4,400	$ 132,000	13	5,200	$ 156,000	22,400	$ 672,000
100	30	Ivory sweater set	$ 50.00	14	5,600	$ 280,000	10	4,000	$ 200,000	7	2,800	$ 140,000	5	2,000	$ 100,000	14,400	$ 720,000
200	15	Low rise jeans	$ 60.00	20	8,000	$ 480,000	14	5,600	$ 336,000	12	4,800	$ 288,000	10	4,000	$ 240,000	22,400	$ 1,344,000
200	15	Boot cut jeans	$ 60.00	18	7,200	$ 432,000	12	4,800	$ 288,000	10	4,000	$ 240,000	8	3,200	$ 192,000	19,200	$ 1,152,000
200	25	Black skirt knee-length	$ 50.00	14	5,600	$ 280,000	16	6,400	$ 320,000	14	5,600	$ 280,000	15	6,000	$ 300,000	23,600	$ 1,180,000
200	25	Navy long skirt	$ 50.00	8	3,200	$ 160,000	7	2,800	$ 140,000	6	2,400	$ 120,000	5	2,000	$ 100,000	10,400	$ 520,000
200	35	Black trousers	$ 70.00	16	6,400	$ 448,000	18	7,200	$ 504,000	15	6,000	$ 420,000	14	5,600	$ 392,000	25,200	$ 1,764,000
200	35	Navy trousers	$ 70.00	12	4,800	$ 336,000	13	5,200	$ 364,000	11	4,400	$ 308,000	12	4,800	$ 336,000	19,200	$ 1,344,000
200	35	Khaki pants	$ 50.00	10	4,000	$ 200,000	12	4,800	$ 240,000	15	6,000	$ 300,000	18	7,200	$ 360,000	22,000	$ 1,100,000
200	45	Khaki shorts	$ 40.00	6	2,400	$ 96,000	12	4,800	$ 192,000	20	8,000	$ 320,000	28	11,200	$ 448,000	26,400	$ 1,056,000
300	18	Blue knit dress	$ 60.00	8	3,200	$ 192,000	10	4,000	$ 240,000	10	4,000	$ 240,000	14	5,600	$ 336,000	16,800	$ 1,008,000
300	28	Black cocktail dress	$ 95.00	4	1,600	$ 152,000	3	1,200	$ 114,000	4	1,600	$ 152,000	3	1,200	$ 114,000	5,600	$ 532,000
		Total		323	129,200	$ 4,767,200	319	127,600	$ 4,606,800	314	125,600	$ 4,441,200	333	133,200	$ 4,629,200	515,600	$ 18,444,400

Figure 3.8 A projected sales plan that has been developed for a student project in a buying class. The merchandise plan and resulting line sheets for an item in this plan illustrate Nicole Bettinger's Excel skills and understanding of the process of buying and merchandising.

demonstrate line planning capability by showing style numbers and flat sketches of styles, computer-generated worksheets and completed line sheets, or catalogs. Work that illustrates process should show your knowledge of the relationship among design, merchandising, and marketing. This work may include presentation of a concept, target market research, and promotional materials such as hang-tags, labels, product announcements, and signage, which may characterize a merchandising project.

As the industry has evolved, so have industry positions. With the addition of a team-based approach to product development and the growth of retail private labels, merchandising roles have been expanded to include positions more directly related to products. These positions often include knowledge of product design needs, brand development, and sourcing, which have direct connections to the marketing and sale of the product to the target customer. Providing evidence from these areas will communicate a comprehensive understanding of the industry and give you the competitive edge over other candidates. Inclusion of a team-based project from school or the workplace will communicate your ability to work both independently and as part of a team. It is essential to explain your role within the team, in addition to your individual contri-

bution toward a project. Company information is typically proprietary; therefore, remember that you must seek permission from previous or current employers before you include the work from a professional stint in your portfolio.

Examples of Focused Portfolios

Focused portfolios need to show that you have a complete understanding of a narrow segment of the industry. The variety of work may exhibit all aspects of the individual industry segment or could actually feature one job target within the segment. Figure 3.8 shows a portfolio focused on buying and merchandising. Note the variety of work that connects together a buying

Merchandise Plan

		March	April	May	June	Total
BOM	Plan	11,918,000	11,517,000	10,658,880	11,573,000	45,666,880
	LY	10,676,954	11,059,370	12,187,506	10,939,603	44,863,432
	% Inc over LY	11.6%	4.1%	-12.5%	5.8%	Ave Inv
Stock/Sales Ratio Plan		2.5	2.5	2.4	2.5	9,133,376
Stock/Sales Ratio LY		2.3	2.5	2.7	2.5	8,972,686
Sales	Plan	4,767,200	4,606,800	4,441,200	4,629,200	Total 18,444,400
	LY	4,642,154	4,423,748	4,513,891	4,375,841	17,955,634
Sales % by Month-Plan		25.8%	25.0%	24.1%	25.1%	% Inc over LY
	% Inc over LY	2.7%	4.1%	-1.6%	5.8%	2.7%
Reductions	Plan	341,812	505,155	240,478	424,996	Total 1,512,441
	LY	462,735	387,816	298,207	320,242	1,469,000
Red % by Mth-Plan		22.6%	33.4%	15.9%	28.1%	Plan Total Red %
Red % by Mth-LY		31.5%	26.4%	20.3%	21.8%	8.2%
Purchases	Plan	4,708,012	4,253,835	5,595,798	5,481,196	Total 20,038,841
Retail	LY	5,487,305	5,939,700	3,564,195	4,751,695	19,742,894
Cost IMU: 54.2%	Plan	2,156,269	1,948,257	2,562,870	2,510,388	Total 9,177,789
EOM	Plan	11,517,000	10,658,880	11,573,000	12,000,000	Stock Turn 2.02
	LY	11,059,370	12,187,506	10,939,603	10,995,214	2.00

Line Sheet

Description

Item #   **151**

White Short-Sleeve Tee

		$	MU on R	MU on Cost
Cost	$	9.50	47.5%	100%
MU	$	10.50	52.5%	111%
Retail	$	20.00	100%	211%

Promotion / Event:		Basic Tees	Promo %:	30%
		$	New MU% on R	
Cost	$	9.50	67.9%	
MU	$	4.50	32.1%	
Retail	$	14.00	100%	

Orig Retail	$	20.00
% Off		30%
Promo Retail	$	14.00

Packs
Inner   4

Master   20

Vendor   Shirts, Shirts, Shirts

Country of Origin   USA

Terms   Payment   2/10/N30

Shipping   FOB LA

Fiber Content   100% Cotton

Details   Short-sleeve white basic tee slightly

fitted at waist, 1/2" band at neck

plan and the merchandising of the line. In addition, this portfolio includes a trend report, target market research, and a visual profile that illustrate pre-process work.

A product-line-development-focused portfolio is shown in Figure 3.9. This segment of the industry is very diverse. This candidate chose to focus the portfolio on product line development. Other options for targeting portfolios within product development could focus on aspects such as technical design or sourcing. The portfolio work in Figure 3.10 is focused on textile product development. The variety of research and images reflect the innovative technology in the area of textiles today. The portfolio showcases specific development strengths of the individual through CAD print and color work.

Fashion marketing is the focus of the portfolio in Figure 3.11. Although this portfolio is primarily text-driven, it also illustrates the creativity and marketability of the candidate. Strong writing skills are valued across the fashion and merchandising spectrum. Including a press release shows a prospective employer your understanding of the importance of publicity and skill in developing a publicity campaign. This combination ensures that the portfolio will be applicable to many positions within a retail company. The focus of this portfolio could be narrowed if necessary by eliminating the creative pages and concentrating more on documents. Either way, it is clear that this candidate did her research on the company before applying.

Figure 3.12 shows an example of a portfolio focused on merchandising.

The work reflects understanding of the career path by showing merchandising plans and strategies, brand development, and visual merchandising. A comprehensive body of knowledge comes across.

Portfolio Supplies

Basic tools are needed to create a portfolio, and supplies may differ depending on the type of portfolio you are creating. This section is divided into different lists depending on the type of portfolio you choose to develop.

Portfolio Styles and Sizes

Portfolio cases can be purchased in a variety of standard sizes at art or office supply stores or online. Necessary supplies for development can vary widely depending on the type of portfolio you create (traditional, custom, or digital). Traditional and custom portfolios will utilize many of the same supplies.

Conventional Presentation Cases

Presentation cases are used for traditional portfolios and are constructed of leather, vinyl, canvas, or nylon.

Figure 3.9 An inspirational project based on the brand essence of Cadillac. This project uses images of fabric, color, target audience, and products identified with this audience to show an understanding of the brand essence. The portfolio's creator designed a line using these images as a conceptual direction and developed marketing collaterals to help sell this line to the target customer.

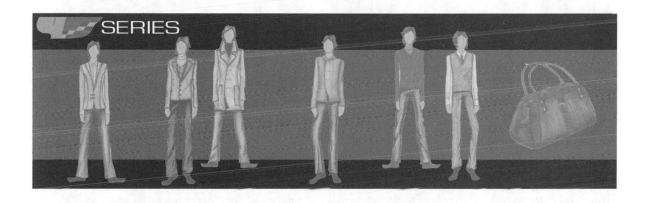

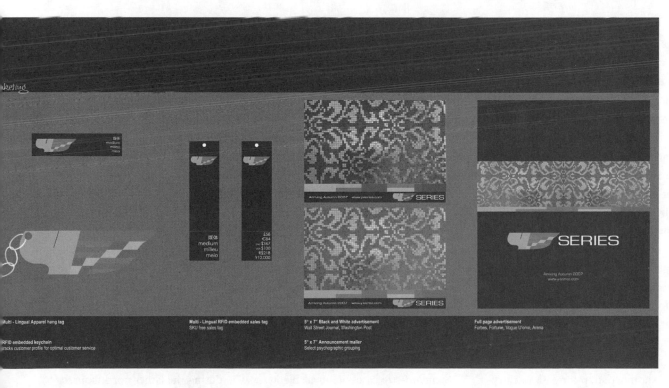

Multi - Lingual Apparel hang tag

RFID embedded keychain
tracks customer profile for optimal customer service

Multi - Lingual RFID embedded sales tag
SKU free sales tag

5" x 7" Black and White advertisement
Wall Street Journal, Washington Post

5" x 7" Announcement mailer
Select psychographic grouping

Full page advertisement
Forbes, Fortune, Vogue L'omo, Arena

Source: Courtesy of Shawn Ormsby, Natasia Moose, and Monica Conner

Figure 3.10 The portfolio shown here is focused on textile development. John Kelly developed prints and fabrics for three different garments to show his skill in designing apparel with U4ia.

The style and details of the case will vary depending on the materials used. The conventional portfolio that looks like a briefcase contains a metal three-ring or comb binder for holding sheets and keeping contents in place. Sheet protectors are available in side-loading or top-loading styles and can be purchased individually or in a package. Sheet protectors that are compatible with the comb-style binder have black paper inserts, which can be used for layout and presentation in the portfolio. Closures will range from zippers that completely close the portfolio to a snap or Velcro tab, to no closure at all. Some cases will provide handles or a shoulder strap for ease in carry-ing. A less expensive alternative is the case that is bound to look like a book. This style case has protector sheets that are constructed of a durable heavy plastic cover (available in a variety of colors) containing top-loading protector sheets that cannot be removed. These can be purchased with 12, 24, or 48 protector sheets to accommodate different presenta-tion sizes and lengths. The colored insertion sheets that come with this style portfolio are not intended for use in presentation and layout and should be discarded. This bound style does not have a handle, so it can be placed into a briefcase or carried under your arm.

Standard-size cases are available in 8.5 × 11 inches, 11 × 14 inches, and 11 × 17 inches. The most commonly used size for merchandising port-folios is the 8.5 × 11-inch version. This size provides practicality, con-venience when traveling, and fits the size of most documents. Indi-viduals involved in creative segments of the industry such as marketing, promotion, visual merchandising, and product development may find the 11 × 14 or 11 × 17-inch portfolio a better fit for their needs. The larger portfolio size provides more room to lay out related contents in a page spread, which can provide greater visual impact. Small presentation boards can also be accommodated when using the larger portfolio size.

Basic supplies for creating conventional portfolios include the following:

- Layout paper
- Decorative papers such as vellum, transparent, or embossed
- Scissors, markers, pens, pencils
- Plastic ruler with graph grid
- PC or Mac computer
- Scanner and printer
- Software for creating work including Microsoft Word, Excel, PowerPoint, and Publisher; Adobe Illustrator; and Photoshop

Innovative Media

Custom portfolios are developed individually to meet the needs of the merchandiser or industry segment, and the book portfolio is the most common type used in this case. When you prepare the book format, you can print and duplicate the pages to allow for multiple portfolios to be assembled, each providing a slightly different look depending on the job interview. These books are generally 8.5 × 11 inches but can also be effective as small as 5 × 8 inches or as

Figure 3.11 A portfolio project that reflects Target's collaboration with recognized architects to develop product lines for their stores. This project is a mock-up of a store event planned to showcase the new line for the store and communicates that the candidate researched the company before applying for the job.

Contact: Jennifer Matthews
Director of Advertising/ Public Relations
718-XXX-XXXX

For Release: August 7, 2006

MODERN BLISS DEBUT

Brooklyn, New York - Sally Mackereth will appear on August 19, 2006 from 2-4:00 pm at Target to introduce her new intimate apparel collection.

An architect from London, Sally Mackereth, has created a women's contemporary sleepwear line. Mackereth has incorporated her modern and simplistic architectural philosophies into fashion forward loungewear. The target market concentrates on women between the ages of 20 and 35.

For more information please contact Jennifer Matthews at 718-XXX-XXXX.

###

Source: Courtesy of Anna Blackwell, Amanda Bockwoldt, Allison Conrad, Nikki Johnson, Annie Moss, and Amy Porter

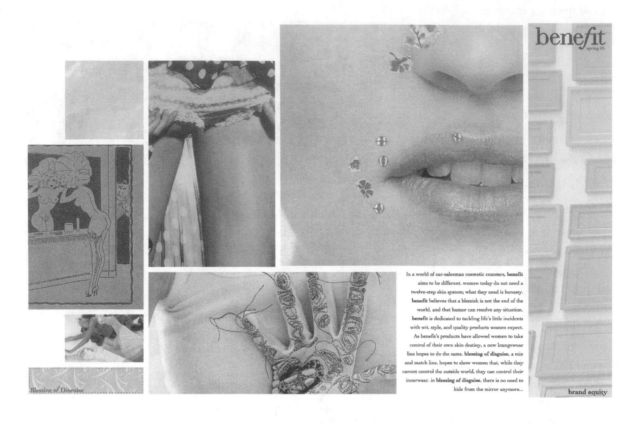

In a world of car-salesman cosmetic counters, **benefit** aims to be different. women today do not need a twelve-step skin system; what they need is honesty. **benefit** believes that a blemish is not the end of the world, and that humor can resolve any situation. **benefit** is dedicated to tackling life's little incidents with wit, style, and quality products women expect. As benefit's products have allowed women to take control of their own skin destiny, a new loungewear line hopes to do the same. **blessing of disguise**, a mix and match line, hopes to show women that, while they cannot control the outside world, they can control their innerwear. in **blessing of disguise**, there is no need to hide from the mirror anymore...

brand equity

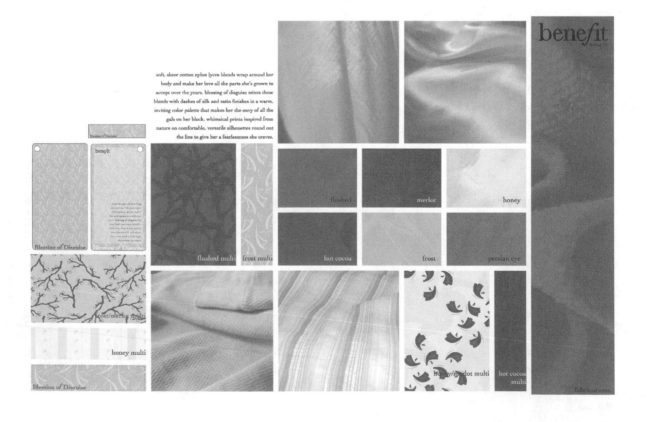

soft, sheer cotton nylon lycra blends wrap around her body and make her love all the parts she's grown to accept over the years. blessing of disguise mixes these blends with dashes of silk and satin finishes in a warm, inviting color palette that makes her the envy of all the gals on her block. whimsical prints inspired from nature on comfortable, versatile silhouettes round out the line to give her a fearlessness she craves.

fabrications

large as 11 × 14 inches. These books must be developed as a cohesive package portfolio and either spiral-bound with wire or plastic or adhesive-bound. A visit to a local copy or office supply store that offers binding services should be helpful to develop a polished presentation. Most cities have bookbinders who will also bind the portfolio in a professional manner. This option allows you to customize a front cover and perhaps a back cover as well. Custom portfolio pages can be computer-generated, scanned into the computer, or color-copied. A custom portfolio allows you to demonstrate packaging, branding, and marketing skills. Carefully and accurately price out each of these options to see how they work with your budget. Individually customized books can be less expensive than most traditional cases but if you begin to produce multiple custom books, it may become expensive.

Basic supplies for creating customized portfolios include the following:

- Matte or glossy print paper
- PC or MAC computer
- Software for creating work including Microsoft Word, Excel, PowerPoint, and Publisher; Adobe Illustrator; and Photoshop
- Scanner and printer
- Presentation and/or drawing software
- Decorative papers such as colored, vellum, transparent, embossed, or foam-core
- Finishing method materials such as lamination or custom sleeves
- Custom case
- Digital camera

Digital Media

Portfolio work that you originally created on the computer is easy to prepare for a digital medium. You will need to scan any other work you

Figure 3.12 This project completed by the student team consisting of Lynn Fry, Joan Markey, Stephanie Otto, and Meredith Smith showcases brand identity and development.

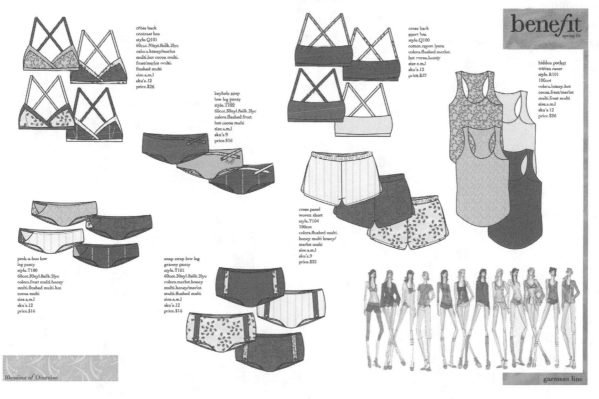

Source: Courtesy of Stephanie Otto, Lynn Fry, Joan Markey, and Meredith Smith

created, however, into a computer program, or you can photograph it with a digital camera and download it onto a computer. It is very simple to burn a CD of the portfolio so you can always have it available to either accompany the paper portfolio or to use as a stand-alone piece. Many industry professionals have strong feelings in favor of or against reviewing portfolio contents on CDs. It is always advisable to check with a prospective employer to see which format they prefer.

When choosing the e-mail attachment option, it is recommended to use PDF formats. The format is fairly universal and most companies have Adobe Acrobat Reader available. You can use page layout programs to directly place your work in sequence so that it reads like a paper portfolio. Be careful that the presentation does not become so large that it is not easily downloadable. The other option is to send the images as individual presentations and custom select images for each attachment. Personal Web sites can accommodate much larger presentations and allow for animation and interaction. These are easily accessible to employers but, as any digital piece, they require the recipient to act in order to view your work, as opposed to you presenting or mailing a conventional or innovative paper portfolio.

Basic supplies for creating digital portfolios include:

- PC or Mac computer

- Software for creating work including Adobe Photoshop; Adobe Illustrator; Macromedia Freehand; Microsoft Word, Excel, PowerPoint, and Publisher; or any other industry-specific application

- Software for presenting work including Microsoft Word, Excel, PowerPoint, and Publisher; Microsoft Front Page; Adobe GoLive; Macromedia Flash; Dreamweaver; or Acrobat Reader.

Activities

Determine which type of portfolio concentration is best for you.

Once you complete Worksheets 3.1 and 3.2, you should know which type of portfolio you plan to create (general or focused). Refer back to Worksheets 2.1 to 2.3 for a compilation of skills that you will need to emphasize for your particular job search. Gather and begin preliminary organization of work samples for the portfolio based on the concentration selected (general or focused) that communicate necessary skills and qualifications.

Determine if you will utilize a traditional, custom, and/or digital portfolio. Acquire the supplies necessary for you to develop your portfolio.

Chapter 4

Organization
and Contents

The essence of a portfolio is its content. This content is a collection of visual material that represents your **qualifications** and presents your capabilities, knowledge, and skills to a potential employer. The manner in which you organize and present your portfolio content is equally important. Organization demonstrates your understanding of the competencies and skills necessary for a given position. Organization also demonstrates your knowledge of the industry and the process of bringing a product to market. The presentation of each page showcases all that you have learned and what you can offer to a particular job opening. The collection of work needs to flow harmoniously and visually represent you, even when you are not present. The work should be organized in a way that is self-explanatory and tells the viewer who you are; the portfolio should demonstrate on its own your thought and work processes. It is essential to include pertinent top-quality work that either stands alone or is part of a development sequence. Identify the work with a brief explanation that informs the reader why the piece was developed.

At the close of an interview, it is not uncommon for you to have to leave the portfolio behind for others to review. Since others may not have the benefit of speaking with you, the portfolio must speak for itself. The development of an individual market-ing piece (IMP) can also be used as a leave-behind portfolio image that remains with the company or can be mailed to assist in obtaining an interview. The Individual Marketing Piece, or IMP as it is referred to in this book, is your compact brand identity presentation. The IMP can be in print or digital form and needs to convey your individual brand essence.

Organization of the Portfolio

Organization is one of the most critical steps in the development of a portfolio and depends primarily on its intended use. If you are a recent graduate applying for entry-level positions in the industry, then your portfolio may be either general or focused, depending on the range or type of work you select to present and the requirements of the positions for which you are applying. If you anticipate a job change within the fashion industry or apply for a promotion within the company at which you work, then your portfolio needs to be focused. If you seek to change fields within the fashion industry, then your portfolio should highlight the new knowledge you have obtained and present evidence of success. It is crucial that you research the qualifications and skills necessary for the desired position so you can demonstrate that you possess the appropriate competencies for the job.

Some companies may not require that merchandising applicants submit portfolios; however, it is becoming much more common for candidates to present evidence of their knowledge and skill base to a potential employer with portfolios. Positions within the fashion industry are highly competitive, so it is in your best interest to present as much evidence as possible to prove you are the best candidate for the position. If you are proactive in your presentation, you will have a better chance of obtaining the position.

Applying for a job demands that you market yourself to a given company, and any marketing effort needs to have a plan. A merchandising portfolio is a fantastic marketing strategy that conveys what you know about the industry in general, as well as the specific company to which you are applying. Once you have researched the company, you should demonstrate this knowledge in your work. The portfolio is a way for you to articulate your understanding of the needs of the position, communicate that you possess the skills necessary to be successful, and prove that you will be an asset to the company.

A merchandising portfolio is also beneficial to students who are applying for internships, co-op positions, or part-time job opportunities in the fashion industry while they are still in school. Industry experience is a major asset to all students because it helps them apply theoretical knowledge to professional practice and assists in determining post-graduation interests. Potential employers consider work experience extremely beneficial because it

exhibits initiative, interest, and the skill development necessary for success in your chosen field. The experience of working at a company provides a clear understanding of positions in the industry as well as a realistic picture of the job requirements. Most positions in the fashion industry require individuals to work long hours and effectively multitask at all times. Due to the extensive number of seasons in fashion, it is not uncommon to be working on two seasons at the same time and have products at various stages in the development process. Although you might have a limited amount of work to show, a portfolio visually conveys what skills you do have and how well you are able to apply them.

You should always include your best work in your portfolio and make sure it is branded so it communicates your identity. The portfolio should contain a minimum of 7 pieces and no more than 20 pieces of work; however, quality is always more important than quantity. A general portfolio is often best for people who are still in school or recently graduated, but a focused portfolio is ideal if the job target is clear and there is sufficient work to develop one. A wider scope of work is necessary for the development of a general portfolio. For example, if the job target or objective is visual merchandising or marketing, a general portfolio would show a body of work that encompasses all facets of the field. You might include trend reports, a conceptual board communicating mood, prototype merchandise, and final plans for either the marketing of the goods or planograms for displaying the merchandise in a store.

A focused portfolio is slightly more complicated to develop and should concentrate on one or more skills specific to a job target or objective. When developing a focused portfolio, you will want to narrow the scope of the portfolio and show depth in each piece. For example, if you have selected visual merchandising as the target, you need to show skill and understanding in more detail than in the general portfolio. Trend reports and conceptualization can still be included but you might also include work that communicates understanding of the elements of design and specifics of styling. You can show photographs of mannequins you have styled, displays you have created, and development process work you prepared for the display. Previous school or industry work can be re-created or modified for inclusion in a focused portfolio.

Using an overall layout plan will facilitate the organization of both the focused and the general portfolio. The merchandising portfolio model offers development steps and guidelines for any type of portfolio developed. It is a model that organizes the portfolio in a logical manner.

Model Format

The merchandising portfolio model was developed specifically to help organize the contents of portfolios directed toward the merchandising, marketing, and **product development** segments of the fashion industry. No single formula is perfect for everyone, but this model offers a general guide to organize the flow of the portfolio and provides endless opportunity for personalization through work and style. Refer back to Figure 2.1 to see the merchandising portfolio model.

The introduction page is an opportunity to tell the viewer who you are and establish a style or brand for the portfolio. It is essential to immediately establish the look of your brand and continue it throughout the portfolio.

The job target and/or job objective page is the first real step in organizing the portfolio. This page states the industry position you are targeting and outlines the required skill set for this position. This page is extremely important and helps to establish the work content that will be included in the bulk of the portfolio. If desired, you can use two pages: one for job target and one for job objective. A job target is specific and can be described on the target page; it could be focused on a specific job opportunity or it could be a generic target that might fit a number of companies. For examples of available positions in the industry and the qualifications necessary for each, check out job postings at specific Web sites (Table 4.1). Conduct research to include other possible jobs that interest you and fit your qualifications.

A job objective is more self-directed since you address the specific criteria required by a particular position. The job objective states skills you would like to learn in a position, responsibilities you wish to assume, and advancement opportunities to which you aspire. The portfolio should provide a clear presentation of the skills and capabilities you can offer a company. The organization of the portfolio also demonstrates communication skills and problem-solving abilities. Table 4.2 highlights examples of job objectives that are applicable, but not exclusive, to the industry.

Table 4.1 Job Targets & Required Skill Sets

Job Target	Industry Job Description	Required Skill Set
Assistant buyer	Assist in the planning, procurement, and evaluation of consumer goods for a specific target market	Retail costing Profit analysis Trend analysis Negotiation skills Planning skills
Assistant product manager	Assist in the development, purchase, evaluation, and performance of a brand-driven, private label product line	Visual concept Color trends Fabric trends Design Flat sketching Merchandising
Planning and distribution	Develop, execute, and communicate strategic financial plans to support merchandising, sales, and marketing goals for profit	Analytical Financial Planning Problem-solving
Visual merchandiser	Create and implement brand-driven visual sets Provide visual and written communication to stores Display key trends	Trend analysis Visual communication Brand equity

Table 4.2 Job Objectives and Required Skill Sets

Industry Field	Job Objective	Suggested Skill Set
Retail buying/merchandising	Opportunity in retail buying and merchandising. Responsibilities include planning, procurement, and promotion	Six-month plans Math skills Market analysis Product purchasing
Retail product development	Seeking a creative/technical position on a branded product development team for a department or specialty store	Creative designs Technical flats and specifications Fabric, color, styling skills
Brand development and marketing	Career opportunity in corporate marketing department focusing on brand identity and development	Graphic, layout skills Target marketing Planning/strategies
Store management	To obtain a position focused on retail sales management	Floor merchandising Staff plan/train Sales planning Communication skills
Textile industry	Career opportunity in the area of textiles	Woven, knit, print fabric development Fabric styling Line merchandising

Organization of Skills Evidence

When you complete the job target and/or job objective page, you will need to determine the required skill set for the position. This skill set is derived directly from the target or objective and is determined by both the job listing posted by the company and by researching the skills necessary for the position. Research similar positions on the Internet, read company literature, and refer to industry reference material. Tables 4.1 and 4.2 offer examples of how skill sets are derived from a job target or job objective. Although you may not specifically list the job description with the job target, by developing the skill set in your mind, you will better communicate your understanding of the needs of the position.

A close examination of job target qualifications reveals that employers view cognitive skills to be as important as manual skills. **Manual skills** are easy to demonstrate since it requires that you complete a task and exhibit it in the portfolio. **Cognitive skills** are more challenging to demonstrate. The best way to demonstrate industry knowledge, problem-solving, and communication skills are through portfolio layout and flow. Process understanding is vital to success due to the complexity of the business and the multifaceted nature of job positions. Many positions in the fashion industry require teamwork to bring a product to market. It is essential to demonstrate an understanding of the responsibilities of others on the team, as well as of the position for which you are applying.

You might consider showcasing manual skills such as demonstrating retail math concepts, apparel assembly, garment quality analysis, specification detailing, and a working knowledge of computer programs. You need to demonstrate a command of word processing programs, spreadsheet programs, and industry-specific product packaging or textile development software. Skills might also include graphic and presentation programs that are utilized for trend boards, conceptual images, and presentations. Single portfolio pieces can demonstrate multiple skills. For example, a Microsoft Excel sheet containing an example of a retail merchandise buy, including cost prices, retail prices, and markup achieved will showcase both the knowledge of retail math skills and the mastery of spreadsheet development. This might also be a good opportunity to include a trend sheet that shows examples of the type of merchandise detailed in a mock purchase order or on a merchandising spreadsheet. Doing research on a merchandise buy showcases trend forecasting skills, graphic layout skills, and knowledge of graphic and presentation software. Figure 4.1 shows an example of a trend forecasting project done in Adobe Photoshop. The project is entitled Catwalk and is inspired by seasonal apparel runway collections and adapts these styling, fabric, and print trends to the home goods market, particularly in bedding. The fabrics selected for the two beds shown in Figure 4.1 were designed on Lectra U4ia software from runway print designs.

The merchandising portfolio model indicates three possible sources for evidence of skills: academic, self-directed, and industry. When seeking an internship, a co-op, or a part-time position, most of your work will be from school projects or even competitions into which you entered. When applying for an entry-level position, your work could be from any or all

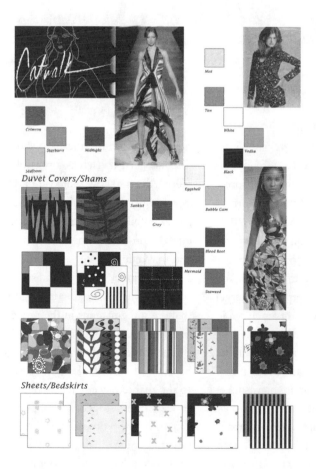

Figure 4.1 Adria Dawood's portfolio shows a trend forecasting presentation from the Catwalk to the home furnishings market, and product and fabric design inspired by the fashion runway.

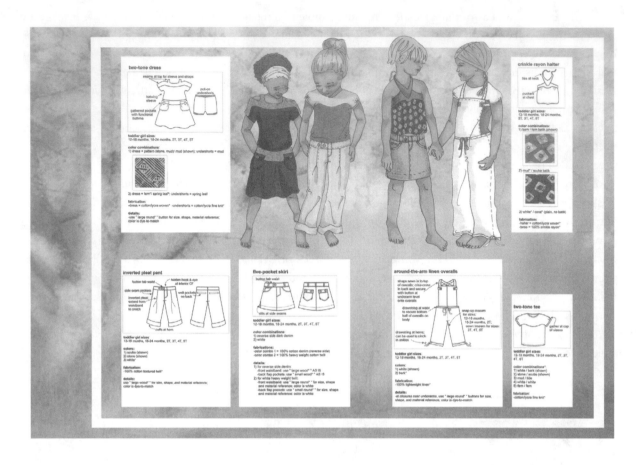

Figure 4.2 Jennifer Dusold's self-directed project is specifically designed for Gap, Inc.

of these areas. If you are currently employed in the industry and are seeking to switch fields or to advance, it is essential to show industry or self-directed work for the majority of the portfolio. Most company executives want to see work you have actually done in the industry, especially if it relates to their needs. Self-directed work may be either freelance work or individual projects you have developed to showcase skills. Ann McAtee, executive recruiter for Gap, Inc., believes it is essential to see self-directed work when reviewing candidates for positions with the company. She wants to see if candidates understand the target customers of each

of their brands. Figure 4.2 shows a project specifically done for Gap, Inc. Self-directed work shows companies that you understand their customers and brand identities (McAttee, 200).

Sometimes you can't show work that you completed for a company or school project in your portfolio. You must therefore reinterpret and target the project for the company in which you are interested. For example, perhaps you created a promotional piece for a branded company in the past, either as a school or an internship project. You might revisit the project and direct it toward a new company or a nonprofit organization. Figure 4.3 shows an example of a promo-

tional invitation for a fashion show that has been chosen as a **portfolio piece**. Always show that you understand not only the artifact (finished piece) but also how it is integrated into the process of merchandising and marketing.

The majority of merchandising students will be working in positions that are integral steps in the process of bringing a product to the consumer. Table 4.3 shows the process necessary to bring a fashion product to the marketplace. Each step in the process offers students an opportunity to develop process work and integrate it into their portfolios. **Process work** is the developmental

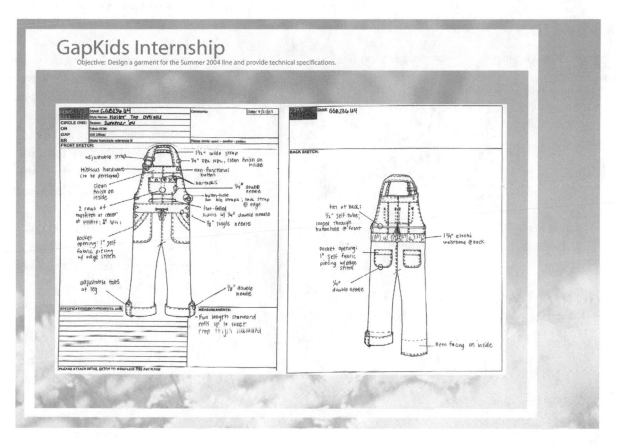

Source: Courtesy of Jennifer Dusad

work that begins when an opportunity is determined in the marketplace and ends when a final line has been developed. Strengths, weaknesses, opportunities, and threats to success are identified and evaluated in what has become known as a SWOT analysis. Individuals conduct pertinent research to aid the development of the line by members of the product team. **Brainstorming** takes place, which helps to produce possibilities or **ideations** for a solution. Brainstorming is the sharing of research, discussion of findings, and free exchange of ideas and implications without commitment to eventual solution. Ideations and multiple possible solutions for development result from this brainstorming.

Source: Courtesy of Catherine Gaddy, Erin Massey, Carrie Roesler, Elizabeth Stinson, Ashley Tondu, and Kirby Young

Figure 4.3 This invitation was designed as a project for class.

Table 4.3 Product Development Process

Product Development Process	Industry Examples
1. Determining opportunity	New merchandising fashion forecast
	Seasonal highs and lows
	Product, market, and territory expansion analysis
	SWOT analysis
	Online extension to brick/mortar
2. Research the opportunity	Previous year's sales, bestsellers
	Trend reports, fabric reports
	Target market profile
	Socioeconomic trends
	Fashion/product trends
	Store layouts, fixtures, locations
3. Concept development	Brainstorming activities
	Trend boards, research reports
	Mood, image inspiration boards
	Target market profiles
	Brand equity and identity reports
4. Ideation	Brainstorming activities
	Line plans, buying plans
	Merchandise buys, marketing plans
	Logo development, display options
5. Development	Technical sketches/specifications
	Patternmaking, product assembly
	Marketing plans, visual plans
	Labeling, packaging, promotion
	Press releases, product launch

These can be documented in either visual or text form and outlined to show the process.

Members of the product team then develop a conceptual direction for the product or product line—always visual and often text driven as well—and come up with ideas about how to bring this product to market in the ideation step. Ideations can be physical drawings, prototypes, or proposals on how to best develop an opportunity. All are then evaluated and a course of action is determined. The development stage is the fruition of all the elements involved in the process.

It is important to organize individual portfolio pieces in the evidence section of the portfolio to show your understanding of how the merchandising process works. This communicates your cognitive skills to an employer. Figure 4.4 illustrates an entire project that followed the process. The conceptual images, target market images, and forecasting information led to a final color, fabric, and trim board proposed for the project. This format could easily be revised for any company or season prior to portfolio presentation. Figure 4.5 shows a portfolio page that highlights key research findings and develops analysis important to consider in product planning.

Selection of Contents/Evidence

You should select the final contents for your portfolio after careful analysis. After determining the position you desire and the skills that it requires, you must produce evidence that shows you can succeed in the position and grow with a company. The content pieces must showcase your skills in the best possible light. Include the strongest and most detailed piece you have for a specific skill. It is not necessary and is undesirable to include earlier work that you are not as proud of just to show how you have grown in ability. This is a common error made by new graduates. You don't have to include all the work you've done; the employer needs to see only the skills relevant to the position he or she is trying to fill.

Layout of the content must show your understanding of the process. Remember that the industry professional thinks in terms of the process. Let's examine the way Barbara

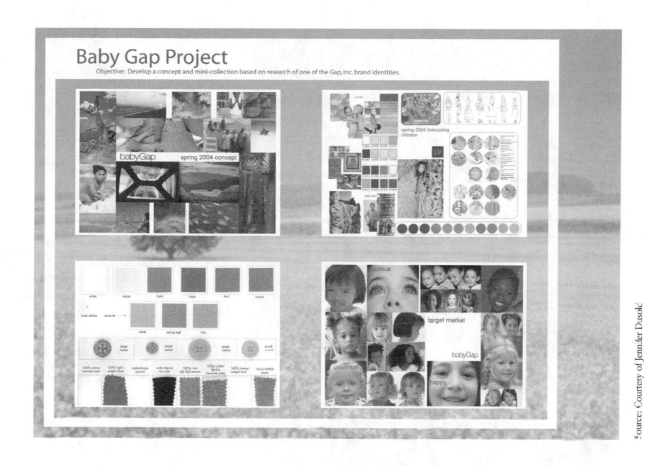

Figure 4.4 Jennifer Dusold completed her entire project for Gap, Inc. and included it in her portfolio to show both skill and process understanding.

Cibulka, Wal-Mart's planning director for women's apparel, describes her job: "We work with buyers who give us the merchandise orders and then we break them down so each store has a representative portion of the order" (Cibulka, 2005).

This planning director needs an assistant. If you structure the portfolio to resemble the process she just described—merchandise buy, store analysis and breakdown, and final store layout—then it proves to this executive that you understand how the process works. It is essential to plan the skills/evidence section to either mirror the process or show

selected groupings of work. Choose two to three pieces that best illustrate your understanding of the integration of process steps.

The selection and layout of the portfolio pieces are extremely important. Worksheet 4.1 will aid in this process, but you must first understand how the job target, skill section, and portfolio pieces relate to one another. For example, if the job target is assistant buyer, then see Table 4.4 for possible examples of work you might include in your portfolio. Now you must sequence the work to direct the flow of the portfolio.

Integrating Evidence of Skills

The merchandising portfolio must work as a collective unit and provide clear examples in a logical order. The pieces you choose to include need to revolve around a central job target/objective and the skills required by this position. *Always open with your strongest piece of work* since this highlights your best strength within the skill set. First, you impress the viewers and encourage them to keep reviewing the portfolio; second, you never know if you will get interrupted during the interview or if the person reviewing your portfolio will get called away. Therefore, make a

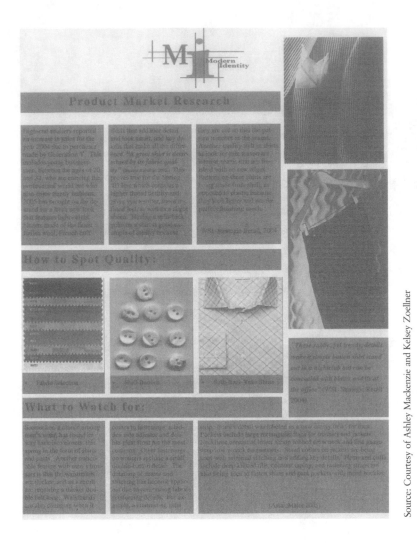

Source: Courtesy of Ashley Mackenzie and Kelsey Zoellner

Figure 4.5 Research analysis can be very text driven, but this page is nicely laid out to include visuals with the information.

Portfolio Plan

Page one: Introduction Page

Page two: Job Target Page

Page three: Market and Trend Research

Page four: Target Market Research

Page five: Color Trend Board

Page six: Ideations

Page seven: Ideation sketches

Page eight: Final line

Figure 4.6 Portfolio plan to assist in portfolio layout.

strong impression and leave an image of who you are—your brand identity—in their minds. The next strongest piece you have completed needs to be the last portfolio page in the evidence of skills section. This allows you to end on a strong note. It also impresses readers who begin to review a portfolio by going to the last page and flipping back to the first. These two pieces of work book-end the portfolio, and process work fits neatly in the body of the book. Figure 4.6 shows a portfolio plan that maps out how it will be assembled. This portfolio plan is for an assistant buyer position and has a job target and skill set similar to that detailed in Table 4.1. Figure 4.7 shows how that plan translates into a sample portfolio.

Items that Appear in Portfolios

You should consider including all work that you have generated through classroom assignments, student projects, contest entries, internships, co-ops, and work experience in your portfolio. Only the best of this work eventually appears in your final portfolio, but you can consider revising some pieces to include at a later date. The majority of the work for an entry-level portfolio will come from classroom projects unless there is considerable work experience. Academic assignments are geared toward skill development and offer targeted projects directed toward the industry. You should consider including these projects because of their content to show process understanding and skill development. You will need to revise much of the work you collect to incorporate brand identity and focus. Evaluate

Table 4.4 Portfolio Plan

Portfolio Order	Portfolio Piece Description
Portfolio piece #1	Socioeconomic visual image
Portfolio piece #2	Research report on socioeconomic trends
Portfolio piece #3	Profit and loss statement for a store department
Portfolio piece #4	Seasonal line plan for fall season
Portfolio piece #5	Merchandising plan for early fall buy
Portfolio piece #6	Specification sheet for merchandise buy
Portfolio piece #7	Clip collage from runway shows
Portfolio piece #8	Marketing plan for fall season
Portfolio piece #9	Brand identity and equity research report
Portfolio piece #10	Brand identity/marketing visual/promotion board
Portfolio piece #11	Target market visual board
Portfolio piece #12	Apparel trend styling board

and edit freelance or self-directed projects so you can include them whenever necessary. Don't forget to consider work that you completed on a volunteer basis—for example, if you assisted with a trunk show, planned a fashion show, or developed a flyer for a special school or community event.

Professionals currently in the industry and preparing to switch fields within the fashion industry may have portfolios that need to be updated with current work. They must include the most recent industry work and review past work closely to ensure that it is still relevant. The brand identity needs to be clear, so they may need to update some portfolio pages. Last, they should take care that the brand image is unified between older portfolio pieces and their most recent work.

Creating the Brand Identity for the Portfolio

Brands rule the marketplace. The stronger the brand image, the more successful the product. Brand identity is critical to differentiating one product from another in the consumer's mind. Each successful brand needs a clear consumer base, lifestyle, market position, and strategy. You are no different. You are your own brand. You are competing with other graduates and industry professionals for a job, the same way products compete with one another so consumers purchase them. You must therefore present work that is uniquely your style, even if the components can be found in another person's portfolio. Your branded portfolio should convey style and format and a brand image is that specific to you and your talents, creativity, and aesthetic.

Creating a brand identity is an essential component of organizing your portfolio and will help you to connect with the right company.

Integrating Brand Identity into Your Portfolio Type

Deciding whether you will put together a general or focused merchandising portfolio is the beginning of your brand choice. When selecting a general format, the brand should reflect a universal appeal. Choose one quality that is present in all of your work and incorporate this into your brand image. For example, there may be a formal, precise, and angular appearance to your work— very clean and minimalist. This should be reflected in your branding elements. A focused portfolio requires a more detailed brand. You must convey a brand image that is consistent with the job target and/or objective you selected, the companies at which you apply for work, and the body of work you have chosen to include.

For example, if you desire to work in the childrenswear industry, this identity could be playful and fun. If you are seeking a position that is focused toward a financial or analytical career, you could establish a businesslike persona through page design and text. You need to incorporate whatever brand identity you select throughout your portfolio and accompanying application materials such as the cover letter and IMP.

Developing a Brand Identity for the Introduction and Divider Pages

The introduction page is the first impression that a prospective employer has of your work. A good

Figure 4.7 *This plan is the one Emily Hensler followed for her portfolio project.*

Source: Courtesy of Aarti Vasudevan

Figure 4.8 This is an example of the introduction page that Aarti Vasudevan developed for her portfolio.

first impression is as essential in a portfolio as it is at an interview. The introductory page needs to establish your brand—your name—and make a connection to the type of work you seek. The page could be text and graphic elements alone or it could present a visual, verbal, or conceptual image. If you are strong at sketching, you might show an original sketch. If you have developed an exciting fabric pattern or color image, you might want to incorporate it into your brand. Figure 4.8 shows a sample introduction page.

Divider pages are the only other pages that have just text messages on them; they should reflect your branded concept or identity but may show a condensed or abbreviated version of the introduction page. It is very important that the image of your name remain consistent throughout the entire portfolio, although it is not necessary that your name appear on every page. Figures 4.9 and 4.10 show examples of graphic signatures that appear on both introduction and divider pages to reinforce identity. Your style and focused image need to be consistent on every page. Your portfolio should be presented as one cohesive project, although individual pieces of work may have been completed under the direction of various mentors or company brands. The text, color, layout, graphic element, and presentation of the introduction page establish a brand image that needs to be consistent with who you are, what your work represents, and what you envisage your future to be in the industry.

Maintaining Brand Identity on Evidence/Documentation of Skills Pages

Once you establish the visual identity on the introduction page by using color, logo, graphic, text, and layout, you need to consistently apply the format throughout the skills and divider pages. Your choice of branding elements is dictated by your brand, whether it is obvious or subtle. The purpose is to connect you to your work and leave a memorable impression with the prospective employer.

Figure 4.9 Aarti Vasudevan uses these portfolio pages to establish continuity throughout her portfolio.

Figure 4.10 Divider pages reinforce brand identity in Aarti Vasudevan's portfolio.

Individual Marketing Piece (IMP)

The Individual Marketing Piece, or IMP, is a dynamic branding piece that will help you in many ways. You can send the IMP as a teaser of your portfolio, along with your resume and cover letter, to entice a potential employer to interview you. You can also use the IMP as a leave-behind marketing tool that serves as a reminder of you and your work. The IMP needs to reflect the essence of who you are as a brand. Your strength might be developing strong marketing and promotional plans for a company. If this is the case, your IMP should be showcased as a promotional piece. If your strength is design and illustration, you should exhibit a compact image of your work. The best way to develop the IMP is to take a page from your portfolio that you believe is either your strongest piece or the essence of your work skills. This could be the front or back of your IMP. The other side should contain your name, contact information, and any information you might like to leave behind. Think of the IMP as a visual business card that identifies you, your skill strength, and how to reach you in the future.

Printed

The printed IMP can be any size or shape but it should be large enough to be noticed and significantly smaller than a portfolio. The layout needs to be clean and uncluttered and to include significant brand identity elements. The printed IMP could be as simple as a business card or postcard or as extensive as a foldout brochure or small mini-portfolio that

Source: Courtesy of Julie Weiner

Figure 4.11 Julie Weiner created a beautiful senior thesis collection that also makes a wonderful CD cover that entices potential employers to review the portfolio CD.

Source: Courtesy of Elyse Perez

Elyse Perez
elyse xxx@internet.com
telephone: 555-555-5555

Figure 4.12 Elyse Perez created this two-sided IMP postcard to leave behind after interviews.

reproduces actual pages from your portfolio.

A printed business card should contain your name, your contact information, and brand identity elements. Be sure to include your mailing and e-mail addresses. You might want to include your home and mobile phone numbers. Remember, by including this you encourage employers to call you. Make sure your voice mail has a professional recorded message. You may use the IMP to help designate your preferred method of contact by only listing your mobile phone and e-mail address. The brand identity elements might be only text or graphic elements, such as a line or symbol, but it could also be a small reproduction of an image in your portfolio. You could also design something for the IMP that you did not include in your portfolio. For example, you might use a piece of work you liked but that did not work into the flow of the portfolio. Figure 4.11 shows

Checklist for Evaluating the Content of Portfolios

List the job target and/or job objective you are considering for your portfolio.

Job Target/Objective

_____

_____

_____

Assemble all of the work that you see as potential portfolio pieces.

Do not be concerned with the order of the pieces because that will be determined later. Print a checklist for each of your portfolio pieces.

Describe each piece for future reference in the Activities section of this chapter.

Portfolio Piece

_____

_____

○ Yes   ○ No   Is the portfolio piece applicable to the job target/objective?

○ Yes   ○ No   Is the portfolio piece ready for presentation?

○ Yes   ○ No   Is the portfolio piece the correct size for the portfolio?

○ Yes   ○ No   Does the portfolio piece need revising for presentation?

○ Yes   ○ No   Does the portfolio piece need revising for content?

○ Yes   ○ No   Was the portfolio piece created in a digital format?

○ Yes   ○ No   If yes, is the work saved?

○ Yes   ○ No   If no, do you want to re-create the piece digitally?

○ Yes   ○ No   Does the portfolio piece show evidence of skills applicable to the job target/objective?

○ Yes   ○ No   Does the portfolio piece show evidence of your knowledge of the process?

○ Yes   ○ No   Would you consider using this piece as the first portfolio piece?

○ Yes   ○ No   Would you consider using this piece as the last portfolio piece?

○ Yes   ○ No   Is this piece part of a sequence showing work process?

○ Yes   ○ No   Is this portfolio piece a stand-alone piece?

○ Yes   ○ No   Does the piece include an explanation of the project?

the front and back of an individual marketing piece that is the size of a CD cover. The IMP can be printed back-to-back as a stand-alone piece or can double as a cover and back for a jewel case that would include a CD of additional work or possibly an entire portfolio. Figure 4.12 shows an IMP that illustrates the student's layout ability and knowledge of CAD and reminds an employer of her business travel line of apparel and accessories. Her contact information is on the reverse side.

Digital

Many of the images contained in a portfolio are developed on the computer. This makes it easy for you to compile a digital IMP and offers the option of leaving a CD of your portfolio along with a printed piece behind for a prospective employer to review.

The most important feature of a digital IMP is its readability. For an employer to review the work either before or after an interview, or to share the work with others, you must make it easy to open and navigate. All of the images should be in a presentation format that all computers would be likely to have. This can include a PDF form for Adobe Acrobat Reader or a PowerPoint presentation format.

Remember that the IMP does not replace your portfolio; it is an extension of your portfolio. Consider developing either a digital or printed IMP that complements your portfolio format.

Activities

The checklists you completed for evaluating the content of portfolios are necessary for the completion of the following activities. There should be a checklist for each portfolio piece you are considering for your portfolio plan.

1. Complete Worksheet 4.1 based on a job target/objective you selected. You may complete multiple worksheets if you are considering multiple job targets/objectives. List each individual skill that is necessary for each position. List the skills in the left column and applicable pieces of work that demonstrate competency in each skill. You may have multiple portfolio pieces for a skill, so you may list a skill more than once.

2. Complete Worksheet 4.2 to develop a portfolio plan. This plan will determine which pieces you will include in your finished portfolio and the order in which you will place them.

Chapter 5

Presentation Formats and Layout

Portfolio presentation is made up of three component parts: encasement, content layout, and page design. Although you develop each part independently from the others, each is inseparable from the whole.

The encasement, or what you put the portfolio in, is discussed in Chapter 3. The size, shape, and material of the case reflect professional style and preference and are the first branding statements you make with the portfolio. The style, color, and material of the portfolio must complement the interior page design and layouts. Brand image begins with the case and is reinforced throughout the contents of the portfolio. The orientation of the portfolio case dictates the appearance and format of the interior pages. If the case is designed to be viewed vertically, then it has a **portrait orientation,** meaning the page height is greater than the page width. If the case is designed to be viewed horizontally, then it has a **landscape orientation,** meaning the page width is greater than the page height. See Figures 5.1 and 5.2 for examples of landscape

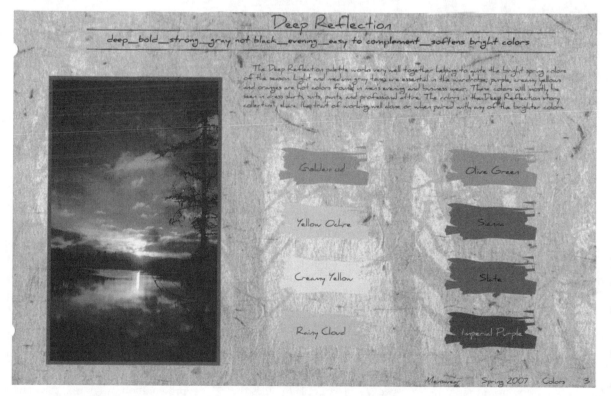

Figure 5.1 Jacqueline Saile chose a landscape layout for her Deep Reflection color trend story.

background blue

swirly bottle

champagne gold

table top

Figure 5.2 Cory Fites chose a portrait layout and dramatic lines to showcase his color trend work.

and flow of the portfolio content tell the story of your work.

The third element of presentation involves the format and layout of each individual piece of work that you are presenting. Each work or artifact is designed to demonstrate skill and knowledge, but each piece must relate to the total and be unified with the layout style. The graphic presentation of every page of the portfolio must connect to the previous page; this total presentation is your brand identity. Remember that every page does not need to look exactly the same. Establishing a brand identity simply means that the pages must have commonality in presentation style, layout grid, text, and content quality. This is achieved through a consistent format and layout that is adapted for the content of each page. This results in a visual impression of you as a brand. The layout design of each page needs to be aesthetically pleasing and functional. The choice of landscape or portrait orientation will dictate the page dimensions but an individual work may have a different orientation and still be included on the page without any revision beyond resizing. The pages may vary in style but need to follow a consistent pattern or **grid** design. The grid is formed by horizontal and vertical intersecting lines on a **page layout**. The grid is used for aligning and layout of all elements on the page—the images, text, and white or negative space. The grid is easy to determine if you do it on a computer (just add grid lines by going to View and selecting Show Grid in your presentation program). You can choose a color for the grid lines, usually a contrasting one so the lines are

and portrait orientation. It is important to decide which orientation best showcases your work.

The second element of presentation is portfolio content. The manner in which you assemble the portfolio

content communicates process knowledge, skill, and competency strengths as well as your individual style. The layout plan guides the viewer through the pages of the portfolio to the resume. Both the layout

obvious, and you should specify how far apart you want the lines to be. The most interesting grids vary the line spacing for emphasis and flow on a page. After you lay out the grid, you can add text and graphics and import images into grid sections. Make sure you lay out all the pages in your portfolio after careful consideration of basic design principles. This includes developing page balance (symmetric or asymmetric presentation), pleasing proportion and scale, and a strong use of color. The composition of each page should be balanced and exhibit depth of line, shapes, and texture. Figure 5.3 exhibits three pages laid out for a portfolio presentation. The first image shows the basic grid pattern before any images have been imported. It will contain images and text that describe and highlight suiting as a trend. The second image

suiting

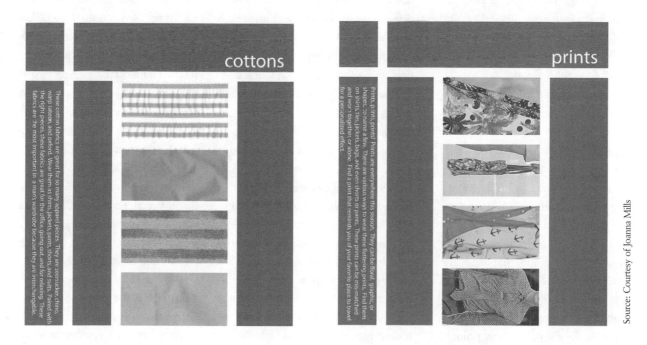

cottons

These cotton fabrics are great for so many apparel pieces. They are seersucker, chino, warp sateen, and oxford. Wear them as shirts, jackets, pants, shorts, and suits. Paired with the right pieces, these fabrics are great for the office, going out, and for relaxing. These fabrics are the most important in a man's wardrobe because they are interchangeable.

prints

Prints, prints, prints! Prints are everywhere this season. They can be floral, graphic or shapes, to name a few. There are various ways to wear these flattering prints. Find them on shirts, ties, jackets, bags, and even shorts or pants. These prints can be mis-matched and worn together or alone. Find a print that reminds you of your favorite place to travel for a personalized effect.

Source: Courtesy of Joanna Mills

Figure 5.3 The grid can be adaptable for many portfolio pages yet still offer continuity for portfolio presentation.

shows a fabric trend page highlighting cotton fabrics for the season. The third page shows the grid that has a print trend page. Once you lay out the grid, you import the images onto the pages so that layout remains consistent throughout the presentation.

Design Elements and Principles for Page Design

The design and layout of each page in a portfolio are critical. Every page is an opportunity to showcase work and exhibit knowledge of design elements and principles. By definition, the **elements of design** are the component parts that combine to make up the whole, known as the design. Elements of design include **point, line, shape, color,** and **texture** and are combined based on **design principles** to develop a cohesive and aesthetically pleasing page design.

A principle is a fundamental truth, doctrine, or assumption underlying a work. Design principles include balance and symmetry, proportion and scale, and context and placement.

Point, Line, and Shape

A point or simple mark on a blank page begins a design. If solitary, it simply marks an orientation to the page and is often referred to as the focal point. The focal point is placed on a page to direct eye movement toward that point. When there are two points, they form a visual line that directs eye movement on the page. Multiple points that are either similar in color, shape, or weight will determine and direct how eyes move around the page.

Figure 5.4 illustrates how points direct eye movement across a portfolio page. Horizontal lines form a

platform or floor on which the models find firm footing, giving the illustration a natural realism that pleases our expectations. Models are positioned as if they are coming toward us, and viewers find this simulated depth of field engaging and natural. In each panel, the patterned pant stands out among a wardrobe of solids.

The eye naturally scans from top to bottom and left to right, and the movement tracks along a diagonal, much like a Z, throughout the page. A contrasting line is often utilized as a point or points to direct the eye and move it around a page. The eyes seek a meaning or relationship for the line and make connections while following a logical course, which is what it means when we say that people *read* an image.

A line has direction and is created by connecting a series of points. It moves the eye from one point on a page to another, creating a visual path. The line directs eye movement, defines space, and encloses images. A line can be straight or curved. Straight lines convey strength, definition, and a sense of order. Curved lines are less regimented and more engaging—conveying softness and calm and sometimes whimsy. The thickness or weight of the line also conveys meaning. A wide line strengthens the emotion or feeling. Furthermore, the direction that a line takes also conveys emotion. A line can be horizontal, vertical, or diagonal. Horizontal lines imply tranquility and rest while vertical lines convey strength and power. Diagonal lines suggest movement and direction; however, they are not as stable as vertical or horizontal lines because they do not align with the grid. A

line can also be implied through the strategic placement of a series of points on the page that draw a visual connection and encourage the eyes to move from one image to another. Lines contribute to the quality and overall feeling of a layout and should be engaging to evoke emotion and reinforce brand identity.

When branding yourself as an analytical merchandiser who has strong mathematics and planning skills, use strong, bold, straight lines on the page. When branding yourself as a creative merchandiser who has strong product development or promotional skills, use curved lines on the page. Figure 5.5 shows a CAD divider page strengthened by the use of straight lines. This project is for a young men's fabric line. Figure 5.6 shows a U4ia divider page that frames the feminine curves of a woman in a triplet that gives us the sense of a photo album from a magazine shoot. The illustrations showcase originality, computer skills, and a fashion-forward sensibility. The project consists of fabrics for the women's market.

Shape is the result of closed lines: an element defined by its outline. The three basic shapes are the circle, rectangle (square), and triangle. Lines create two-dimensional or flat shapes. When shapes are three-dimensional, they are called forms. A drawing is a flat shape and a garment is a form. Space is defined by shapes and forms. **Positive space** is where shapes and forms exist; **negative space** is the space around the shapes and forms. Negative space is often referred to as **white space,** even if the page is not white. White space is a powerful tool in the design of a

Figure 5.4 John Kelly utilizes color and lines to guide the eye throughout the page.

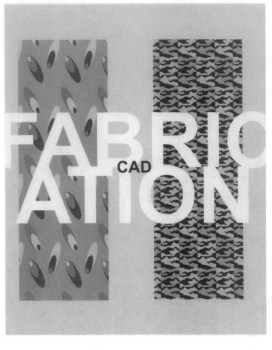

Figure 5.5 This CAD portfolio divider page utilizes bold lines and sturdy columns for a masculine impression.

Figure 5.6 This U4ia portfolio divider page showcases fabrics developed for a women's ready-to-wear line.

page, giving the eye relief from images or text.

The portfolio divider page in Figure 5.6 makes excellent use of negative space to direct the eye to the important text on the page, as well as to the images. Geometric lines contrast with feminine curves. There is an architectural feel and strength to the shape of these marketing elements.

Color and Texture

Color is created from light rays moving in a straight path from a light source. Within the light rays are all the rays of color in the spectrum. When the light rays hit an object, our eyes respond to the light as it is bounced back and we see that color.

When we refer to color, we refer to hue, value, and intensity. The name of each color is its hue—red, blue, yellow; the value is how light or dark the color is; and the intensity is how bright or dull it is. Colors are often used in schemes to create design and page impact. These schemes are based on the color wheel. The combination of colors on a page can convey harmony, discordance, coolness, or warmth. See how color moves your eye through in color plate 2.

Texture is the surface quality of an object. Words such as rough, smooth, pebbly, and sleek are used to describe surfaces. The texture of an image gives it dimension and authenticity. The yarns that go into fabrics have inherent qualities and

textures from the fibers that form them. These yarns can be made of wool, cotton, silk, or synthetic fabrics. The yarns are then woven or knit into fabrics. The resulting fabric has a texture as well, or many textures depending on knots and stitching. Digital renderings of fabrics give them surface terrain and depths that make them appear realistic. Figure 5.7 shows the textures of actual fabrics that were scanned. Figure 5.8 shows fabric textures developed through digital rendering. The textural quality of the image was developed through the use of U4ia software. Texture can also refer to the material from which something is created and could have tactile as well as visual texture. Textured paper is

Figure 5.7 Megan Ault developed a strong fabric storyboard by scanning actual fabrics.

sometimes utilized in a portfolio for a specific branding element. This engages the senses more and leaves a lasting impression. Note the use of texture and pattern in the color plate 4 story board.

Balance and Rhythm

Balance is the arrangement of one or more elements in a design or on a page so that they visually equal one another. Balance depends on the distribution of visual interest on a page. Different objects, sizes, colors, shapes, and fonts create different degrees of interest. Balance is usually desirable in page design but there are instances when an unbalanced page is preferable. The tools for achieving balance are symmetry and asymmetry. When items are symmetrically balanced, they are mirror images of each other, and when they are asymmetrically balanced, they are uneven or disproportionate. **Symmetrical balance** is achieved by placing equal visual weight on either side of a visible or invisible line or axis. The weight is the important element and is achieved by equally balancing proportions of size, shape, color, and positioning. Symmetrical balance is also referred to as formal balance and gives the feeling of permanence, stability, and order. Formal balance can also be achieved by arranging elements equally around a central point, like the center of a flower and its petals. This is called radial balance.

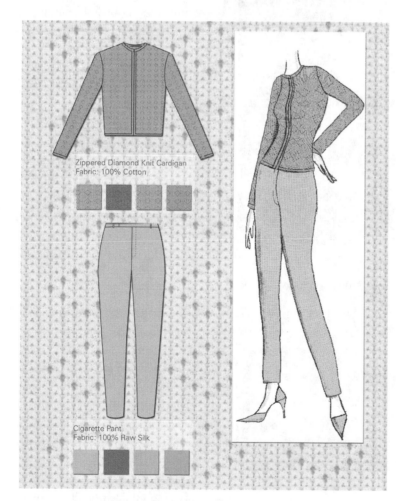

Figure 5.8 John Kelly developed fabric textures for garments digitally using Lectra's U4ia software.

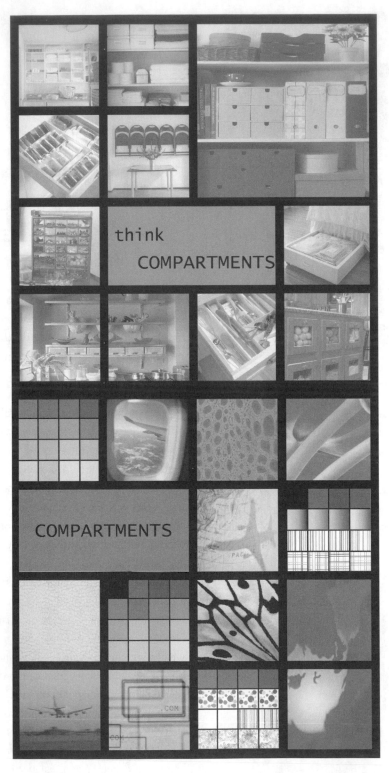

Symmetrical balance occurs from left to right on a page and from top to bottom. The left and right sides of a page are equally balanced around an invisible center. Top to bottom balance, however, requires a visible or invisible horizontal line that is usually not centered on the page. Most pages appear more stable if the bottom seems slightly heavier than the top, so images may be visually heavier at the bottoms of pages. Figure 5.9 shows an example of symmetrical page balance. Notice the axis that runs horizontally across the middle of the page, dividing it in half. Sometimes this axis is invisible, but the weight on either side is always balanced. This image has the weight perfectly balanced top to bottom and side to side, which embodies and articulates the concept of a sturdy system of compartmentalization. It also suggests the job candidate is highly organized and can multitask.

Asymmetrical, or informal, balance is much more difficult to achieve but is generally more appealing to the eye. Component parts of an asymmetrical image are not balanced around a visible axis but allow for objects of varying visual weight to lay out a pattern surrounding an invisible line or point. This creates a page design that is often more visually interesting and kinetic and that moves the eye from the heavier image to the lighter one. Examples of **asymmetrical balance** are found in Figure 5.10a and b. The first example is weighted at the top left and drops down the diagonal to the right. If placed on the left-hand side of an open portfolio spread, this creates a pleasing angle toward the center. There is also a quirky off-balance, but

Source: Courtesy of Kyle Koerner

Figure 5.9 Kyle Koerner shows symmetrical balance in this page for her Compartments project.

centered, horizontal line across the page; the product line anchors the bottom of the collage, and the top half of the page speaks for the product line's edgy modern style and philosophy. This layout is both intellectually stimulating and pleasing to the eye.

The second example in Figure 5.10 shows a slight visual axis down the center of the page that divides the weight of the dissimilar box sizes. Although the color blocks on the right and the images on the left are of different weights, they are graphically equal and the eye finds balance.

Rhythm is created when the eye moves across the page in a pattern. It is a visual tempo and the beat is created by the placement of visual elements. The rhythm controls the pace of visual awareness and should alert the viewer when key elements demand additional examination. The rhythm creates a dynamic interest in the page and the elements contained within the page design.

There are several types of visual rhythm. A **regular rhythm** uses repetition and creates a predictable pattern. An **alternating rhythm** is more complex and employs the use of many visual elements to alternate and vary the pattern design. **Progressive rhythm** builds or decreases in size, shape, color, or intensity. Rhythm utilizes many elements of design and is a powerful graphic tool.

Look at the example of varying rhythms in a portfolio layout shown in Figure 5.11. These are pages from a luggage line that was developed to ease the hectic pace of business travel by offering organized and compartmentalized luggage. The first page is the concept board that shows a

Figure 5.10a
Josie Graham creates an interesting page using an asymmetrical layout for her graphically driven image for Smack cosmetics. This line was her final academic capstone project and shows her logo image.

Figure 5.10b Meredith Smith combines multiple board images for one strong portfolio page. The left side of the page is heavier than the right, but the collage ties together her work and personality.

strong repetitive rhythm. The next page shows the customer with the finished line. The job applicant has shown a complete understanding of the product line development process, from concept to execution. This board is visually busy, using multiple images to create the illusion of moving figures that subsequently direct the eye around the page. The grid is loose and some images are significantly larger than others, which varies the pace. Rhythm is created in many ways on a page but it always creates a feel and vision that is unique to that page.

Proportion and Scale

Proportion is established by the balanced relationships of visual parts to the whole. It is the relationship between sizes, shapes, **space**, quantities, and color. It is essential in a page layout to consider the right size for each object, text, and visual space *and* to determine how those elements relate to one another. The viewer's eye will first look at any element on the page that is out of proportion to the rest of the elements. Objects are considered in proportion or out of proportion to the whole and to one another. It is this relationship of one element with the other that directs the eye and conveys the visual message. On a page, specific text is often larger than the rest and the viewer's eye will gravitate to this text first. Proportion is used for emphasis and relies on the viewer's sense of scale.

Scale is defined as the size of the object and its relationship to other objects on the same page. The scale of objects on a page relates to the total image of the page and relate to

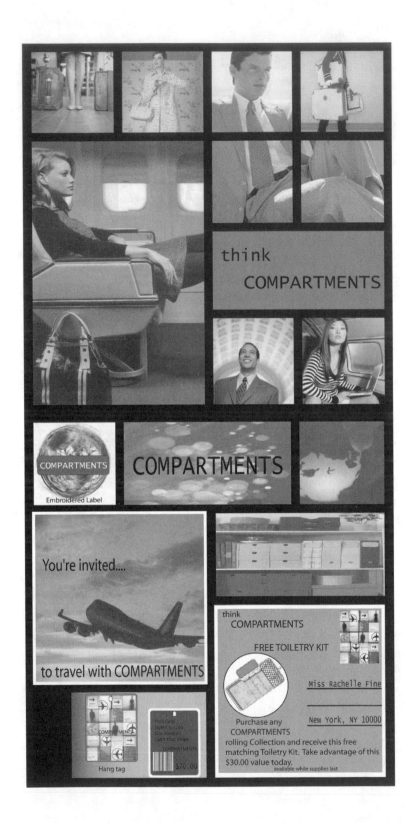

Figure 5.11 Pages from Kyle Koerner's Compartments project show many different page rhythms. This portfolio shows an understanding of the product line development process, from concept to execution.

Source: Courtesy of Kyle Koerner

mine size scale appropriateness for an object. If the scale is deemed incorrect, the object is considered out of proportion. This creative tool directs the eyes and can produce a focal point or emphasize a point on a page.

Figure 5.12 shows a series of pages in a portfolio presentation. The pages are a self-directed campaign for a new seasonal line for Diesel. The creator of the campaign wanted to draw visual attention and used scale and proportion in an effective way to attract that attention and communicate freshness. The first page shows a close shot of a face that is out of scale with the page and with the text on the page. The oversize eyes of the model become the focus of a face that has already drawn our attention because of its size. The second page shows the same face, this time with images that further identify the target customer. These are more in proportion to the page scale but not in proportion to the scale of the face.

The third page pulls the face of the target market from an earlier thumbnail and represents it in a larger scale on the page than the viewer would expect. The styles are superimposed on the face, and the viewer becomes intimately engaged with the ideas for garments that are displayed. The final image, a fabric page, utilizes scale in the form of text. The text is set all lowercase but larger than would be expected. It functions as signage to announce the product. The background fabric is maximized on the page so details show. Finally, the square fabric swatches are a standard size and shape, so the contrast of scale and proportion continues to engage the viewer.

individual visual elements. Manipulation of scale by the page designer creates dynamics that work to add emphasis and rhythm to a page. Humans use their own bodies and elements of nature to visually deter-

Placement, Pattern, and Unity

Visuals, text, and white space must be carefully laid out on a page. A repeat pattern can be created as a guideline for the eye and for emphasis of objects on the page. The way you place patterns of repeated objects, whether you increase or decrease the size of objects, and the final pattern you create connect one portion of the page to another to form a unified design. **Unity** is achieved when all visual elements contribute to an aesthetically pleasing whole. This is the first assessment or test the viewer gives the page before examining the individual parts of the whole. The colors, shapes, and sizes need to belong together yet engage other principles to direct the reader toward the desired interpretation of the page. Symmetrical images offer a strong sense of unity on a page but unity can be achieved through the use of all of the design elements and principles.

Many companies use logos or taglines in their advertising as part of their strategy to build brand recognition. These logos and taglines remain consistent in content and placement on printed materials, television ads, and Web sites. The pattern or shape is often subtly repeated throughout the pages, which creates unity to the advertising page. Target is a perfect example. The store chain consistently uses the bull's-eye in all their marketing. Figure 5.13 illustrates the use of pattern and placement in a portfolio that was directed toward Target stores. The candidates in a group project understand that glamour can be affordable. This would be a good presentation for the visual merchan-

Figure 5.12 Jamie Pentak's project for Diesel haunts us with its images. The scale of the background, in proportion to the foreground, gives the presentation great depth and human interest.

dising applicant, as it communicates the ability to take available building blocks and organize them in an appealing way.

Factors to Consider When Selecting Page Layout

Once you have decided on the encasement of the portfolio and its

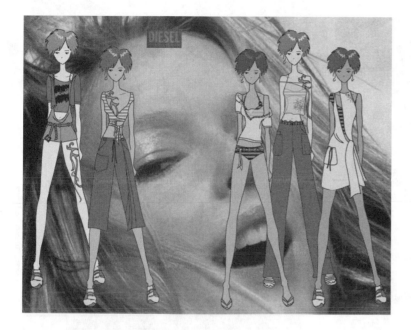

Source: Courtesy of Jamie Pentak

images that lets people know you can "think outside the box."

Page design is the organization of visual and written material and negative or white space. This involves sizing images and placing them on the page in an organized and planned format. You will also incorporate appropriate text and brand identification. The page should be balanced and formatted and have a rhythm that moves the eye through the page and engages the viewer in its content. Most graphic design guidelines recommend an even balance of page elements for portfolio presentation. This is referred to as the **rule of thirds**—a third of the page is text, a third of the page is visual or graphic content, and a third of the page is dedicated to negative or white space. This may involve some reformatting of projects to ensure there is a consistent brand image throughout the portfolio. A portfolio should showcase a variety of work; however, the presentation of individual components should complement the whole by providing continuity and cohesiveness.

Page layout begins by designing a grid or underlying structure for a page. This is much like plotting on graph paper. The grid provides a pattern that allows for the organization of images and written material. A branded image, graphic, or text should be designed and placed on every page, or every right-hand page of the portfolio. A portfolio is read like a book, so the bottom or top of each right page is an excellent place to include the branding image. You may choose not to vary the placement of the brand image so that it appears in the same location on every page, which gives you the

general format and style, you can design the individual pages. The presentation of each page showcases the work that you have decided to include in the portfolio and demonstrates your process and industry knowledge. Each page needs to be laid out in a

format that is aesthetically pleasing and informative to a potential employer. A tailored garment distributor will look for a classic and balanced portfolio. An innovative electronics merchandiser might prefer a memorably disproportionate grouping of

Source: Courtesy of Chinae Alexander, Whitney Holder, Amy Jackson, Stephanie Layne, Bethany Lewright, and Lauren Whalen

Figure 5.13 Pattern placement is evident in this group project done for Target.

flexibility of reorganizing the portfolio without having to rework the pages. You need to consider the overall presentation of the portfolio when determining page layout so you can adapt it to each individual page design.

When planning page layouts for individual portfolio pieces, you will need to consider three factors: the position of the piece in relation to the overall portfolio plan, the overall grid pattern (format) and brand image for the portfolio, and the content of each portfolio piece.

Position of Page in the Portfolio Plan

You will need to complete Worksheet 4.2 before beginning page layout. This will determine the order of the portfolio pieces and help in planning the page layout. When you are ready

to lay out the portfolio pages, you need to select either facing or double-sided pages. Always avoid a layout that contains single-page presentations that face a blank portfolio page. A combination of facing and double-sided pages can also be used to change the tempo of the portfolio layout. For example, the introductory page and the divider pages will usually be stand-alone pages and will utilize a two-page spread (facing pages). Evidence or examples of work pages can be facing pages to add variety and also portray process work and creative problem solving. If the pages are facing, they need to complement each other. For example, Figure 5.14 shows two pages of trend research accented with images that personify the concepts being addressed. These

candidates master the delivery of information in an engaging spread that captures and holds the attention—which is important when one needs to present a lot of text. The student chose images of coins to symbolize the economy, and mounted these research boards for the effect of a visual aid that might accompany a talk at a conference or a presentation at a meeting. This portfolio is professional and academic, so it has a broad range of possibilities.

Worksheet 5.1 will assist in planning the flow of your portfolio and how each spread might be laid out. Using the examples you have seen, choose the layout that expresses who you are while doing justice to the concepts, products, or research you have worked on developing.

The introductory page is extremely important and may be as simple as a branding statement that sets the tone for the portfolio. This page could also include conceptual images that help direct page development throughout the entire portfolio. The introductory page showcases design principles and provides color, text, and page layout formatting that will be reflected in all the other pages. Divider pages, if utilized, should echo the format of the introductory page to provide continuity.

The **portfolio plan** should organize the strongest evidence or samples of work at the beginning and at the end. This may be work that has visual evidence to accompany written text. The page should be strategically laid out so the visual image catches the eye and guides it to the written content on the page. In a situation where a visual image was not included as part of the project or work, consider adding one to create page interest. The final pages of the evidence of work section should be a strong double-page spread that is clearly directed toward the job position or objective you have chosen. It is essential to create a flow for the portfolio that leads to this final statement. Because you are showcasing individual strengths and skills throughout the portfolio, the last evidence presentation needs to show integration.

Overall Grid Pattern

The purpose of page presentation is to communicate your work and thought process. A grid provides the framework for designing portfolio pages to best showcase your work and allow the portfolio to appear cohesive. Grids provide structure and help to organize images, text, and negative or white space. All of the pages do not have to be identically laid out because the grid allows for selection in the placement of design elements while maintaining balance and continuity. Grid components are made up of margins, content area, and branding identity. Margins are generally considered to be the outside border of the page; however,

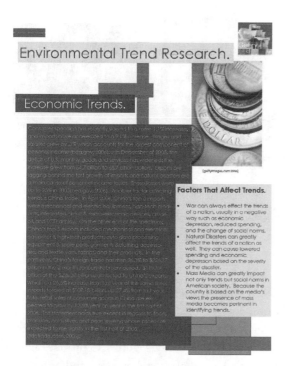

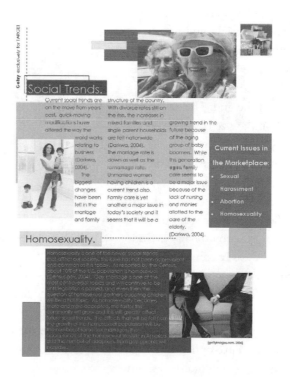

Source: Courtesy of Chinae Alexander, Whitney Holder, Amy Jackson, Stephanie Layne, Bethany Lewright, and Lauren Whalen

Figure 5.14 A team project, based on the work of Frank Gehry, shows key image placement. The team included members Chinae Alexander, Whitney Holder, Amy Jackson, Stephanie Layne, Bethany Lewright, and Lauren Whalen.

margin spacing can also be planned between grid lines or components. The outside margin acts as a frame for the internal content, just as a matte works to enclose fine artwork. Be mindful of the size of the outside margins in relation to the inside margins that might contain a fold or binding. When the portfolio pages are bound directly into the presentation, you must consider the space needed for binding. For example, measure the side margins of a bound book and notice that the margin that is bound is wider than the unbound margin. This is so the page appears evenly balanced to the eye. Typically a quarter to a half inch of the right margin is reserved for binding use. A portfolio can also be bound at the top.

The content area is divided into columns and rows and can be set at any width or height but must be consistent from page to page. Page design can be created by using an individual grid section or multiple sections of the grid. The design will depend on the size of the image, text box, and negative or white space. When you create the portfolio entirely on a computer, it is important that you set up a grid for all of the pages before you place images and text on the page. Grid patterns are easily constructed with presentation computer software such as PageMaker or Microsoft Office Publisher. When using word processing software, you can form the grid by using the Table option or using the Drawing option to establish grid lines. When you use the grid from the Drawing option of the program, the lines are visible while you place text and images, but they do not

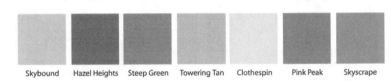

Figure 5.15 Brittany Krotts shows many different grids in her forecasting pages yet they all work together in an inclusive book.

print on the final copy. When you manually format page layout, you must cover the grid lines with page content or erase them after you complete the layout. You can also use tracing paper with grid lines to help guide you with the image and text placement. *The grid is used only as a guideline for content placement*

and should not be visible on the finished page.

Evaluate each page for content and clarity. Figure 5.15 provides samples of several different grid options to use in developing a portfolio page. In this portfolio, white space actually acts as a frame around the different images. You can incorporate a diverse

t a l l
fabric
Patterned Wool

Patterned, lightweight wool is a nice touch to the tall man's outfit. A patterned jacket places attention on the upper half of the body, which is another lengthening illusion. Plaids are especially important in the upcoming season and are seen in a variety of fabrications, from jackets to shorts. Herringbone, houndstooth, and, of course, stripes are also integral players in this fabric story. The key is to keep these fabrics as lightweight as possible for comfort and elegance.

h a n d s o m e
style trend
Profound Piping

Clean, bold lines are key style elements for the upcoming season, and a fine attention to detail makes for very becoming garments. These lines and details are major components to handsome clothing. A way in which these components are apparent is through the use of bold, interesting piping, whether it be to emphasize the rounded edges of a jacket or to accentuate the cuffs of a sleeve. This profound piping is especially strong for Spring 2007 in contrasting colors or decorative embroidery.

Source: Courtesy of Brittany Krotts

array of work and branding styles into the flow and still have consistent page design and layout based on a grid system. The grid helps to achieve continuity and makes for aesthetically pleasing pages.

Content Layout for Individual Portfolio Pieces

The content of each page contains four elements—visual images, written text, negative or white space, and brand identity. Each component of the page plays a critical role in the overall aesthetic appearance and identity of the portfolio.

Visual Images

Images used in a portfolio must be clear, clean, and balanced in relation to both text and spatial arrangement. If the images are not centered on the layout, then they should be weighted toward the outside edges of the page. Figure 5.16 shows different examples of page balance with portrait (vertical) orientation. For landscape (horizontal) orientation, you should weight the images slightly heavier at the bottom of the page for balance. Scanned images should be crisp and clean, and original drawings need to be easy to interpret. Depending on the job position or objective you select, you may or may not have visual images to showcase. In the latter case, you may wish to add related visuals to a page of written text to create interest and impact. For example, if you are including a buying plan or a merchandising spreadsheet, enhance the page with imported images of stores or representative merchandise that you have obtained permission to use. Always make sure to credit the sources that you have used for images. Citations should appear below the images or at the bottoms of the portfolio pages. In a situation where you actually helped merchandise a retail floor for work or a school project or created a mockup of a store display in class, photograph the merchandise and include it in the page layout. When you do not have the opportunity to include images, colorful lines or graphic shapes can also be used to enhance portfolio pages. Utilize these elements with care and make sure they complement both the written work and your brand identity.

Written Text

Written text is also placed within the page layout grid and may fill one or more grid spaces or be placed along grid lines. The typeface you use becomes part of the composition and needs to integrate with the other elements on the page. Typefaces can be divided into two main categories—**serif** and **sans serif**. Serif type has letter strokes that end in cross strokes or accents, such as Times New Roman or Garamond. These are best used for lengthy text boxes because the typeface leads the eye across the page and provides ease when reading. Sans serif fonts do not contain cross strokes and are more dynamic and stand alone. Sans serif typefaces, such as Arial or Century Gothic, are best used for one word statements, headings, or headlines. Text style can also be formatted to create greater impact by using bold, italic, underline, or even capitalized or lowercase letters (Figure 5.17). The casual font expresses the style of an upcoming menswear line. The font you choose can say much about the fashions and merchandise that are on display. The styles should be complementary. Remember, fonts should remain consistent throughout the portfolio. Although you can use more than one font, it is suggested to limit typeface, style, size, and line weight to no more than two formats. Use of a wide variety of any of these elements can break continuity and project a less than professional image.

Written text should include a title or headline of the page and captions to describe the work being viewed. This rule holds true whether the content is visual or written. The work is treated separately from the written text. In the example of the merchandising buy, you should include captions to let the viewer know that the visual merchandising shown is an example of the merchandise allocated in the plan. The text needs to work

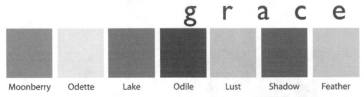

grace

| Moonberry | Odette | Lake | Odile | Lust | Shadow | Feather |

A major theme for Autumn/Winter of 2006/2007 is Grace, inspired by the beauty of Swan Lake. With soft, sheer fabrics, a cool color palette, and an emphasis on whimsical ornamentation and movement, the allure of the swan can be adorned in all its glory. Indulge and become Odette for the day in a feathered top with a floor-sweeping skirt, and dance to the music of Tchaikovsky.

poise
style trends
Emphasis on Waist

The waist is an integral part of the ballet dancer and is also a key component in this coming season's Poise-inspired trends. Over the past couple seasons, the waistline has increasingly risen and has reached a beautiful point at the very center of the waist. Emphasis on the waist combines the silhouettes of ballet dancers and Audrey Hepburn. Whether accentuated with sashes, belts, buckles, or bowes, the waist is the center of attention in all articles of clothing for Autumn/Winter 2006/2007.

SAMBA TIME

This versatile jacket and 2-n-1 lightweight pant are perfect for Katie as she travels. She will be able to stay comfortable while on the cool plane, and then immediately transform into cool comfort on arrival in Manaus.

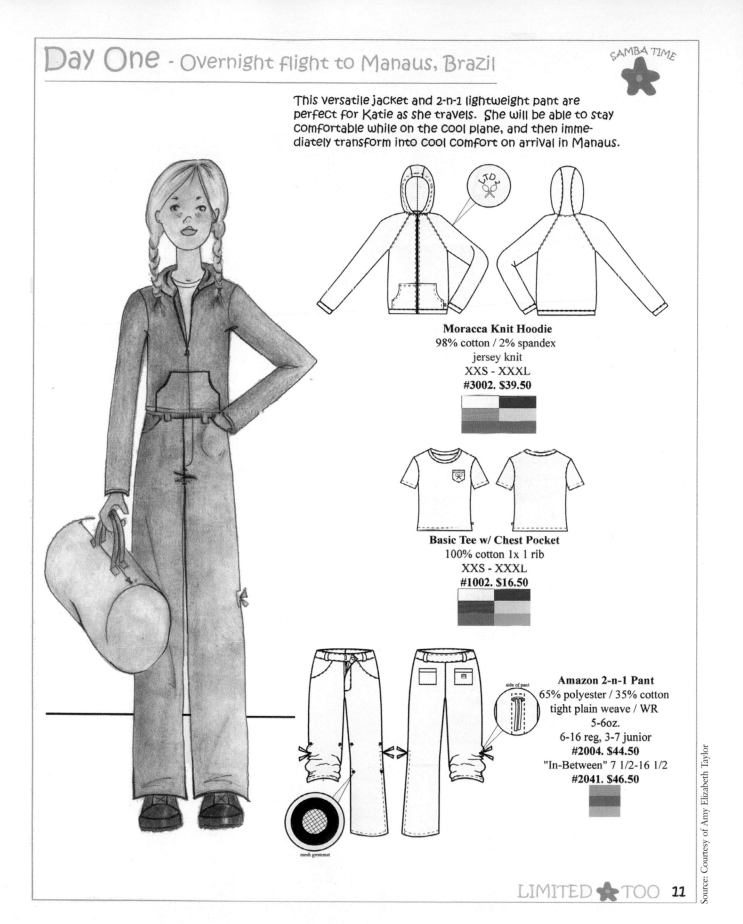

Moracca Knit Hoodie
98% cotton / 2% spandex
jersey knit
XXS - XXXL
#3002. $39.50

Basic Tee w/ Chest Pocket
100% cotton 1x 1 rib
XXS - XXXL
#1002. $16.50

Amazon 2-n-1 Pant
65% polyester / 35% cotton
tight plain weave / WR
5-6oz.
6-16 reg, 3-7 junior
#2004. $44.50
"In-Between" 7 1/2-16 1/2
#2041. $46.50

side of pant

mesh grommet

LIMITED ✹ TOO 11

Color Plate 1 This self-directed project for Limited Too not only demonstrates illustrating and flat sketching skills but shows merchandising and layout proficiency as well. The page is part of a team project in which a group of students developed a line of merchandise for a fictional weeklong visit to Brazil.

DENIMBAR

DenimBar is a clothing store that contains two lines—Blueprints and DenimBar.

Concept board showing inspiration for the lines. Ideas draw from colors and shapes of today's architecture and home fashions.

Media:
Illustrator
Photoshop

denimBAR

Color Plate 2 Jennifer Daggy's layout incorporates her visual image for a new store, Denimbar, with her CFDA/Target award-winning collection, Blueprints. Note the layout consistency, media identification, as well as conceptual and merchandising skills on the facing pages of her portfolio.

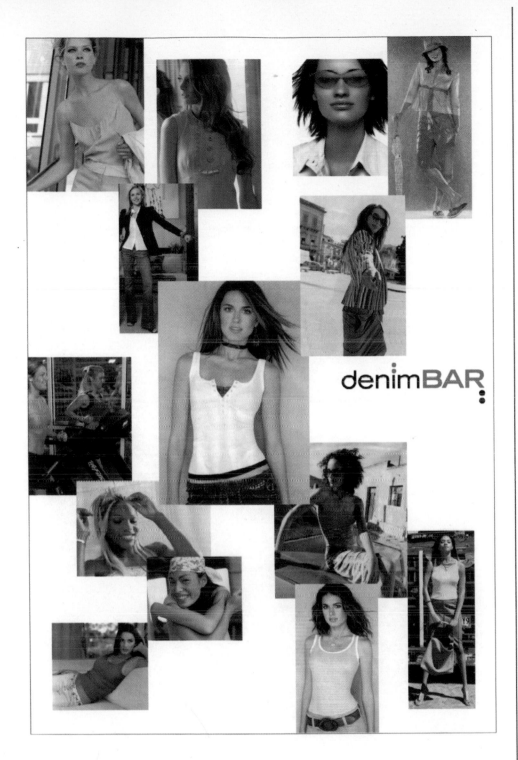

denim**BAR**

DenimBar target market board, targeting busy, self-discovering young women between the ages of 21-30.

Media:
Photoshop
Illustrator

Source: Courtesy of Jennifer Daggy

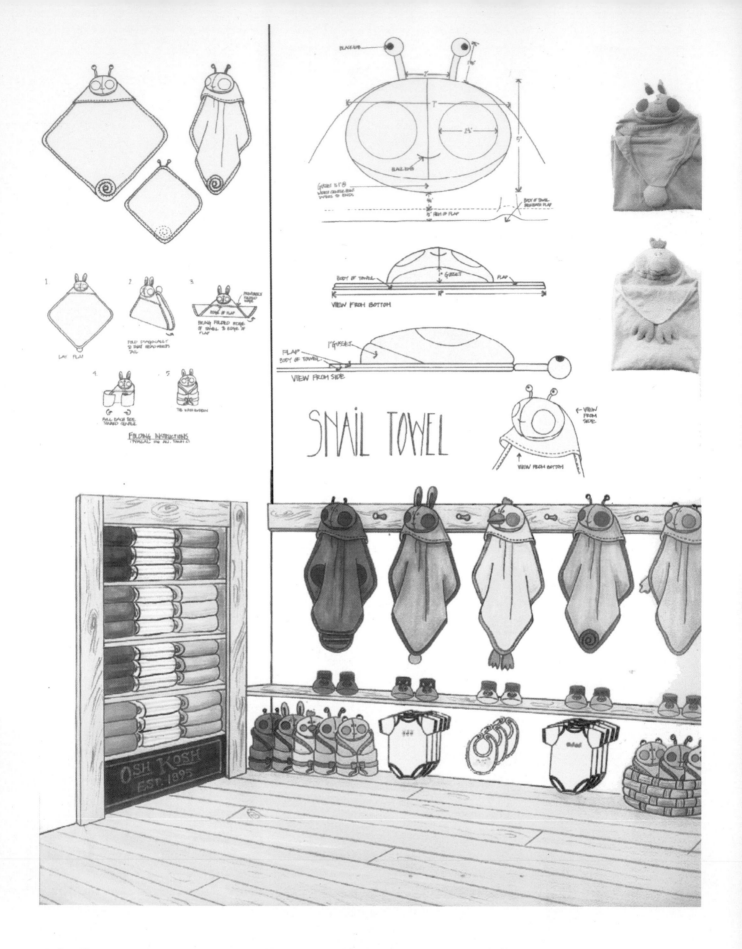

Color Plate 3 Industry work is the focus of these two pages from Nancy Friedman's portfolio. The lay-out of the project pages demonstrates her expertise in store layout and merchandising, apparel design and merchandising, and drawing and computer illustration, as well as her experience working in the industry.

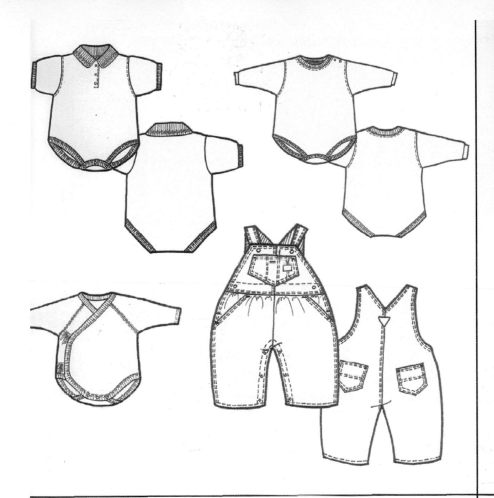

OSHKOSH®
EST. 1895

As a co-operative education student, I worked for Oshkosh B'Gosh Design Studio for two quarters. Some of my responsibilities included illustrations and flat sketches for the infant and newborn clothing lines.

During my first quarter of work, I designed a series of hooded towels as part of the Oshkosh Happy Baby newborn line. These towels were produced to complement the Spring 2004 line of clothing.

work experience

January-March 2003
June- September 2003
January-March 2005

Color Plate 4 *The basis for the work on these two pages was a team product development project for Nordstrom. The presentation shows an understanding of the product development process, from target market identification and selection of trend and line concept direction to illustrated flat sketches of the line and retail price points. Text-driven documents can be exciting when page layout and color application are carefully planned. A strong color story creates impact and ties the presentation together.*

Market Analysis II

JUSTIFICATION FOR LINE

The purpose of developing Rennie Mac was to create a European inspired line of children's sportswear for girls ages 3-8. The inspiration came from the art nouveau architect, Charles Rennie Mackintosh. We have closed the gap between toddlers and adolescents clothing by creating an adaptable line which offers a variety of coordinating separates that permit children to dress themselves with ease. Rennie Mac provides quality clothing with prices at the better range and will be sold exclusively in Nordstrom stores and online.

The line will be introduced in Spring 2007. The unique style, pattern, and colors of the garments will appeal to the target customer because they are looking for just that, something unique. Rennie Mac will be a profitable option for Nordstrom because the clothing line is different from any other competitors' style. This particular line of clothing has been developed to fill a void in children's wear. Each garment was constructed with full intention to establish an adaptable piece that will allow children to create a fun and fashionable style on their own.

Rennie Mac is positioned in Nordstrom because this allows for all target customers to be reached. Nordstrom's carries a wide range of products targeting similar customers.

DESCRIPTION OF LINE

The overall goal for this label is to provide unique and quality children's clothing at reasonable prices. This was achieved by using fun fabrics, colors and styles that will appeal to the wearer and the buyer. Our line will range in price from $12.50 for a tank top to $32.50 for a sundress. These prices are relative to the spring 2007 line. When developing lines for other seasons prices will change based on fabrication and labor, but will stay relatively close to the current price point. Rennie Mac will be known for the creation of cute, comfortable fashions for girls ages 3-8. In creating the line we took into consideration what a child might name the colors of their clothing. For spring 2007 the basic colors will be peanut butter, olive juice, sunshine, sky, jelly, rose bud, and rosey cheeks. As stated, comfort was a major factor in the development of the line. One hundred percent cotton fabrics were chosen for the line and range from broadcloth to cotton knit jersey

The line will consist of two skirts, one dress, one pant, one short, one sweater, and five tops. The first skirt, the puff skirt, is 100% cotton broadcloth in a floral print with the colors peanut butter and olive juice, retailing for $28.50. The drawstring skirt is 100% cotton broadcloth in olive juice and retails for $26.50. The sundress is 100% cotton broadcloth and is patterned with colorful polka dots in all colors of the palette and retails for $32.50. The pants are made from 100% cotton bottom weight twill and are offered in peanut butter; they retail for $32.50. The shorts are 100% cotton bottom weight twill in jelly and retail for $26.50. The sweater is 100% cotton knit jersey in sunshine and retails for $26.50. The peasant top is 100% cotton batiste, offered in both rosebud and peanut butter and retails for $24.50. The polka dot top is 100% cotton broadcloth and retails for $24.50. The cap sleeve tee is 100% cotton jersey in sky, jelly, and sunshine, and retails for $14.50. The ruched tank is 100% cotton broadcloth and is offered in rosey cheeks, sky, olive juice, and sunshine. It retails for $14.50. The jersey knit tank is 100% cotton and is offered in jelly. It retails for $12.50.

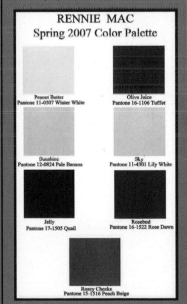

RENNIE MAC
Spring 2007 Color Palette

Peanut Butter Pantone 11-0507 Winter White	**Olive Juice** Pantone 16-1106 Tuffet
Sunshine Pantone 12-0824 Pale Banana	**Sky** Pantone 11-4301 Lily White
Jelly Pantone 17-1505 Quail	**Rosebud** Pantone 16-1522 Rose Dawn
Rosey Cheeks Pantone 15-1516 Peach Beige	

Source: Courtesy of Catherine Gaddy, Erin Massey, Carrie Roesler, Elizabeth Stinson, Ashley Tondu, and Kirby Young

IDENTIFICATION

Name: Concrete Jungle
Born: May 2006
Citizenship: United States
Marital Status: Style and Performance
Occupation: Multi-functional Jackets
Hair: Fabric Technology
Eyes: Forward Styling
Retail Cost: $220 - $780
Shop Online: www.concretejungle.com

·10% off!
your entire first purchase
expires January 1, 2008

*enter this code at time of purchase: B593HJ3
*each code can be used one time only

[top: back of sample mailer coupon]

FIRST CLASS MAIL
U.S.POSTAGE
PAID

[place address label here]

[left and right: front of sample mailer coupon / two options]

[style that performs]
Presented is The Big Apple Collection
see more online...

[style that performs]
Presented is The Emerald City Collection
see more online...

[style that performs]
Presented is The Big Apple Collection
see more online...

Source: Courtesy of Emily Hensler

Color Plate 5 Emily Hensler's portfolio page lays out a marketing campaign for her self-directed line of jackets, Concrete Jungle. The portfolio page at the top and detail of a mailer below demonstrate layout and design skills as well as her promotional ideas.

g r a c e
style trend
Whimsical Ornamentation

Source: Courtesy of Brittany Krotts

Figure 5.16 Brittany Krotts created forecasting pages that show different examples of balance on each page.

for navigating a page. The open, negative, or white space on a page is used to separate images and text. White space not only provides a place for the eye to rest but also directs and guides how the viewer sees the content of the page. Use of this space can create a dramatic focal point or simply be used to direct eye flow. Too much space can make the portfolio page uninteresting while too little space can confuse the viewer and not properly showcase the work.

Page Design

The fourth and final element of page design is your personal branding image. This could be an image, a graphic line, or a shape that appears in the same place on every page, or it could be your name or even initials. If the brand is an image, it must portray the look and feel of the portfolio and indicate your intended career path. If you are interested in the accessory field, an example of this could be an icon of an accessory, such as a shoe or handbag. An example of a simple, yet powerful, branding element could be a consistent line or series of lines. Line conveys color, shape, and emotion and also serves to connect the portfolio page by page. The use of your name is an excellent way of reminding the viewer who you are and at the same time allows for you to put a signature on each page. This signature also portrays an image of you through the text, color, and size you use. The branding element should never dominate a page, nor should it be so small that it is not noticed. All the elements on each page need to be balanced and project a strong and cohesive message.

with the images, not dominate them. A page title may or may not be important, depending on the page layout style adopted. If a title is included, it can be either literal ("merchandise planning") or creative ("let's stock the store"). Remain consistent in style and substance throughout the portfolio for unity and clarity.

Space

Space is the third element of page design but often the most important

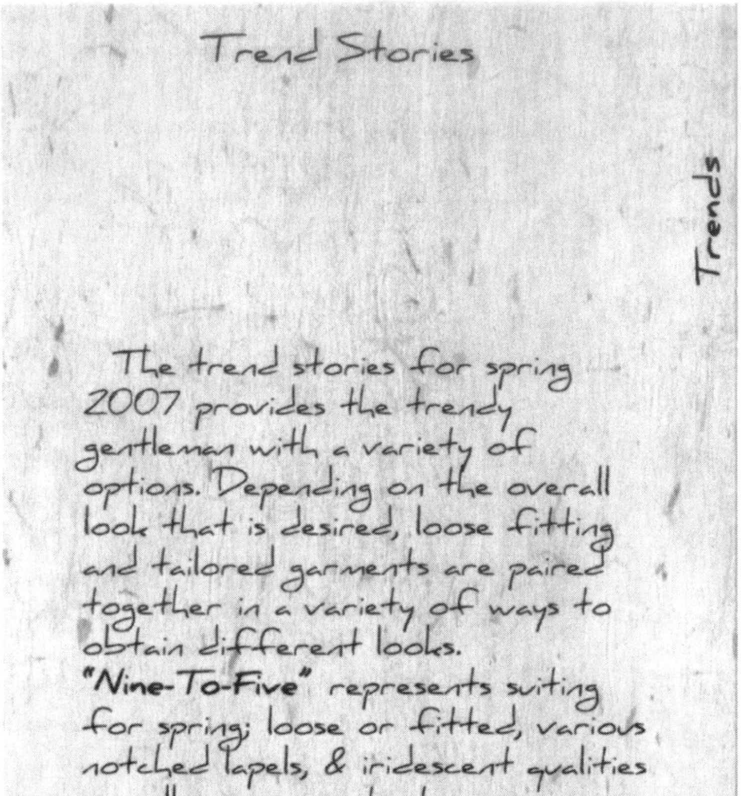

Trend Stories

The trend stories for spring 2007 provides the trendy gentleman with a variety of options. Depending on the overall look that is desired, loose fitting and tailored garments are paired together in a variety of ways to obtain different looks.

"Nine-To-Five" represents suiting for spring; loose or fitted, various notched lapels, & iridescent qualities are all very important.

"Outerwear" consists of vests and lightweight jackets that are worn for the practicality they provide or the look they add to an outfit. "After Hours" provides casual clothing that is coupled with dressier pieces for more effects.

"Run About Savvy" consists of layering effects and simple, comfortable fabrications.

"Adornments" provide the guy with even more unique details to further personalize his look.

Menswear   Spring 2007   Trends   10

Source: Courtesy of Jacqueline Saile

Figure 5.17 This trend storyboard by Jacqueline Saile uses a casual and unique font to express the style of an upcoming menswear line.

Activities

1. Complete Worksheet 5.1 to help you create the page layouts that could best present your work. The first eight layouts are examples to help you begin to develop your own style in the blank boxes offered on the second page. When you have completed this exercise, you should select the style(s) you wish to use in your portfolio pages.

2. Complete Worksheet 5.2 to help you select the best layout for each piece of work that you wish to include in your portfolio. Following this, you should be able to lay out each page in the order in which it will appear so you can visualize the flow of the portfolio.

3. You will need to develop a brand image that communicates your personal style. This brand image needs to appear consistently throughout the portfolio as well as on your resume and cover letters. The brand needs to capture the essence of you—your professional style and your identity that is carried out throughout your work. You should develop your brand by using color, lines or shape graphics, and text.

   a. Develop 10 possible branding image ideas.

   b. Choose 5 final design ideas from the original 10 or from hybrids.

   c. Design and print, with correct color and text, the 5 final ideas and place each on sample layout pages. Review and select your final brand image.

Chapter 6

Use of Technology in Portfolio Development

Technology is an integral part of our lives in today's fast-paced society. Most fashion industry professionals spend hours on their computers sending and answering e-mails, researching trends and product information, developing plans for marketing and merchandising, or updating product data management systems that are utilized in day-to-day business. The constant interface of fashion professionals with their computers has become the norm. In many instances, the development of digital portfolios provides the quickest way to reach these professionals and offers an easy and efficient way for them to review your job credentials. In the quick-paced fashion industry, jobs need to be filled in a timely manner. With the exception of the larger companies, most companies do not hire in advance into a training program. Many companies simply hire when a position becomes open in the company and often are in need of someone well qualified to fill the position and work independently. Digital portfolios allow a company to review work quickly and proceed to the interview.

The easiest way to create a digital portfolio is simply to make a CD of your portfolio pages. Today, most students and industry professionals prepare papers and projects on computers. Doing so ensures that files are readily accessible and easily organized into your paper portfolio. Since your portfolio is saved electronically on CD, you can easily keep its focus the same or easily change it from focused to general. Resumes, cover letters, and various design, merchandising, and marketing projects today need to have the precision of computer development so they are also easy to include. This type of portfolio just becomes a compilation of your work that you can duplicate easily and send to numerous companies without having to pay much, if anything at all. The beauty of working with a computer is that you are not limited to saving just computer-generated work electronically; you can also easily scan projects that you complete by hand and save them in their original form or enhance them with whatever software programs you have. Figure 6.1 shows a portfolio page that Emily Hensler created entirely on the computer. The page shows conceptual images that relate to a target customer for a store. The images were downloaded from the Web and reformatted to create this page. Figure 6.2 shows design sketches and fabric swatches developed for a childrens-wear line. The sketches were completed by hand and scanned into the computer. The fabrics and image were scanned as well and now can be part of a digital portfolio presentation. Digital files are readily retrievable, easily reformatted and saved, and easy to compile into a focused presentation to a targeted employer.

Figure 6.1 This computer-generated page layout by Emily Hensler shows a conceptual image board developed in Adobe Photoshop.

Web-based portfolios have also become an essential tool in portfolio development. This portfolio format showcases not only a candidate's work but also a candidate's ability to create a digital presentation that can be viewed online. Web pages can be developed for placement on a multitude of employment Web sites geared toward the fashion industry. University placement offices often offer this service as well. Sarah Donovan was a 2005 graduate of a small university in the Midwest and wanted to work as a merchandiser for a New York–based company. Sarah knew she could not travel to New York to interview on her own so she decided to showcase her work on the Web. She created a PDF portfolio that she posted on her school's Career Placement Web site. Her Web portfolio was only 10 pages long because she was restricted by the school's site limitations, but she included her strongest work. Sarah researched 10 companies in New York and looked up the human resources contacts in their respective Web sites. She e-mailed each contact a copy of her resume and a cover letter. She briefly stated her job target and described a little about herself and directed the person to her attached resume and her Web site. The resume and cover letter were branded with her brand identity, as were the images on the Web site. Five of the companies contacted her and three of them conducted phone interviews with her. She was offered a position in the merchandising department for a branded manufacturer. Sarah found her dream job and did so by completing the entire process over the Internet and the phone. She flew to New York a month before she was to begin work to sign all the necessary papers and to find an apartment. Her use of the merchandising digital portfolio proved successful for her interview process. It is recommendable to ask human resources contacts if digital portable portfolios are acceptable before you submit them to the companies you solicit.

E-portfolios, or portfolios sent via e-mail, can also be highly effective in securing a position within the industry. If you just want to show some of your work to an employer, attach an e-portfolio to your resume and they can view it immediately. This allows you to show your target work to a potential employer and demonstrate your technological skills at the same time.

Source: Courtesy of Krista Dugan

Figure 6.2 This figure shows hand-sketched and rendered images that were scanned into the computer.

The merchandising professional has many technology options to choose from in portfolio development. The most important part of developing a digital portfolio is to make it user-friendly. The CD-ROM and Web site need to be easily navigated and well presented. The portfolio should guide the viewer from page to page effortlessly. Digital portfolios can be updated easily and accessed from any location and sent anywhere. This will be an extremely strong professional asset that leads to successful job placement.

A digital portfolio offers a unique way for you to brand yourself. If accompanying a printed portfolio, the images need to be compatible and have one to three elements in common such as a logo, a signature, or an image. The digital portfolio offers more options to show presentation and technology skills that may set you apart from the competition.

Platforms and Software

The first decision you need to make is the platform that is best for your needs. The two main platforms are Microsoft Windows (PC) and Macintosh (Mac). It is important for you to research both and determine which is best for you. The majority of software used in the fashion industry is available in both platforms with only slight differences. Most people have a definite preference for one or the other and become proficient in that platform. If you choose Mac, then your files will open easily on the Mac but you may have some problems when you try to open them on a PC. Files created on a PC (using Windows) will open in both. You can solve this type of problem by saving your documents in a transfer format that is compatible with both platforms. This would include formats such as JPEG, GIF, TIFF, and PDF.

A **JPEG** is a format that condenses color image files for easy transport and is named for the group that developed the standard for the format—the Joint Photographic Experts Group. JPEGs display images well but can become pixilated when enlarged. A **GIF** is a compressed file for drawings and Internet images. The name stands for Graphics Interchange Format, and it allows for images to cross formats and be viewed. Files that are not compressed can actually be too large for a potential employer to open and for timely transmission, so this format helps to solve that problem. **TIFF**, or tagged image file format, is one of the most popular compression formats. It is most effective in compressing solid color graphics and less effective for photo images. Since a TIFF does not apply as much compression as a JPEG, it requires more storage. A **PDF** file is a Portable Document Format created by Adobe Systems that can be easily viewed on Adobe Acrobat or Acrobat Reader. You can download the software easily free of charge if it is not already available in your computer software package. PDF files allow you to present work in any size without dealing with the quality issues of the JPEG; moreover, you can present your work in a sequential manner, similar to a paper portfolio. It is easy to tell which format a file is saved as by the file name. For example, two different files could be stored in two different formats—stored in the original Adobe Illustrator file or stored in the more portable PDF or TIFF format that allows you to easily transport the files. The file extensions indicate the file format—targetmarket.ai for Adobe Illustrator and/or targetmarket.pdf for the Adobe Acrobat format. Excellent software systems are sold by a number of manufacturers. Illustrator by Adobe Systems and Macromedia Freehand are excellent for design, drawing, and artwork. Adobe Photoshop is used universally in the industry for conceptual images, photography, and presentation.

Industry-specific professional software is also available to companies and universities, and the work generated on these software programs is excellent to include in your portfolio. This would include Lectra Systems U4ia for fabric design and both Lectra's **PLM** and Gerber's **PDM** for product planning and development. Presentation software or other programs that can create slide shows are

the most universal for viewing. Adobe Acrobat can be utilized to develop PDF files for page-by-page viewing. Your "book" can be viewed page by page, from the cover to the resume, and still be contained in one file. This is a very easy format for an employer to view and can be burned onto a CD even though it's a large file. Video player software, such as QuickTime and Windows Media Player, allow for continuous slide presentation. PowerPoint is also used frequently because so many people are comfortable with it. PowerPoint is not the best program for digital portfolios, but it may work just fine if the visuals are not highly graphic. PowerPoint is best for the combination of text-driven and image-driven portfolio pages.

Using the Computer to Execute Portfolio Page Design

It is important to remember that a digital portfolio must follow the same criteria as any other portfolio. It must have a cohesive branded design and flow in a logical sequence. The strongest images should appear first to garner a good first impression and entice the viewer to keep reviewing. There need to be a few connected process projects followed by a strong finale. The digital portfolio lets viewers zoom in on images so they can view details carefully. For example, flat sketches can be viewed in detail for stitch placement and proportion. Figure 6.3 shows a page of flat sketches developed on the computer in Adobe Illustrator. The precise lines of the stitch detail are

Figure 6.3 Melissa Bodner created this line of flat sketches using Adobe Illustrator.

greatly enhanced by the computer tools. These flat sketches can be further enhanced and detailed for specification packages for apparel production. Figure 6.4 shows flat sketches that are done by hand but scanned into the computer and enhanced with the tools in Adobe Photoshop. These flats are referred to as stylized flats and used for presentation purposes, not for product specification package sheets. Fabrics can be seen in detail so use of fabric design software such as U4ia is truly beneficial. Figure 6.5 shows a digital presentation of fabric swatches created with U4ia software. These portfolio pages become more appealing to potential employers who seek candidates with technical know-how

because they see the original concept shown alongside the U4ia examples. These portfolio pages were saved in both PDF and TIFF formats for multiple uses. This is necessary because not all companies have U4ia and not all computers have U4ia on their desktops. All computers can read PDF and TIFF file formats. Sometimes it is necessary to go back and add to projects that you have completed to show multiple skills and competencies. In general, however, you have the ability to exhibit a greater quantity of work in a short time with the digital format, but the challenge is finding the best platform and software for your work.

Well-executed computer-generated portfolio pages are professional, pol-

ished, and graphically strong. You can play around with page design by using the tools in your computer software. The best pages are those that combine simple graphics and images with interesting, professional text. You can align text left, center, or right; easily establish column widths; and format paragraphs, bullets, and headlines. Once the template is set for graphic or work pages, it is simply a matter of inserting text and images. It is usually beneficial to alternate page format for facing pages in a hard copy book, but digital page formatting can remain repetitive because the pages or slides are visually sequential, not alternating. You can download interesting fonts from Internet sites such as

Figure 6.4 Meredith Smith illustrated her stylized flats and scanned them to create both a portfolio page and an image she could reduce and use on other pages.

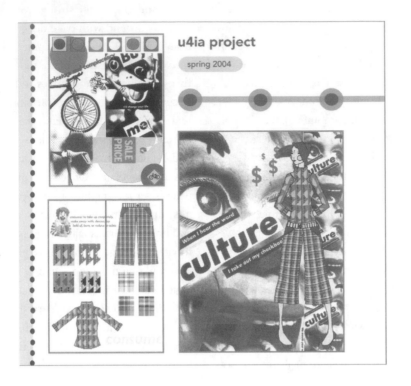

Figure 6.5 Lisa Bruemmer's U4ia project showcases her print and fabric development. Note the presentation of her objective—this communicates her skills very effectively to potential employers.

www.fonts.com and you can even include **clip art**. There are many sites for clip art and images such as www.doverpublications.com, www.images.com, www.imagebank.com, and www.gettyimages.com. Clip art or images can enhance a text-driven page and offer images for conceptual emphasis. Images can be easily inserted from personal files, scanned or downloaded from digital photography, or downloaded from the Internet. A professional layout is accomplished easily by utilizing grids and rulers to design text and images. Digital images can be manipulated and altered with only the limits of the imagination. Figure 6.6 shows an example of a downloaded special font that was crucial to the execution of this portfolio page.

When scanning in work or creating digital files, remember to pay careful attention to digital **resolution**. Images that are taken from print form to digital often appear blurry or pixilated. Scanning is done at a high or low resolution or **dpi** (dots per inch). The higher the resolution, the larger the file, so this could become a problem when transmitting the image. A large file may be difficult to e-mail due to the time it will take to open the file and the amount of space it will take up on a receiver's computer. A lower dpi allows for easy downloading and storage but often lacks in clarity and sharpness. Most scanning of graphic image work is done between 72 and 300 dpi. Line art may become jagged when scanned, so it is often best to scan at higher resolutions and compress the file. Photographic work often works well at 300 dpi. Today, almost everyone has digital cameras,

Source: Courtesy of Emily Hensler

Figure 6.6 Emily Hensler uses bold text and texture to communicate the brand essence of her project.

Presenting your work digitally gives you more control over your presentation, since you do not need to depend on the potential employer's access to a computer. Each presentation can be custom made for each interview and you can store additional work or burn any particular piece or pieces easily if the potential employer wants to review it at a later time.

so taking your own photography for use in your images pieces is highly recommended. If you are not sure what resolution is the best for each media, ask a professional printer or seek help from your computer graphics center, if you are still in a university setting. Trial and error will usually help you to determine appropriate dpi resolution for scanning printed images. If you created the image on the computer and printed it for hard copy presentation, then the colors do not always appear the same. Therefore, featuring these images in a digital portfolio may be preferable to including them in a paper portfolio. The dpi may need to be increased to provide a crisp, high-quality printed image. Practice with scanning and printing is recommended so that you can determine the best resolution for your work. Obviously, if you use good-quality scanners, then the quality of your scans will be better. Always make sure the scanner bed is free of any dust or scratches and that your work fits precisely into the designated scanning area. If the work scans in slightly off balance, then you should import it into a program such as Adobe Photoshop to align the edges. There is software available for pur-

chase that enables any merchandising professional to present interview-ready pages for a hard copy portfolio, access portable digital portfolios, or create Web sites that showcase the work.

Digital Portfolio Formats

There are numerous formats you can use for digital portfolios. **Companion** or portable formats complement traditional portfolios and can be utilized in an interview, left behind as marketing pieces, or e-mailed or mailed to prospective employers. These portfolios generally have the same or similar pieces as the traditional hard copy portfolios. Online portfolios are ideal because potential employers have easy access and can review material at their leisure. There are several options to choose from in both categories and often a combination of more than one may be the ideal. If you choose to present only a digital portfolio, it is necessary for you to bring a laptop to your interviews to ensure that you will be able to present it. Supplying your own laptop for a presentation is the best method for total control of your presentation and might be the only option if the interviewer does not have immediate access to a computer.

Companion or Portable Formats

Companion formats are designed to accompany a traditional paper portfolio and/or reinforce and replicate the material in the main portfolio. Companion portfolios are ideal to send in the mail to companies that are far away or to leave behind after an interview. You can include the material in your paper portfolio or you can create a more targeted portfolio presentation that includes additional work specifically targeted to a company and position. Today, many employers are eager to see work presented digitally because it is the medium with which they feel most comfortable and it demonstrates technological skills. There are still many people who prefer not to view the work digitally or definitely want a hard copy to review.

CD-ROM

The CD is the most acceptable form in which to present portfolio material. Burn the portfolio onto a CD-RW so you can rewrite and change the content easily. Various versions of the portfolio or a Web site can then be burned onto a CD-R that is read-only to protect the work and prevent any alterations to the portfolio content. The CD is

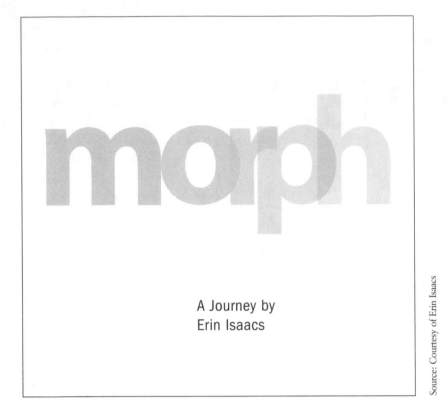

A Journey by
Erin Isaacs

Source: Courtesy of Erin Isaacs

Figure 6.7 Erin Isaacs creates the name Morph with overlapping text and a sheer texture to reflect a light mood and modern approach to design.

inexpensive, which allows you to create multiple copies that you can easily distribute. You may also choose to add voice, music, and animation to the disk.

The external packaging of the portable format is a branding opportunity that introduces you and your work to a potential employer. With a CD cover, there are both front and back visual spaces in which to continue the branding graphics or elements that were developed within the portfolio pages. The CD cover should be enticing and offer a glimpse of what is inside. Your name should appear on the outside, just as it does on the resume and any portfolio page (color, text, brand graphic), and it is usually beneficial to include contact information. Often the best cover is the same work you developed for an introduction page, just graphically altered to appear in the square cover. Figure 6.7 shows an interesting graphic for the cover of a student's CD and a hint of the content inside.

Online Formats

Industry professionals access the online portfolio format on their own computers whenever they choose to review your work. Always reference online formats in your resume and direct the reader to the portfolio work. This is quickly becoming a very popular format with many new graduates in the fashion industry. More and more schools are address-ing the need for this in their portfolio classes, and many schools offer host sites where students may post their projects and portfolios, which facilitates potential employers to review work by job candidates. One drawback is that while potential employers can review one candidate's posted portfolio, they can certainly review everyone else's portfolios on the same site.

Today, e-mail is a way of life for all students and industry professionals. Having an online portfolio available via e-mail is a quick, easy way to distribute your work and credentials. There are a number of different types of online portfolios, and you need to select the one that is most beneficial to you and to a potential employer.

E-portfolio

The e-mailed portfolio or E-portfolio is usually an attachment to either an online cover letter or introductory application. You may choose the software for this attachment but it is recommended that you use a common software that is found on most computers or send the pages as a PDF file that can be read by Adobe Acrobat or Acrobat Reader. If at all possible, save your portfolio so that potential employers can view it as a total presentation and not as individual files that leave the flow of the portfolio out of your control and that may take longer to open.

Web Pages and Web Sites

The most ideal formats for online portfolios are Web pages and Web sites. Microsoft's Front Page will help you create a simple Web site. Everyone can access a Web site, and it gives you total control over how the site is designed and navigated by viewers. It allows you to showcase either a small or an extensive amount of work. You can personalize the site however you wish, which gives you an excellent branding opportunity. If you are not comfortable with designing your own site, there are companies that will assist you in designing the perfect Web site to showcase your work.

Many schools and businesses offer classes in Web site design as well. You can also become part of a group presentation of work on a common Web site shared by multiple users who each showcase his or her work. Companies offer these sites by profession and cover a wide range of clients. This is an easy and inexpensive way to present your work to potential employers. There is a common template that is used for all portfolios, and layout and typography are already formatted for you. The downside of this, of course, is that your portfolio is shown along with others and may lose individuality, but it is certainly a beginning step to developing your own Web site.

Comparison of Digital Portfolio Formats

The companion or portable formats and the online formats are totally compatible and may be used individually or in conjunction with one another. The portable formats can

be sent by regular mail or hand-delivered. They can also be e-mailed and used as introductions, as companion pieces at interviews, or as follow-ups to previously seen work. They can also be easily adapted to fit each job opportunity, and multiple copies can be made for distribution. They are inexpensive and easy to maintain and change.

The online portfolio has the most accessibility. You can e-mail an online portfolio easily. The Web page offers a location for a potential employer to view your resume and any thumbnail or linked images that you choose. The Web site is the most extensive digital version and truly needs to be done well for it to impress an employer. It must be visually pleasing, easily navigable, and very often competes with much more sophisticated sites that can alter a viewer's perception. Unless you have a tremendous amount of work to showcase, the Web site may not be the best choice for you—a Web page or portable format is most ideal.

Copyright Issues in Digital Portfolio Development and Use

It is extremely important to be aware of copyright and intellectual property legalities. Just as you want your work to be protected, so do others. The issue of fair use determines that some use of intellectual property does not violate copyright issues. Most commercial sites that offer clip art or

images state their usage policy on their sites. You also need to be extremely careful if you utilize music in your presentation. Most music sources are copyrighted and you need to be cautious when downloading music for use in a personal presentation.

In most cases, you may use downloaded images for online or personal use but you may not use them for profit. If your work was created on the job, the work belongs to the company and can be shown only with their written permission. If you did the work as part of a team, give credit to those who assisted and try to isolate your own contribution to the project.

To protect your own work, lock PDF files so the work cannot be copied. Whenever possible, make all files read-only so that nothing can be saved onto another computer. All digital files by their nature are vulnerable, however. A hard copy portfolio is taken with you when you leave an employer. Any other format, mail-away, leave-behind, CD, or Web site, renders your work vulnerable. It is important to weigh the advantages and disadvantages of using the digital format for your portfolio as well as the development of that portfolio. Some form of digital format is highly recommended today, so select the option that is best for you.

Activities

Create a sample page layout to use as an e-mail attachment to a digital resume.

1. Select three pieces of work from your portfolio that show a composite of your skills and abilities and are representative of what an employer might desire in a job candidate. Select an underlying grid pattern for your page.

2. Copy and paste your name and contact information onto the page from your resume. You may later decide to alter the size or color of this signature, but begin with the exact copy.

3. Scan the three pages onto the portfolio page and scale them down to fit into three different grid openings. Lay them out on the page with an eye for accompanying grid space in which to insert text that explains the project.

4. Develop an e-mail portfolio page that displays:

   a. your name and contact information

   b. three work examples appropriate for the position you have targeted

   c. three text boxes that explain or highlight the work

Develop a digital portfolio.

1. Choose any format discussed in this chapter and develop a digital portfolio. This portfolio can be developed from your hard copy portfolio pages, scanned, or imported into a CD or Web page. You may also choose to develop the digital portfolio using only some of the work contained in your portfolio and/or additional work that you did not include in the hard copy.

Chapter 7

Portfolio Presentation

The overall presentation of the portfolio, whether printed or virtual, is a reflection and extension of you. The portfolio, resume, correspondence, and application materials, when used by a job candidate, can help establish that person's brand and reinforce his or her marketability as a potential contender for a given position. Creating a positive, memorable visual image can help you stand out in a prospective employer's mind. You want to be the one who they remember. Your work is strong; you have carefully laid it out in the way that best presents you. Now, by establishing yourself as a brand, you will remain a clear and unified image in the minds of all those in the company who reviewed your portfolio. Careful planning and execution will ensure the strongest presentation of you and your brand image.

Branding Yourself

A **brand** is the consumer's perception of a product, service, or company. An image is what the public perceives a brand to be. When this perception becomes common among consumers, it defines a brand's essence or identity. Companies develop brand strategies that allow them to market their brands to a target audience. This strategy can work for individuals as well as products. Consider yourself a brand just like other branded products in the marketplace. Your brand should communicate how you want others

to perceive you. It is crucial to build a brand identity into your job search. Employers do not have a huge amount of time when interviewing potential candidates and the stronger the image you leave them with, the more likely it will be that they will remember you and your work. You have to present your work as a visual connection to who you are. By branding yourself, you help others to quickly grasp your brand essence and assist them in connecting the portfolio work to you as a person. Perception of a brand lies in the minds of individuals; therefore, you should focus on articulating what differentiates you from the competition. It is imperative to always be yourself, convey a consistent image, and be true to your talents, strengths, experiences, and ethical standards. It is important not to mislead the viewer. Do not try to create an image of something you are not, because people will see right through it, whether it is immediate or over an extended period of time. Complete Worksheet 7.1 to see a comparison of how you describe yourself and how others perceive you. This list will prove helpful when you develop a personal image and brand identity for your portfolio and accompanying job application materials.

You are the brand for which an identity must be created. The perception of you—your brand—has already been established in the minds of others. How do others refer to you when introducing or describing you? Do they describe you as creative, spontaneous, dependable? Do they see you as a leader or a rebel? This is as much a part of your brand essence as how you prepare and present yourself for a job interview. Brand identity should be believable, credible, and professional, and communicate important characteristics through the visual elements you select. The brand logo as part of brand identity will help cement your brand in the mind of the employer. Much like advertising, you want to make a memorable, lasting impression in the mind of the potential employer. Brand identity should match your personality and character traits while conveying a sense of who you are, to establish this link in the employer's mind.

Establishing a brand identity is not an easy task. It will take time, careful thought, and planning to capture the essence of you as a brand. You are marketing this brand essence, so it is essential that you understand it.

Developing a Brand Essence

There are three elements that together build a **brand essence**. These elements are the benefits a brand has to offer, the brand's position in the marketplace, and a branding visual that represents and communicates who you are.

Brand Benefits

Your **brand benefits** are the skills and capabilities you bring to a potential job position. These are the specifics that you offer a company that has advertised a position that requires these very skills. You use your portfolio to prove that you have these skills and capabilities by the work

experience you list on your resume and the work you show in your portfolio pages. For example, you might have worked at two different retail stores through college doing customer service, interacting with the consumer and selling products. You probably know the process for bringing new goods onto the floor, setting up a store set, and managing the product sales through the point-of-sale system. This is a part of you. Experience becomes part of your knowledge and understanding base and permeates your brand essence. Part of your brand essence is that you have a unique body of experience and knowledge, which makes you an ideal candidate. Is it the good coffee and the support of coffee growers around the world that make you choose Starbucks? Or is it more than just these perks? That something extra of a brand essence that persuades is brand position.

Brand Positioning

Your **brand position** is the segment of the industry where you wish to work. Starbucks' brand essence positions them as a lifestyle—the friendly coffeehouse encourages acquaintances to sit in comfortable chairs, listen to music, buy first issues of new CDs, and take home some coffee so the lifestyle travels with you. Think of yourself as a lifestyle brand and identify where you want to work, for whom you want to work, what you want to be doing in that job position, and how you want to build your career. You have chosen merchandising as your field and have taken classes within a fashion merchandising program or a related fashion major. You can identify your

job target through your education and work experience and after completing the worksheets from Chapter 2 of this text.

Maybe you want to be an assistant store manager for a specialty store chain. You know you have job experience, organizational skills, and the personality necessary for success in this job. You also have a strong interest in women's apparel and accessories, so you want to position yourself for this job target in the women's segment of the fashion industry. This is a defining part of your brand essence and one you want to develop with a clear direction. This is similar to a branded product's portfolio of intangible assets that lead up to its lifestyle image. The most important element of a brand's essence is its position. Companies that take risks are the ones that reap the rewards because the customer connects with and remembers them. This part of the brand can sometimes be summed up in a product's tagline. Nike's "Just Do It" targets consumers who are active explorers and who put all their effort into whatever they do. Target's "Design for All" positions the brand as creative and innovative yet affordable. Mazda's "Zoom, Zoom, Zoom" just makes us want to get in that car and go. Mazda has positioned its product to capture the market that wants the feel of speed and a stylish image and is not necessarily bothered with details but demands customer satisfaction. Captivating taglines and the striking visuals associated with them are the essence of each of these brands. Figure 7.1 shows a student's visual concept for the General Motors

Figure 7.1 This is Shawn Ormsby's visual conception of the Hummer brand and a self-directed concept design for a new car brand called the Silverback.

Hummer brand. This presentation of the brand emphasizes its strength in the marketplace and captures the attention of a demographic that values quality construction for safety and a rugged, outdoorsy appeal.

Brand Visualization

The visual presentation of your brand is similar to a product's brand logo and advertising campaign. The visual manifestation of a brand's essence is what ultimately lives on in a consumer's mind. Nike's text signature and the swoosh logo show on-the-go movement and have become iconic for athletic excellence. The Target bull's-eye and even Target Dog and the company's cutting-edge advertising truly portray all that the

brand means to the customer. Mazda's advertising campaigns show people watching the car speed by and maneuver past them through gorgeous scenery. Advertising's basic rule of three says the average consumer needs to be exposed to an advertisement three times before a memorable connection between the brand and the product is made. Repetition of the brand logo through out the portfolio will help establish a strong visual connection between brand identity and all elements. The materials (i.e., portfolio contents and presentation, cover letter, resume, and IMP) will provide consistency and continuity and strengthen the association between you and your work. Brand identity should match

your personality and character traits while conveying a sense of who you are, to establish this link in the prospective employer's mind. Remember, you may have only one opportunity to sell your brand to a specific employer, so you must find many ways to reinforce it.

You will succeed if you develop a visual identity for your brand and thread your identity throughout your portfolio. The stamp of your brand essence on all portfolio materials communicates dedication, skill, and determination to make your dream career a reality. Figure 7.2 shows two examples of brand logos. The first is the Armani Exchange logo that was included because the project targeted that company, and the second shows

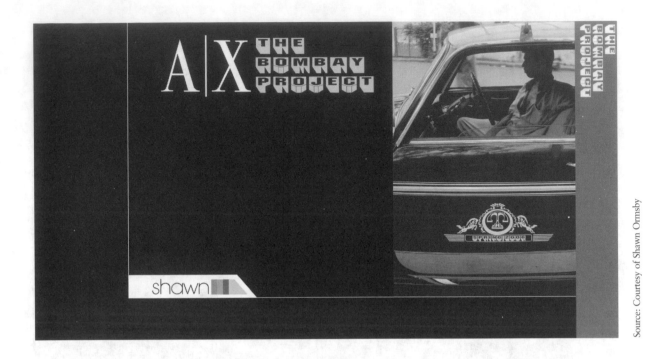

Figure 7.2 Shawn Ormsby's portfolio page shows his portfolio brand image, shawn, and his incorporation of the Armani Exchange logo in a self-directed project for his portfolio.

Source: Courtesy of Shawn Ormsby

the *shawn* logo—the personal portfolio logo of Shawn Ormsby.

Developing a Brand Image

Developing a personal brand image is similar to developing a brand image for a product. Your unique set of skills and capabilities, just like a product's brand, has distinctive qualities that win admiration when marketed to a target audience. Product qualities allow the target market to differentiate between your product and other products and to identify with one brand more than another. Your brand benefits, brand essence, and presentation all contribute to your branded image. You will market this branded image to potential employers—your target market. Knowing who you are and who you want to reach will help you develop a portfolio that strongly

conveys your personal image and allows employers to connect with you. Distinctiveness, individuality, uniqueness, style, and personality are areas to consider when deciding the best way to create and present your personal image.

Branding the Portfolio

Developing a branded merchandising portfolio begins with identifying your skills and capabilities, otherwise known as your brand benefits. You identified these clearly earlier while laying out your portfolio plan and choosing the work that best represents these skills. These pages are in your portfolio plan and have been nicely laid out so that each piece is strong.

Next, you decide how to showcase your individual style and position your brand to target the job you desire within the fashion field. The last element involved in branding your portfolio is a specific visual presentation of yourself as a merchandiser, or your brand essence. This presents you to the marketplace. It is important to brand your merchandising portfolio so that employers have a sense of who you are and so that you rise above other candidates on the list. The aesthetic appeal you choose to develop, coupled with the contents of the portfolio, will demonstrate competencies, capabilities, and qualifications, as well as convey personal style and character traits through the overall presentation. Personality traits include being organized, detail-oriented, meticulous, methodical, and professional. Other traits make an individual creative, talented, and innovative. Your brand may be modern, traditional, or eclectic. Contemplate the words others use to describe you and consider how you can convey this information through the visual presentation, organization, and execution of the portfolio.

Although our merchandising portfolio model is suggested as the basis for organization, there are endless possibilities for making the portfolio presentation your own. The style, size, texture, and design of the encasement, page design and graphic layout, and palpable brand essence define and personalize your presentation. The dimensions of a virtual presentation are more standardized than its printed counterpart; however, you may add original graphics and stimulating broadcast elements to personalize the portfolio and make the user experience unforgettable.

Continuity and Flow

The merchandising portfolio model, discussed in Chapter 1 and Chapter 4, provides a logical format in which contents should be organized to help facilitate the presentation's overall flow. Whether you choose to develop a general or focused portfolio determines content organization and flow within the portfolio. General portfolios possess a broad range of content and follow the logical sequence of events to bring a product to market. Alternatively, focused portfolios follow the specific sequence of events for only one or two narrow segments. The manner in which you organize the content will highlight points made in your resume with various supporting portfolio materials and elements.

The placement of contents within the portfolio determines continuity and flow. With the exception of the first and last pages of the portfolio, all the other pages are facing pages or spreads. You need to carefully consider the content of facing pages. There needs to be a logical connection or relationship between the two pages. Placement of unrelated contents in a page spread can break the logical organization and flow. Blank or empty pages should never be planned in the presentation. Blank pages can appear as if you forgot to insert material. In case you do not possess content for a page at the end of a section, you should create a piece to complement the content on the facing page or remove one of the pages. The manner in which you create and lay out divider pages impacts the number of pages within a section. Some people choose to use a two-page spread to introduce each section of the portfolio, while others use one page. A page is not considered blank or empty if it contains a carefully planned element such as a line, brand logo, text, or image.

Brand identity, page design, layout, and overall organization of contents establish continuity between elements in the presentation of the portfolio. Continuity of components and a harmonious flow from one element to the next reinforce an individual's logical thought process, industry knowledge, and brand identity.

Consistency Among all Portfolio Elements

Consistency and continuity are important when building recognition of yourself and your brand identity. Marketers work to establish and maintain a consistent image in the consumer's mind that relates to the quality of products and services offered. Market yourself in the same way. Focus on your strengths, valuable skills, and the experiences that make you unique. Tailor the presentation to the desired employer to show what you can do for the company and to position yourself as the most ideal choice for the position. Be consistent in how and where you place the brand logo throughout the portfolio, and make sure typeface, style, size, and color schemes, coupled with smart page design and layout, are uniform so there is continuity in the presentation. Using the same typeface and brand identity image on the resume, cover letter, and IMP will provide consistency among all of the portfolio elements and correspondence associated with your job application.

Important Details

Train your eye to notice details, however small they may seem. Avoid the mistake of thinking that someone will overlook a stray mark on a page, a dog-eared edge, or an image placed haphazardly on the page. Attention to detail is *critical* to the presentation of the portfolio and yourself. If the presentation is sloppy, you will be perceived as sloppy. Remember to align elements using a grid to prevent uneven placement. If you are not very detail-oriented, consult a professor, an industry professional, or a friend who has an eye for detail and will point out things you need to address. Openness to criticisms is an essential personality trait of people working in collaborative environments. Take the initiative, invite feedback, and you will get great results.

Portfolio Presentation Do's and Don'ts

Do

Be professional.

Carefully develop a brand logo that truly represents your brand identity.

Link your brand identity to all correspondence with employers to reinforce your suitability for the position.

Carefully consider how you will design and lay out the pages.

Utilize the design elements and principles to complement your work and showcase your strengths.

Proofread all text for grammar, including spelling and punctuation errors.

Pay attention to the details.

Use a grid to develop page design and layout to prevent images and text from being misaligned.

Always cite sources when you borrow or reuse images and text.

Don't

Use overly decorative papers or typefaces that draw attention away from your work.

Use kitsch icons or symbols for establishing your brand logo.

Misrepresent yourself or your work.

Include work about which you are unsure. It is better to omit it or create a new piece to replace it.

Forego using a grid to design and lay out pages to save time. (Images and text placed haphazardly on the page negatively impact the professionalism of the overall portfolio and make you look sloppy.)

Use slang terms and imagery that could be construed as offensive.

Use music in a virtual presentation without obtaining written permission.

Use a different typeface for each piece of work you present. (Doing so breaks the continuity and flow.)

Above all, be sure to match your skills with those the potential employer seeks. You are positioning yourself as a winning prospect, so it is up to you to show why you should be hired instead of the other candidates.

Professionalism

Employers want to hire individuals who will represent their companies in a professional manner. All correspondence with industry professionals and contacts should be professional in language, format, presentation, and timing. Verbal and written communication must be persuasive and polite. Avoid using slang and images that could be interpreted as offensive or disrespectful. You also want to make sure you are not using company-specific lingo—use terminology that is widely known by industry professionals or provide enough information, either visual or textual, to help the viewer understand what they are reading or viewing. Remember, you are in control of the message they receive. Proofread text to ensure there are no grammar errors, including spelling, punctuation, and sentence structure mistakes. Running spelling and grammar check on the computer is not enough; there may be words that are spelled correctly that you did not intend to use (e.g., form instead of from).

Always showcase work of which you are proud in your portfolio. The quality of work you include should meet or exceed industry standards and expectations. Every aspect and detail should be carefully planned and executed to the best of your ability. Never include proprietary work or projects completed for another company without approval first. On a similar note, citation must be included for any information and images used from another source. If you conduct yourself in an ethical, truthful, and professional manner, this is sure to permeate all aspects of your work and lead to you being hired.

Integrated Presentation

Determine how you will integrate your body of work into a portfolio to convey important skills, experience, and accomplishments. It is critical for your work to represent and showcase your level of expertise. Remember, you want to convey to the employer specifically what you can do for them, and your goal is to support this promise with evidence of your ability to deliver results. Color plate 1 shows multiple skills to an employer. When organizing your work, stop and ask yourself some key questions. What are the most important skills required by the position to which you are applying? (Refer to Worksheets 2.1 through 2.3 in the appendix.) What examples of work do you possess that showcase these skills? (Refer to Worksheet 4.1 in the appendix.) Do you need to develop self-directed pieces to show evidence of capabilities that are not currently represented by the work samples you have? Incorporate work that combines skills and competencies that are tailored to the companies at which you are interviewing. Show them that you understand their philosophy and mission. Every element of the portfolio should work together to create a logical, cohesive presentation that leaves the prospective employer certain of a match between the company and you. Color plate 5 shows a strong brand image to an employer.

Checklist for Evaluating Portfolio Presentation

○ Yes ○ No Does the portfolio represent individual identity?

○ Yes ○ No Did you clearly convey the skills/capabilities/ qualifications/accomplishments for the desired position throughout the portfolio?

○ Yes ○ No Does the portfolio contain blank/empty pages?

○ Yes ○ No Do page design and layout complement the work presented?

○ Yes ○ No Is the portfolio organized in a manner that best complements and conveys the candidate's marketability?

○ Yes ○ No Are all portfolio elements consistent?

○ Yes ○ No Is the portfolio organized to provide continuity and smooth transitions among skill sets?

○ Yes ○ No Do elements within the portfolio need further explanation for the viewer to understand what they are viewing?

○ Yes ○ No Is brand image consistent throughout the portfolio?

○ Yes ○ No Is your brand image consistent with the perceptions others have of you?

○ Yes ○ No Does the portfolio complement and strengthen the skills/experience documented in the resume by providing evidence of stated capabilities and competencies?

○ Yes ○ No Is the portfolio general?

○ Yes ○ No Is the portfolio focused?

○ Yes ○ No Is the presentation integrated in a way that provides a logical flow of contents?

○ Yes ○ No Is the individual's personal style conveyed and integrated into the portfolio (through the encasement, page layouts, selection of work, and brand identity)?

○ Yes ○ No Is the execution and overall appearance of the portfolio professional?

Activities

1. Complete Worksheet 7.1 in the appendix to assist in the development of personal style and brand image.

2. Determine how you will adapt your work to the portfolio and if you need to alter any pieces to fit the unified style of the presentation.

3. Evaluate a classmate's or friend's portfolio or an online sample utilizing the Checklist for Evaluating Portfolio Presentation.

Chapter 8

Resume Development

It is natural for people to allow first impressions to form, especially at job interviews. The merchandising portfolio model enables you to capitalize on this opportunity and successfully communicate your brand identity. Making a positive first impression is vital, whether someone is visually evaluating the appearance of you, your resume, your portfolio, or your accompanying job application materials. According to Michelle Sterling of Global Image Group, "Within the first three seconds of a new encounter, you are evaluated . . . even if it is at a glance. . . . Within the first few seconds, people pass judgment on you—looking for common surface clues. Once the first impression is made, it is virtually irreversible" (2006). The power of a first impression should never be underestimated because it is often a lasting one. Once a prospective employer forms an opinion of you, it is extremely difficult to change it. Resumes are an integral part of any job application, as well as an essential part of any portfolio. A resume is often the first opportunity a candidate has to make an impression on a potential employer. Therefore, the layout, organization, and information a candidate includes must provide a strong synopsis of his or her competencies and potential. The information should be presented in an easy-to-read format. Although you send your resume to potential employers via online submission,

e-mail, fax, or regular mail, you should also include it as an integral part of the portfolio. Qualifications and competencies should be clearly delineated on a resume and further reinforced by the inclusion of supporting portfolio materials.

Consider how much information is conveyed through a 15- or 30-second commercial on television, a 2- to 3-second look at a billboard, or a glance at a stranger. Opinions are formed quickly. Human resources departments receive hundreds, sometimes thousands, of resumes each week. The authors spoke with college recruiters and other HR personnel and discovered that recruiters and HR personnel may initially take anywhere from 4 to 22 seconds to review a resume and determine whether a candidate has the right experience for a position. They look at resumes placed in the yes pile more carefully and evaluate them against other candidates' applications to determine who possesses the strongest credentials for the position. Only the strongest individuals are brought in for interviews. Depending on the office policy, they might scan resumes placed in the immediate no pile and add them to their resume files.

Some companies scan resumes into their computers or have all applicants submit their resume information online. In this case, hiring personnel run an initial database search and the computer retrieves candidates' resumes that possess the specific skills, qualifications, and experience. They further review selected resumes to determine who they will contact for an interview. Companies that use application-tracking systems may require the candidate to list a few keywords at the bottoms of their resumes. Recruiters use keywords to help them retrieve resumes that contain the specific qualifications required by the positions they are trying to fill. Therefore, it is important that you integrate key terms used in the job posting into your resume to increase your resume's chances of being retrieved during an electronic search.

The most successful resumes are easy to read and communicate information clearly and in a professional manner. Recruiters should be able to gather the information they need in a few seconds to determine if they should look any further into a candidate's qualifications. What makes the fashion merchandising resume stand out is the stamp of brand identity that has been established in the portfolio. Remember to carry this through visually and contextually as you strive to attain your professional goals.

Resume Formats

There is not necessarily a right or wrong way to format a merchandising resume; the information just needs to be organized in a manner that best markets an individual's experience and qualifications for a given position and communicates his or her brand identity. You must convey the brand identity that you build into the merchandising portfolio in your resume and accompanying application materials, such as the cover letter and IMP. When develop-

ing a merchandising resume, there are several different formats that you can use. These include the chronological, functional/skills, targeted, and creative themes. Chronological, functional/skills, and targeted resumes are the most commonly used formats. The least frequently selected, and most individualized, format is the creative resume, which veers from the norm and needs to be carefully developed to be effective. This is also the most difficult type of resume to develop in a professional manner. Each of these resume

formats will be discussed in this chapter followed by sample resumes, general resume rules, and resume do's and don'ts. Use Worksheets 8.1 through 8.4 in the appendix to document and organize information that you will include on your resume, whether you are creating your resume for the first time or updating an existing one.

Chronological

Chronological resumes organize information in sequential order of employment, beginning with the most recent

Chronological Resume Format Selection Profile

Jane Taylor is graduating with a bachelor's degree in merchandising with a product development focus. Jane's academic program covered all aspects of the supply chain, qualifying her for many co-op and internship opportunities. During college she completed six required co-op work experiences. Jane also worked as a part-time seasonal retail sales associate for a local independently owned store where she gained valuable experience in visual merchandising and display. Jane gained experience in a variety of segments within the fashion industry, ranging from co-ops in textile design, apparel product development, and buying to retail sales and visual merchandising. Jane is passionate about both product design and buying and would like to create one resume that she can use when applying to a few different job targets. She is trying to determine which resume format would be the best choice for her job search.

The chronological format would be a great choice because she has worked for seven different companies and would like to have a resume that she can use to apply for a variety of positions. The functional/skills resume would be acceptable as well. This format would highlight the variety of skills she possesses but may convey a lack of focus in one specialty. The targeted resume should not be considered, due to her wide range of experience and broad job search. The factor that clinches it? Jane is updating her general merchandising portfolio, which will pair best with the chronological resume.

position. This format is ideal when an individual wants to emphasize a pattern of work history that relates directly to a desired job target or position. It can also be utilized to document a combination of related and unrelated work experience. When you use this format, you should be sure there are no major gaps in your employment history. This format is also recommendable when you've had only a few jobs. If you have frequently changed jobs or spent limited time in the positions you've had, it can imply a variety of negative things, including a lack of interest, staying power, or loyalty, or limited capability to perform job-related duties and responsibilities. Always emphasize your most current work experiences that relate to the position you desire. Work history should include years of service, company name, company location (city, state), job title, and brief statements describing responsibilities, demonstrated competencies, and results obtained for each position. It is important to focus on specific quantities, percentages, and numbers to indicate the level or types of responsibilities and results obtained within specific positions held. This information is helpful to a potential employer, as it will indicate more specific accomplishments and competencies that you possess. It is important for a prospective employer to clearly ascertain responsibilities and results obtained for each position held. See Figures 8.1 and 8.2 on pages 115 and 116 for examples of chronological resumes.

Functional/Skills

Functional or skills resumes highlight the abilities of an individual that directly relate to the available position. The focal points of this format are related skills, and they are usually divided into groups and listed in order of importance to the job target. Use a title to designate the types of skills outlined in each grouping. Individuals who have limited practical work experience related to the job target often choose this resume format. Since the focal point of a functional resume is the skills section, it allows people to emphasize what they can do and downplay gaps in their employment history or limited experience related to the position they seek. Work history and volunteer or community service activities are often listed following the skills section to provide a record of employment and service. Work history should list years of service, company name, location (city, state), and job title. A brief statement describing responsibilities may be required if a job title is not descriptive on its own. See Figures 8.3 through 8.5 on pages 117 to 119 for examples of functional/skills resumes.

Targeted

Targeted resumes are purely focused on work experience, competencies, and results related to a specific job position or job target. Each resume developed using this format is created exclusively to address the qualifications and individual requirements of

Functional/Skills Resume Format Selection Profile

Samantha Wright is a merchandising major at a four-year institution and is applying for her first internship position. She is seeking a position with a trend forecasting company. Samantha has held various part-time jobs that range from a retail sales associate to hostess and server positions in restaurant establishments. Samantha has learned her most valuable skills for application to this internship in school through various industry-related hands-on assignments and projects. Samantha is preparing her resume to apply for this opportunity and is trying to decide which resume format would best communicate the skills that she has to offer. The strongest choice would be the functional/skills resume format so she can draw attention to the skills she does possess but that she has not yet applied in a job setting. Since her work experience is limited and in a variety of areas, the targeted format is definitely not an option. The chronological would be acceptable, but it is certainly not the best selection to communicate what she has to offer. Samantha is creating her first merchandising portfolio and has chosen a general format. She is not sure yet which segment of the industry she would like to pursue. The general portfolio format coupled with the functional/skills resume is a great combination for her.

The format you select will depend on your experience. Both styles are followed by work experience, professional affiliations, memberships, and service directly related to the job target. People who have more than two to three years of related work experience and use the targeted resume format should list education at the bottom.

Targeted Resume with a Qualifications Section

If you include a **qualifications section,** you should place it directly following the job target. Prepare brief one- to two-line statements to convey your capabilities and accomplishments that specifically address the credentials required by the job opening. Qualification statements should contain information regarding experience that relates to the job target or job objective. Summarize knowledge and skills related to the position, as well as any personality traits or personal characteristics that would enhance your performance on this job. Be sure to include keywords for which the employer is looking when drafting qualification statements. The number of qualification statements typically ranges from three to eight. Bullets are recommended to organize and highlight each statement. Use of nouns and adjectives are preferred for this application rather than action verbs (See Box 8.1 at the end of the chapter). See Figures 8.6 and 8.7 on pages 120 and 121 for examples of targeted resumes with qualifications sections.

Targeted Resume with Capabilities and Accomplishment Sections

In this format, a **capabilities section** is listed under the job target and

a particular company or position. Use of a targeted format requires an individual to modify the resume to suit the needs of each employer or position. Individuals who have established a strong record of employment and possess expertise and proficiency in a particular area of the industry often use this resume format. The job target will always be listed at the top of the resume, using terminology specific to the position within the selected company, or it can be slightly more general to encompass the same type of job that would be found in several different companies. There are two ways this resume style can be organized—one has a qualifications section and the other has sections for capabilities and accomplishments.

followed by the section for accomplishments. Prepare brief one- to two-line statements to convey each capability and accomplishment. **Capabilities** should include the skills and competencies that will allow you to perform in the targeted position. These statements will tell an employer how prepared you are for the position and indicate what contributions the person will make when given the opportunity. The number of capability statements may range from four to eight.

Accomplishments should communicate results achieved that validate and substantiate the capabilities indicated in the section above. Employers want to know a candidate's job performance. It is your job to clearly communicate how you will perform at a job and back up claims with evidence of results and accomplishments. An example would be recognition for most valued employee of the month based on sales. Accomplishments typically range from three to five brief statements. Action verbs are recommended rather than nouns and adjectives for these sections (see Box 8.2 at the end of the chapter). Again, bullets are recommended to organize and highlight each statement.

Work experience follows the qualifications or capabilities and accomplishments sections. Documentation of work experience is handled differently from the chronological and functional/skills resumes. The years of service, name of the company, location of the company (city, state), and job title are typically all that are listed in this section, although some candidates may include specific responsibilities for each position held. See Figures 8.8 and 8.9 on pages 122

and 123 for examples of targeted resumes with capabilities and accomplishments sections.

Creative

Creative resumes may utilize a chronological, functional/skills, or targeted resume format for the organization of information. What distinguishes this type of resume from others is the overall appearance and nontraditional approach to getting a potential employer's attention. The authors recommend this format for unique situations, as it is sometimes considered too informal. If you fail to execute a creative resume properly (in a professional manner), it can damage your chances of obtaining a position with a company. Remember, first impressions are often lasting. However, this format, when done correctly, can demonstrate your cleverness and creativity and make you stand out from the rest of the pack. This format should be reserved for candidates applying for positions in creative segments of the industry. The intention of a creative resume is to exhibit ingenuity and ability.

You should apply the basic design elements and principles you used in your portfolio page layouts, discussed in Chapter 5, to your resume, regardless of its format. Give careful consideration to the overall appearance and placement of information and your branding element so that the resume is a cohesive component of the portfolio that complements and reinforces a consistent image of you. The resume is a vital component of the application materials, as well as an extension of the portfolio. Composition elements including text, a

brand identity image, graphics, scale, and white space are important factors that you must carefully lay out to maximize your strengths and minimize clutter.

When you develop a creative resume, use the recommended format to organize information and then stylize (brand) the aesthetic appearance with color, typeface, layout, and packaging. It is particularly important that you carefully plan and apply the design elements and principles when developing this type of resume and its unique packaging. Creative resumes are often underutilized and can be a strong marketing tool for candidates who seek positions within creative segments of the fashion industry.

General Guidelines for Resume Development

Microsoft Word offers a few templates that you can use to format your resume (e.g., elegant resume, contemporary resume, and professional resume). These templates give you a quick way to organize your resume without having to invest much time and thought. Simply type in your information in the designated fields and the resume is done. You can also use the Resume Wizard option in Microsoft Word, which allows you to create a new resume template. Although this option allows you to select between entry-level, chronological, functional, and professional formats, you are still restricted to selections from the elegant, contemporary, or professional resume templates. Additionally, there are various Web sites that let you download different resume templates for a fee. When you need a resume

Important Factors to Consider When Selecting Format

You should always carefully consider resume format. The format you select should be visually attractive and sell a potential employer on your experience. For help selecting the format that best suits your level of experience, answer the questions below. A suggested resume format is listed next to each yes or no answer. Circle your answer along with the resume format indicated for all of the questions listed below.

1. Are you seeking your first job or internship/co-op?

   YES—functional/skills or chronological
   NO—chronological or targeted

2. Is your past work experience within the same field?

   YES—chronological or targeted
   NO—functional/skills

3. Are the skills you possess reflected in past work experience?

   YES—chronological or targeted
   NO—functional/skills

4. Are you clearly focused on a specific job target?

   YES—targeted
   NO—chronological

5. Have you changed employers frequently?

   YES—functional/skills
   NO—chronological

6. Does past work history demonstrate significant growth and development?

   YES—chronological or targeted
   NO—functional/skills

7. Are the names of past employers significant?

   YES—chronological or targeted
   NO—functional/skills or targeted

8. Do you want an all-purpose resume?

   YES—chronological or functional/skills
   NO—targeted

9. Are you seeking employment in a creative segment of the industry and looking for a nontraditional resume format that will make an impression even before it is read?

   YES—creative
   NO—chronological, functional/skills, or targeted

Now that you have answered all of the questions, it should be clear which format has come up most frequently and is best for you. If two formats occur equally as often, choose whichever format you believe is most ideal. Get some feedback from your peers. Check the Internet for even more examples of resumes and pinpoint what you like and dislike about each one. You can personalize resumes to best suit your needs by combining formats.

template and have limited time to create one, this option can be a temporary solution. The disadvantage of using resume templates such as these is that your resume will look generic. When you spend time developing a personalized resume format that reflects your brand identity, it will be well worth the investment because you communicate a consistent brand image to potential employers. Another disadvantage of using generic resume templates is that it is difficult to update your information. You constantly work against the preset template's formatting; therefore, the authors recommend that you don't use these templates, especially since it is even more difficult to integrate your personal branding elements into the resume. **Branding elements are the visual cues** that help establish the overall brand identity of the portfolio and its supporting materials.

Begin formatting the resume by adjusting the page margins to 1 inch at the top, sides, and bottom. The minimum margin allowance is one-half inch while the maximum is 1 inch. A 10- or 12-point font is recommended for the general content of the resume. A larger font can be used for your name but should not exceed 22 points. Select a simple, standard font for a clean appearance and readability. Times New Roman, Garamond, Helvetica, Courier New, and Bookman Old Style are good choices. Font selection will have bearing on how much space is allocated for each letter on the page. Some fonts are more compressed, enabling you to include more information on a page. Times New Roman, Helvetica, and

Garamond are examples of more compressed fonts. If you have less information to include on the page and are looking for a font that occupies more space per letter, then try Courier New or Bookman Old Style. The font selected for the resume should be the same or closely complement the font used in the merchandising portfolio. Your brand identity should be incorporated into the resume to establish a strong link between your portfolio and the supporting job application materials. Boldface and italics are recommended instead of underlining for highlighting headings, company names, or job titles. However, these should be used sparingly. Capitalizing words can also be utilized to add emphasis. Be consistent with the font style you use for your name and for the section headings and titles on the resume. For example, if you capitalize your entire name, then you should capitalize all of the section headings (education, experience, skills, etc.). This will provide continuity and balance that will enhance the overall aesthetic quality of the resume. Lines can be inserted to separate the resume into sections, but should be used sparingly. It is not certain they will display exactly as you intended if an employer should open your resume electronically. Consider the design elements and principles here when determining page layout.

General information that you should include on a merchandising resume is contact information, education, work experience, and your branding identity element. Contact information should include name (your formal name rather than a nickname), street address, city, state, zip

code, phone number with area code, and e-mail address. Avoid using an e-mail address that is suggestive or unprofessional. Think twice before including the e-mail address from a current employer when you seek a position with another organization. Does this show company loyalty? Create a new e-mail address for professional correspondence instead of using your current job one. In addition, always make sure your voice mail message is professional, as this also communicates attentiveness and savvy to potential employers. Sometimes it is necessary to list two addresses on a resume, one that is transitory, which you identify as *present, local,* or *temporary,* and one that is permanent, which you identify as *permanent* or *home.* Obviously, use this dual address block only when you are applying for positions or conducting job searches while in the process of moving from one place to another. The format and layout of the contact information and branding element established on the resume will become the letterhead you use for the cover letter and should complement the portfolio, IMP, or additional supporting components of the application.

A job objective is not required on a resume. However, it can immediately identify for which position you are applying. The objective statement should include functions and responsibilities of the job, and opportunities and activities you would like your ideal job to offer. See Table 8.1 for sample job objective statements. If the job objective is too vague, then you should not include it. Examples of poorly written objective statements include the following:

Table 8.1 Sample Job Objective Statements

Industry Position	Job Objective Statement
Allocator	Merchandise allocator for a retail store with the ability to use Excel to facilitate order allocation, review product deliveries, and maintain warehouse stock to meet shipping target deadlines, and manage communication with stores.
Buyer	Buying and merchandising for a retail store with opportunities to define customer needs, procure merchandise, and grow sales and profits.
CAD designer	CAD designer for a mill, manufacturer, or retailer with the opportunity to utilize U4ia software to create fabric designs that integrate forecasted trends with the philosophy of the brand and to develop prints appropriate for specific target markets.
Brand manager	Fashion marketing with the opportunity to develop and grow brand identity and image, while coordinating marketing efforts for a branded manufacturer or retail company.
Product developer	Analyze product and market research, interpret trends, and create a product that represents the manufacturer or retail brand for a specified target market.
Promotion coordinator	Coordinate promotion for a retailer or branded manufacturer with the opportunity to analyze the effectiveness of past promotional strategies, research market trends, and act as a liaison with marketing to increase awareness and sales.
Public relations specialist	Public relations for a specialty retailer or branded manufacturer with the opportunity to coordinate and execute special events, correspond with magazine editors and press, and prepare press releases to build brand awareness.
Sourcing manager	Manager of the sourcing department for an apparel manufacturer with the opportunity to apply knowledge of sourcing, garment construction, and production; ability to employ bilingual verbal and written skills to negotiate quality and delivery with vendors to increase profitability.
Trend forecasting analyst	Trend analyst for an apparel manufacturer or retailer with the opportunity to interpret forecasted trends related to a company's image and target consumer; create storyboards and facilitate presentations to design development divisions; and research forecasting services and competition.
Visual stylist	Visual stylist for a retail store with the opportunity to be creative in implementing visual cues, and increase sales through effective merchandising techniques that silently sell merchandise.

1. To obtain an internship
2. To obtain a position with the opportunity for advancement and growth
3. To gain a high level of knowledge and experience through trying new and diverse work environments and by performing a variety of tasks
4. To obtain an internship that will allow me to build on and strengthen my skills in the fashion industry, while preparing me for a lifelong career in the world of fashion
5. To obtain a position in marketing, product development, or buying

The first example does not tell the employer in which area within the company you seek an internship. The second example is equally vague, although it does specify a desire to grow with the company if given the opportunity. The third example is very vague. The fourth example is much like the second one. The last example provides too many areas of interest and may communicate a lack of focus or that the candidate is uncertain about where his or her skills would be valuable.

A job target is required when you use the targeted resume format. It immediately identifies the position you are seeking. Some may choose to include a job target and/or a job objective when preparing a resume in the chronological, targeted, or functional/skills format.

There are general rules for ordering and listing education. List education at the top of the resume when you are working toward a degree and have not yet earned it, possess fewer than two years of related work experience in the designated career

field, or have earned a degree within the past two years. However, if you possess more than two years of work-related experience or have earned a degree that does not relate to the desired career field, you should list it at the bottom of the resume.

When documenting work history, it is important to place emphasis on the most current positions held. Depending on the resume format selected and amount of work history accumulated, you may choose to document only the selected work experience that directly relates to the position you are seeking. List the years of employment, the name of the company/organization, location (city, state), job title, and description of responsibilities and contributions, competencies, and accomplishments. Bullets are recommended to organize job responsibilities. In the case of internship or co-op employment, it is appropriate to just list the year and write "Internship" or "Co-op" as the job title. You may wish to specify the department or division in which you worked. It is understood that internship and co-op positions typically last 6 to 10 weeks (about a semester). However, listing the months and year is also acceptable. Information describing responsibilities, accomplishments, and results for each position should be organized in order of importance, starting with the most significant. You can also list the specific time frame of an internship or a co-op experience (e.g., 10-week internship). Use action verbs in this section (see Box 8.2). It is important that you choose the correct verb tense. As a general rule, present tense is used to summarize descriptions of currently held posi-

tions, capabilities, and accomplishments, while past tense is used for previous employment descriptions.

Affiliations/memberships in professional organizations, academic associations, or social groups can be listed at the bottom of the resume. Once you have been out of school for a year or two, it is advisable to drop any membership/affiliation from the resume unless it directly relates to your career field. List the years involved, the name of the organization, membership title (i.e., member, president, or committee chair). If you were an officer or a committee chair, you may choose to provide a brief description of your responsibilities (use bullets to organize this information).

Updating the Resume
Reevaluating Resume Format
Once you have established a solid, consistent work history, it is important to reevaluate the resume format you have decided to use. The style you used in the past may no longer be appropriate or the best choice to allow your experience and qualifications to stand out. Go back to page 104 and answer the questions again to determine if the current resume format used is still appropriate. Individuals who possess a greater amount of work experience most frequently use the chronological or targeted resume formats.

Many people often choose to change the aesthetic appearance of the resume to provide a fresh presentation of information and to avoid a dated look. Keep in mind that your resume needs to reflect the image of your brand and maintain consistency and continuity between all of the market-

Resume Do's and Don'ts

Do

- Limit resume to one page.
- Emphasize accomplishments and results.
- Write clearly and concisely. Make every word count.
- Use action verbs when describing responsibilities, capabilities, and accomplishments.
- Use a thesaurus to help select words that best describe capabilities, accomplishments, and experience. A thesaurus also assists in word selection and it is advisable to vary your terms instead of using the same words repeatedly. Be aware of usage and context when choosing words.
- Use nouns and adjectives when describing qualifications on a targeted resume.
- Use present tense to summarize current position descriptions, capabilities, and accomplishments.
- Use past tense for former employment descriptions, capabilities, and accomplishments.
- Write the resume yourself. You know your experience and accomplishments best. Resume services can be expensive and may not provide you with a personalized style to help build and reinforce your brand.

- Ask a well-respected professor or professional to proofread the resume and give you feedback.
- Place emphasis on the most current positions and related experience.
- List years only when listing different employment experiences. Inclusion of the specific month and date employment began and ended should be reserved for the job application.
- Use declarative statements (e.g., refocused division and increased sales by 20 percent the first month).
- Use numbers to support accomplishments and results.
- Use appropriate terminology to describe skills and experience.
- Carefully proofread for grammar, including spelling and punctuation, and formatting errors.
- Print resumes on quality paper using a laser printer or use a professional copy service.
- Store a few extra copies of the resume in the back pocket of the portfolio in case you need them during an interview.

Don't

- Use personal pronouns "I" or "me." It is understood that the information included on the resume refers to your experience; therefore, it is not necessary to make reference to yourself.
- Be dishonest or deceitful.
- List a GPA below 3.0.
- Use abbreviations (except for state and degree).
- Use passive language or make heavy use of dependent clauses (e.g., Sales the first month *were increased by* 20 percent, *which was a result of* refocusing the division).
- List references on a resume or print "references upon request" at the bottom of a resume.
- Use overly decorative, vibrant, or dark papers as

they may be difficult to read or may not lend themselves to scanning.
- Use stylized fonts or colored text that may be difficult to read.
- Include a photograph of yourself.
- Include personal information that is not relevant to the job (i.e., birthplace, age, marital status, ethnicity, and so on).
- Include acronyms or terminology not understood outside a particular company.
- Use self-serving or opinionated words unless you can back them up with facts (such as specific numbers or percentages used to accompany accomplishments).

ing tools used for the job application. When changing the appearance of your brand, it is important to streamline all components from the resume and cover letter to the organization and aesthetic appearance of the merchandising portfolio, the IMP, and even the thank-you letter that you send after sitting through an interview. If you portray a consistent image, the potential employer will recognize all of your individual marketing tools as one package, which will make a greater impact.

Stating Qualifications and Results

First, you must realize your worth and value—then translate this into a format and style that become strong marketing tools for your job applications. You must believe in yourself and be proud of your accomplishments. It is your responsibility to let an employer know why you are the best choice. When a potential employer reviews your resume, he or she already knows the basic responsibilities of the position. You need to focus on statements that reflect your accomplishments. Qualifications let employers know what you can actually do for them based on your experience. Language is your persuasive tool. It is important to communicate competencies and capabilities specific to the job target in a way that convinces an employer that you will add value to the staff. Use quantifiable statements to emphasize accomplishments and results you have achieved. Provide specific numbers, percentages, and time frames when possible to qualify and highlight significant achievements. Document specific results you have obtained to support why an employer

should hire you. Matching the documented competencies and achievements you possess to the level of expertise for which an employer is searching can increase your odds of getting the job. Think about why the following statements would be effective in a resume; afterward, practice writing some of your own.

- Reversed a 3-year negative sales trend to a 20 percent increase within the first 10 months as an associate buyer for men's sportswear.

- Promoted to visual manager after only 10 months as a visual stylist.

- Streamlined and increased efficiency of output of color approvals.

- Conducted competitive shopping research to determine market segment opportunities that led to the launch of a new line that has produced a gross profit of $1.2 million the first year.

- Applied advanced knowledge of CAD software to train team members to increase efficiency and output.

- Received the undergraduate award for Outstanding Achievement three years in a row.

- Achieved $2.8 million in annual sales as an account executive for a growing specialty retail chain.

- Redefined core target market for private label brand and created a promotional strategy that increased brand awareness and sales.

Activities

1. Work through the Resume Development Worksheets 8.1 through 8.4 in the appendix to assist with the documentation of information that you use to create or update your resume. Review Worksheet 2.1 and work through Worksheets 2.2 and 2.3 to determine which skills you possess for the specific job target/job objective desired.

2. Create or update your resume using the information from Worksheets 2.1 through 2.3 and 8.1 through 8.4, and the recommended format (chronological, functional/skills, or targeted). Remember, the creative resume has contents similar to the above listed formats; the presentation and aesthetic appearance, however, will veer from the traditional presentation.

Checklist for Evaluating Resumes

○ Yes ○ No Are margins within half-inch to one-inch tolerance?

○ Yes ○ No Is the font easy to read?

○ Yes ○ No If a job objective is stated, is it clear, concise, and well developed?

○ Yes ○ No Is proper tense used (current job uses present and former jobs use past tense)?

○ Yes ○ No Do you have grammar mistakes, including spelling and punctuation, or formatting errors?

○ Yes ○ No Does the selected resume format best highlight qualifications for the position you seek?

○ Yes ○ No Is the job target listed on a targeted resume?

○ Yes ○ No Do you have continuity and consistency between the formatting/style of headings and your name?

○ Yes ○ No Do you use boldface, italics, and capitalization sparingly to effectively highlight/emphasize information?

○ Yes ○ No Is information aesthetically balanced (space used profitably) on the page to avoid large areas of empty space and other areas of densely covered space?

○ Yes ○ No Are qualifications and capabilities written specifically to address the description of the job for which you are applying?

○ Yes ○ No Does the resume clearly communicate what you can do for the potential employer?

○ Yes ○ No Does the resume effectively provide proof of your skills and accomplishments?

○ Yes ○ No Does the overall appearance of the resume create a desire to read it?

○ Yes ○ No Do important qualifications and experiences stand out?

○ Yes ○ No Did you eliminate irrelevant or redundant information?

○ Yes ○ No Do you use action verbs to describe capabilities, accomplishments, and responsibilities?

○ Yes ○ No Does the overall appearance of the resume reflect a consistent brand image that relates to your portfolio?

Box 8.1 Nouns and Adjectives for Qualification Statements
Nouns

Ability	Delegate	Instruction	Publication
Access	Director	Integrity	Publicity
Account	Discretion	Interest	Purchase
Adherence	Display	Interview	Receiving
Advocate	Document	Invoice	Recognition
Analysis	Draft	Knowledge	Result
Application	Effect	Language	Routine
Arrangement	Enthusiasm	Leadership	Scenario
Assurance	Evolution	Majority	Schedule
Attention	Executive	Merchandise	Shop
Authority	Expansion	Network	Show
Authorization	Expert	Observation	Skill
Award	Expertise	Opportunity	Solution
Balance	Expression	Outcome	Source
Beginning	Factor	Outline	Speaker
Benefit	Fashion	Ownership	Specialty
Boost	Feature	Package	Stable
Budget	Field	Partner	Standard
Business	File	Passion	Strategy
Capacity	Focus	Percentage	Style
Category	Foresight	Phase	Success
Client	Frequency	Pioneer	Supervision
Communication	Function	Pitch	Supplement
Concept	Gains	Placement	Support
Conduct	Goal	Plan	Synthesis
Consideration	Guide	Preparation	Transaction
Construction	Help	Priority	Transition
Contract	Impact	Procedure	Travel
Conversation	Importance	Production	Venture
Correspondence	Improvement	Profession	Warehouse
Creator	Increase	Progress	
Customer	Influence	Projection	
Decision	Innovation	Promoter	

Able	Conventional	Genuine	Practical
Above	Credible	Global	Proficient
Accurate	Critical	Graduate	Profitable
Active	Current	Handy	Prominent
Annual	Daily	Heavy	Published
Another	Decrease	Helpful	Punctual
Applicable	Desiring	Highest	Receiving
Appropriate	Direct	Honorary	Reliable
Approximate	Distinct	Ideal	Representative
Attentive	Distinguished	Immediate	Resourceful
Authentic	Diverse	Immense	Responsible
Authoritative	Double	Important	Self-made
Available	Dual	Incomparable	Skilled
Aware	Dynamic	Industrious	Steadfast
Beneficial	Eager	Influential	Subjective
Best	Earnest	Informative	Subsequent
Beyond	Economical	Inherent	Successful
Bold	Educated	Intense	Suitable
Brilliant	Effective	Knowledgeable	Superior
Broad	Effortless	Latest	Supported
Busy	Elevated	Logical	Supporting
Capable	Eligible	Lucrative	Teaching
Celebrated	Enterprising	National	Timely
Characteristic	Entire	Noteworthy	Traveling
Charitable	Expanded	Official	Tremendous
Clear	Expert	Original	Typical
Combined	External	Perceptive	Ultimate
Compatible	Fair	Periodic	Viable
Complete	Favorable	Persistent	Vital
Complex	Flexible	Personable	Voluntary
Comprehensive	Fluent	Persuasive	Wholesale
Concise	Fundamental	Planned	
Contemporary	Further	Potential	

Box 8.2 Past Tense Action Verbs

Abided	Articulated	Composed	Detected	Executed
Accelerated	Assembled	Conceived	Determined	Exhibited
Accepted	Assessed	Concluded	Developed	Expanded
Accommodated	Assigned	Condensed	Devised	Expedited
Accompanied	Assisted	Conducted	Directed	Expressed
Accomplished	Attained	Confirmed	Discovered	Facilitated
Accounted	Attended	Constructed	Discussed	Figured
Accrued	Audited	Consulted	Dispensed	Filed
Accumulated	Authorized	Contained	Displayed	Finalized
Achieved	Averted	Continued	Disseminated	Financed
Acknowledged	Balanced	Contracted	Distributed	Fired
Acquired	Blended	Contributed	Documented	Flourished
Acted	Broadened	Controlled	Doubled	Focused
Activated	Budgeted	Conversed	Drafted	Followed
Adapted	Built	Converted	Earned	Forecasted
Added	Calculated	Convinced	Eased	Formulated
Addressed	Calibrated	Coordinated	Edited	Founded
Adjusted	Categorized	Corresponded	Educated	Furthered
Administered	Certified	Counseled	Elevated	Gathered
Adopted	Challenged	Crafted	Eliminated	Gauged
Advanced	Chaired	Created	Emerged	Gained
Advocated	Changed	Customized	Emphasized	Generated
Advised	Charted	Decided	Employed	Granted
Allocated	Checked	Decreased	Enabled	Greeted
Amended	Circulated	Defined	Enacted	Grouped
Analyzed	Collaborated	Delegated	Enforced	Guided
Answered	Collected	Delineated	Engineered	Handled
Appealed	Combined	Delivered	Enhanced	Headed
Applied	Commanded	Demonstrated	Equipped	Heightened
Appraised	Committed	Deposited	Enriched	Helped
Apprenticed	Communicated	Derived	Established	Hired
Apprised	Competed	Described	Evaluated	Identified
Approved	Compiled	Designated	Examined	Illustrated
Arranged	Completed	Designed	Exceeded	Impacted

Box 8.2 Past Tense Action Verbs (cont.)

Imparted	Mediated	Proved	Resolved	Submitted
Implemented	Mentioned	Provided	Resourced	Succeeded
Improved	Merchandised	Publicized	Responded	Summarized
Incorporated	Mixed	Published	Revamped	Supervised
Increased	Modernized	Purchased	Reviewed	Supplied
Indexed	Modified	Pursued	Revised	Supported
Influenced	Monitored	Quadrupled	Revitalized	Surmised
Informed	Motivated	Qualified	Rewrote	Surpassed
Initiated	Moved	Quantified	Routed	Surveyed
Innovated	Multitasked	Quoted	Satisfied	Synthesized
Installed	Negotiated	Raised	Scheduled	Targeted
Instituted	Nominated	Ranked	Searched	Taught
Instructed	Observed	Rated	Secured	Tested
Interested	Obtained	Received	Selected	Thrived
Interpreted	Operated	Recognized	Separated	Tracked
Interviewed	Ordered	Recommended	Served	Trained
Introduced	Organized	Recorded	Set up	Translated
Invented	Oversaw	Recruited	Showed	Traveled
Inventoried	Participated	Reduced	Simplified	Trimmed
Investigated	Performed	Referenced	Skilled	Tripled
Issued	Personalized	Referred	Sold	Unified
Judged	Pioneered	Refined	Solved	United
Justified	Planned	Regarded	Specialized	Upgraded
Launched	Positioned	Regulated	Specified	Used
Led	Prepared	Reinforced	Sponsored	Utilized
Located	Presented	Related	Standardized	Validated
Lowered	Prevented	Relayed	Stated	Valued
Maintained	Prioritized	Relocated	Stocked	Verified
Managed	Processed	Renegotiated	Streamlined	Volunteered
Maneuvered	Produced	Reorganized	Strengthened	Widened
Marketed	Programmed	Repaired	Structured	Won
Mastered	Projected	Reported	Studied	Worked
Maximized	Promoted	Represented	Styled	Wrote
Measured	Prompted	Researched	Stylized	Yielded

Jennifer F. Green

2122 Wyndham Dr. ▪ Arlington, TX 76063 ▪ 682-XXX-XXXX ▪ candidatename@yahoo.com

Buyer for Diamonds

Buy and develop private label diamond jewelry with the opportunity to use GIA certifications to procure merchandise and grow sales and profit.

Education

2003-present	**Gemological Institute of America**	Carlsbad, CA

- GIA Certified—Diamond Essentials and Diamond Grading course and lab
- GIA Certified—Colored Stones Essentials and Colored Stones course and lab
- Completed GIA Gem Identification Lab

1998-2002	**Texas Christian University**	Fort Worth, TX

- Bachelor of Science in Fashion Merchandising; General Business minor—*Magna Cum Laude*

Experience

2004-present	**Bailey, Banks, & Biddle**	Irving, TX

Associate Buyer for Color, Gold, & Silver, 2005-present
- Developed and implemented new gold assortment for FY07
- Assist in product development of private label sterling silver jewelry line
- Negotiate RTVs in gold and semiprecious departments

Merchandise Planner for Designer & Pearls, 2004-2005
- Assisted in sell-off of 29 stores and the movement of $24 million in aged inventory
- Created FY06 Designer plans by building a bottom-up-by-store-by-designer plan
- Achieved and maintained a 90% in-stock rate in the core pearl business
- Developed order projection worksheets for core designer and pearl items

2002-2004	**Neiman Marcus**	Dallas, TX

Merchandise Planner for Designer Sportswear, 2004
- Prepared preliminary Spring 2005 plans
- Assisted in presentation for General Managers Meeting

Assistant Merchandise Planner for Precious Jewels & Watches, 2003-2004
- 2003 Neiman Marcus Assistant Merchandise Planner of the Year Award
- Created core programs for top performing vendors including Cartier and Franck Muller
- Supervised closure of precious jewels salons in Beachwood and Biltmore
- Analyzed and proposed markdown opportunties to liquidate aged merchandise
- Generated vendor analysis for European market trip
- Keyed monthly projections

Assistant Merchandise Planner for Precious Designer Jewels, 2002-2003
- Managed open-to-buy and created purchase order system for designer precious jewelry area
- Developed vendor and trend analysis for best sellers and market recaps
- Drafted product and location plans and managed owned inventory by initiating transfers, redistributing merchandise and creating new buy and markdown books
- Visited and negotiated with vendors regarding advertising, RTVs, and receipts
- Trained new Assistant Buyer in duties and responsibilities for the position
- MDP Curriculum—Computer training, group projects, and presentations

2001-2002	**Pottery Barn**	Fort Worth, TX

Sales Associate
- Assisted customers with purchases and restocked inventory, and created visual displays

2001	**Neiman Marcus**	Fort Worth, TX

Intern, 10-week internship program
- Exposed to delivery department, visual merchandising, public relations, loss prevention, and HR

2001	**Zale Corporation, Bailey, Banks, & Biddle**	Irving, TX

Buying Office Intern in Watch Division, 10-week internship program
- Gained working knowledge of buying office operations
- Assisted with marketing and vendor meetings
- Participated in visual merchandising for new store and on-site setup

Figure 8.1 Jennifer Green's chronological resume with a job target and focused objective for a diamond buyer position.

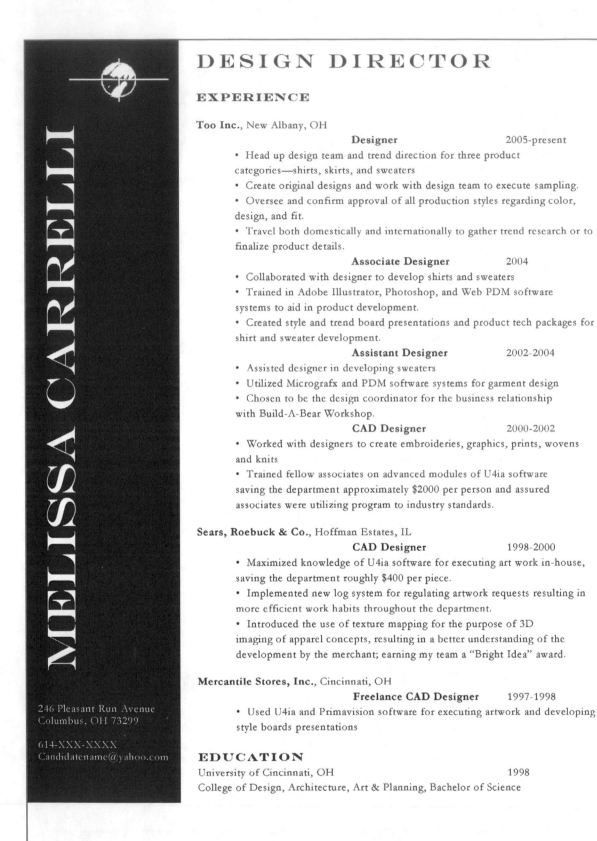

DESIGN DIRECTOR

MELISSA CARRELLI

246 Pleasant Run Avenue
Columbus, OH 73299

614-XXX-XXXX
Candidatename@yahoo.com

EXPERIENCE

Too Inc., New Albany, OH

Designer   2005-present
• Head up design team and trend direction for three product categories—shirts, skirts, and sweaters
• Create original designs and work with design team to execute sampling.
• Oversee and confirm approval of all production styles regarding color, design, and fit.
• Travel both domestically and internationally to gather trend research or to finalize product details.

Associate Designer   2004
• Collaborated with designer to develop shirts and sweaters
• Trained in Adobe Illustrator, Photoshop, and Web PDM software systems to aid in product development.
• Created style and trend board presentations and product tech packages for shirt and sweater development.

Assistant Designer   2002-2004
• Assisted designer in developing sweaters
• Utilized Micrografx and PDM software systems for garment design
• Chosen to be the design coordinator for the business relationship with Build-A-Bear Workshop.

CAD Designer   2000-2002
• Worked with designers to create embroideries, graphics, prints, wovens and knits
• Trained fellow associates on advanced modules of U4ia software saving the department approximately $2000 per person and assured associates were utilizing program to industry standards.

Sears, Roebuck & Co., Hoffman Estates, IL

CAD Designer   1998-2000
• Maximized knowledge of U4ia software for executing art work in-house, saving the department roughly $400 per piece.
• Implemented new log system for regulating artwork requests resulting in more efficient work habits throughout the department.
• Introduced the use of texture mapping for the purpose of 3D imaging of apparel concepts, resulting in a better understanding of the development by the merchant; earning my team a "Bright Idea" award.

Mercantile Stores, Inc., Cincinnati, OH

Freelance CAD Designer   1997-1998
• Used U4ia and Primavision software for executing artwork and developing style boards presentations

EDUCATION

University of Cincinnati, OH   1998
College of Design, Architecture, Art & Planning, Bachelor of Science

Figure 8.2 Melissa Carrelli's chronological resume with a job target for a design director position.

CHINAE ALEXANDER

1504 W. Century Dr.
Dallas, TX 76109
972.XXX.XXX
studentname@hotmail.com

OBJECTIVE

Internship at a major fashion publication with the opportunity to work in an editorial department that would allow for correspondence with designers and retailers to procure merchandise for editorial spreads

EDUCATION

2003-present   Texas Christian University, Fort Worth, TX
Fashion Merchandising major, General Business minor

TECHNOLOGY SKILLS

- Proficient in CAD U4ia and KaledoStyle software programs
- Working Knowledge of Adobe InDesign and Photoshop, and Microsoft Word, Publisher, Excel, and PowerPoint software programs
- Determining garment specifications and costing

WRITTEN COMMUNICATION SKILLS

- Writing fashion stories
- Preparing press releases and press kits
- Developing content and layout of promotional materials
- Conducting, compiling, and analyzing market research
- Preparing comparison shopping reports

CREATIVE & VISUAL SKILLS

- Developing original textile prints, weaves, knits, and technical flat drawings
- Creating concept boards and page layouts for presentations
- Developing product lines
- Creating and styling visual merchandising displays
- Designing promotional materials

EMPLOYMENT SUMMARY

2005-present   Pappadeaux Seafood Kitchen, Fort Worth, TX
Server

2004-2005   The Alternative, Fort Worth, TX
Fashion Editor/Advertising Representative

2004   Armstrong Wealth Management, Fort Worth, TX
Personal Assistant/Secretary

2003-2004   Merle Norman Cosmetics, Mission, TX
Beauty Consultant—Full Commission Sales Associate & Team Leader

PHILANTHROPY

2005   DIFFA Dallas Collection Charity Fashion Show & Auction—*Featured Designer & Volunteer*
Hurricane Katrina Disaster Relief Efforts, *Volunteer*
Salvation Army Fort Worth, *Volunteer*
2004-2005   Presbyterian Women's Night Shelter, *Volunteer*
2003-present   Links to Literacy, *Volunteer*

ACTIVITIES & MEMBERSHIPS

Pi Beta Phi Fraternity for Women, *Pledge Class Social Chair & T-shirt Chair*
Brachman Residence Hall, *President and Hall Council Member*
Residential Hall Association, *Interest Group Leader*

Figure 8.3   Chinae Alexander's functional/skills resume with a focused objective for an internship.

KACEY GRAGG

6500 Empress Lake Dr. • Fort Worth, TX 76133 • (817) XXX-XXXX • studentname@hotmail.com

OBJECTIVE   Enter JCPenney's Merchandising Trainee Program with the opportunity for promotion into an allocation position to support a buying team.

EDUCATION
2007   **Texas Christian University**   Fort Worth, TX
                  Bachelor of Science in Fashion Merchandising; GPA 3.7

                  Minor: Psychology
                  • Participated in New York and Paris Study Abroad Programs
                  • TCU Scholar

ANALYTICAL SKILLS
                  • Preparing merchandise plans and purchase orders
                  • Planning open to buys, reorders and assortment plans
                  • Creating vendor analysis
                  • Calculating store markup
                  • Costing apparel and soft home products

RESEARCH & SOFTWARE SKILLS
                  • Proficient in Microsoft Excel, PowerPoint, Outlook, Access, Word, AutoCAD
                  • Conducting and preparing market research and completive retail reports
                  • Analyzing trend forecasts

COMMUNICATION SKILLS
                  • Preparing professional correspondence
                  • Ability to articulate thoughts in both verbal and written forms

EXPERIENCE
2006-present   **Charmed by Melissa**   Southlake, TX
                  Merchandising Assistant Sales Associate
                  • Assist owner with merchandise selection during vendor visits
                  • Checked in new merchandise, priced, and merchandised sales floor
                  • Assisted with merchandising sales floor; Created window and interior displays
                  Intern, *10 week internship program*

2003-2004   **Gap Inc.**   Midland, TX
                  Seasonal Sales Associate

2003-2004   **MGM Oil & Gas Company**   Midland, TX
                  Seasonal Assistant Office Manager

MEMBERSHIPS
2003-Present   The National Society of Collegiate Scholars, Member

Source: Courtesy of Kacey Gragg

Figure 8.4 Kacey Gragg's functional/skills resume with a focused objective for a trainee position.

Amanda Bockwoldt

29 Rebecca Dr. Dallas, TX 76248
studentname@hotmail.com
817-XXX-XXXX

Objective

To obtain an internship with Gap Inc., in product design and development that would provide the chance to assist in creating concept boards, line development, sourcing fabrics, and compiling product packages.

Education

TEXAS CHRISTIAN UNIVERSITY   **2007**   Fort Worth, TX

Bachelor of Science in Fashion Merchandising; Major GPA: 3.6
Minor in Advertising and Public Relations
- TCU Scholar: Fall 2005; Dean's List: Spring 2004 and Fall 2005
- TCU Scholarship recipient
- Member of Phi Upsilon Omicron Honor Society—Beta Zeta Chapter

Related Skills

CREATIVE & TECHNICAL
- Research, analyze, and interpret trend forecasts for identified target markets
- Create trend, mood, and line storyboards
- Design products, create technical flat drawings, and fabricate apparel lines
- Determine garment specifications and calculate product costs and store markup
- Preparing merchandise and assortment plans
- Planning open to buys and reorders

MARKETING & COMMUNICATION
- Proficient in Microsoft Office applications—Excel, Word, PowerPoint, Publisher
- Strong verbal and written communication and presentation skills
- Conduct market research in relation to brand and target market
- Develop promotional strategies and materials to increase brand awareness
- Competent in Italian language

Work Experience

BANANA REPUBLIC   **2004-present**   Fort Worth, TX

Assistant Manager   [2006-present]
- Oversee Banana Republic Card enrollment
- Co-manage new merchandise roll outs and manage daily store operations

Visual Specialist [2005- 2006]   Fort Worth, TX
- Earned *Banana Republic Visual Excellence Award*   Chesterfield, MO

Sales Associate   [2004-2005]   Fort Worth. TX
- Sales leader in St. Louis and Fort Worth stores   Chesterfield, MO
- Earned *Star Performer Award*

MAIN STREET GYM   **2002-2003**   St. Charles, MO

Supervisor
- Managed all weekend business and maintained appearance of gym: Opened new memberships

Figure 8.5 Amanda Bockwoldt's functional/skills resume with a focused objective for an internship.

Jessica J. Weiss

27 Ramsey Place   Hoboken, New Jersey 07030   (212) XXX.XXXX   candidatename@yahoo.com

Job Target: Design Director

Qualifications

- Expertise in Design and development of branded seasonal product lines – Hosiery, Handbags, Belts, Scarves
- Proficient in computer applications - Word, WordPerfect, Excel, Internet, Filemaker Pro (Hosiery spec program), Photofinish, Lotus (spread sheet). Experience with using Adobe Illustrator CS and Photoshop CS
- Skilled in developing product specifications, illustrating flat sketches, and merchandising product lines
- Experience working with Mills and collaborating with Sourcing & Quality Control to ensure high quality products at targeted prices
- Utilize communication skills to build strong relationships with domestic and overseas venders
- Ability to interpret apparel trends for branded seasonal lines and develop complementary accessories

Experience

Polo Ralph Lauren Hosiery, New York, New York   2001-Present
Associate Design Director

- Design and develop men's and women's Polo lines per season. Men's line includes: Purple Label, Polo Blue Label, RLX, Polo Jeans, and Polo Boys. Women's line includes: Blue Label, Lauren Ralph Lauren, Polo Jeans and Active. Assist with design and development for Club Monaco, Lands' End, J. Crew, and Hot Sox Men
- Supervise team of 2 designers to execute all designs and ideas using graphic program *Pointcarre*
- Meet with Jerry Lauren and team each season to present sample lines for final approval
- Partner with Polo apparel for inspiration regarding each line per season
- Travel domestically to work with mills on development
- Maintain strong, dynamic relationship with domestic and overseas vendors
- Build life size concept rigs to represent each group per season
- Finalize all styles per line per season using hosiery spec database *Filemaker Pro*
- Meet seasonally with Sales and Production teams to merchandise the lines
- Work jointly with Sourcing and Quality Control team to ensure the best product for the best price

Liz Claiborne, Inc., New York, New York   1998-2001
Associate Designer: Handbags, 2000-2001

- Contributed designs for Fall and Holiday 2000, Spring 2001 with full involvement from initial concept through production
- Illustrated and created specs for hardware and handbag designs through flat sketches
- Worked closely with overseas offices to receive samples in time for meetings and Market Week
- Partnered with the V.P. of Design developing new piece goods and approving lab dips
- Participated with setting up the showroom for market presentations
- Shopped market for trends and ideas/inspiration

Design Assistant: Belts and Scarves, 1998-2000

- Assisted designers with all aspects of design development for each season
- Scanned and manipulated sketches using *Photofinish*
- Created and updated spec sheets for design development seasonally
- Received and reviewed strike offs with designer to make color corrections and design comments
- Sourced new fabrications and novelty items with overseas vendors

Garan, New York, New York   1998
Design Assistant: Toddler Boys, Boys 4-7

- Participated in initial development and design research and assisted in all aspects of writing and correcting specs
- Designed plaids, stripes, and motifs using *Adobe Illustrator 7.0*
- Created presentation boards for buyers

Education

The Shannon Rodgers and Jerry Silverman School of Fashion Design and Merchandising   1997
Kent State University, Kent, Ohio
Bachelor of Arts in Fashion Design, Minor in Fiber Arts

- Dean's List 1996
- Steven Stipleman Illustration Workshop Scholarship August 1996

Figure 8.6 Jessica Weiss's targeted resume with a qualifications section for a design director position.

Nicole Mertz

3414 Alexander Drive · NE Atlanta, GA 30326 · 404-XXX-XXXX · candidatename@yahoo.com

Visual Designer

Summary of Qualifications

- Seven years experience in Visual Merchandising & Display—Marketing & Promotional Events
- Proven experience in detailed planning, resourceful budgeting, and organization of visual promotions and allocation of resources. A well regarded manager of corporate resources.
- Skilled in interpreting and communicating trends for maximization of sales.
- Experience managing and merchandising large format specialty stores with 25-30 departments, smaller specialty boutiques, and individual model homes.
- Skilled in protocols of hiring and managing employees, as well as building customer/vendor relations. Possess strong written and verbal communication skills.
- Manage, create and maintain all aspects of in-store and window displays, vignettes, museum cases, lighting, fixtures, signage, merchandise, and floor sets—Accountable for reaction to and impact of merchandising and its direct relation to sales volume and loss prevention.

Experience

2006-present **Beazer Homes, Interior Design Division**   Alpharetta, Georgia
Designer
- Select and purchase all elements to merchandise interiors of model homes nationally. Maintain budgets for each home.

2004-2006 **Anthropologie**
Visual Manager   Atlanta, GA
- Managed entire store team of 15 associates. Trained and developed department managers and assistants in all aspects of merchandising.
- Improved loss prevention through careful planning of floor sets and merchandising of fixtures within departments decreasing theft/loss of products.

2002-2004 **Nordstrom**
Visual Manager   Frisco, TX & Charlotte, NC
- Hired and managed team of visual stylists and freelancers. Managed merchandising of 25-30 departments.
- Managed visual merchandising budgets from $700-$10,000

Visual Stylist   Dallas, TX
- Merchandised and maintained 12 departments. Managed over 50 freelancers and employee volunteers as Lead Stylist for Holiday trim Installation.
- Recognized and awarded for various Design of Department promotions/events.

Figure 8.7 Nicole Mertz's targeted resume with a qualifications section for a visual designer position.

DANA C. SMITH

4607 Timber Road · Dallas, TX · (214) XXX-XXXX · candidatename@yahoo.com

Product Development Manager

CAPABILITIES

- Expertise in private brand product development management - national and international experience.
- Ability to improve cost effectiveness by accurate forecasting, sourcing and material selection, and decreasing overstock levels. Possess a natural talent for perceiving style, fabric trends, quality and value.
- Proven track record of developing apparel lines and complete decorative hard and soft lines for home.
- Create product packages including fabric and trim detail selections and size specifications.
- Collaborate and execute design ideas with Asian, Indian, and domestic suppliers.
- Aptitude for developing season color palettes and evaluating lab dips for color approval.

ACCOMPLISHMENTS

- Received the Outstanding Achievement Award - First person in St. John's Bay to receive this honor.
- Designed entire best selling activewear line for St. John's Bay - Spring 2002
- Reversed a 2-year negative sales trend to a 17.6% increase within the first year as Assistant Brand Development Manager for Duo Maternity.
- Collaborated with technical designer to improve and update maternity wear fit to decrease returns.
- Implemented technical fabrics to enhance active wear quality, style and detail selections.
- Redefined active wear customer base and expanded product mix to compete with current trends.

EXPERIENCE

Home Interiors & Gifts, Inc.,	Carrollton, TX	2002-present

Product Line Manager – HI Kids, Accessories, Clocks, Furniture, Bathroom Accessories, Garden
- Hired to manage and grow new HI Kids Line.

JCPenney Co.	Plano, TX	1998-2002

Assistant Designer – St. John's Bay (Women's) – 2002
- Promoted into newly created private brand design team to assist designers of knits, wovens, sweaters, and active wear.

Assistant Product Manager – St. John's Bay Active – 2001-2002
- Transferred to assist in reviving the troubled private brand active wear line with regard to trends, specific styles, details, technical design, materials and sourcing decisions.

Assistant Brand Development Manager – Duo Maternity – 2000-2001
- Transferred to brand development. Personally selected by Merchandise Development Manager to groom for future private brand corporate liaison with NY based trend manager.

Catalog Inventory Analyst – Maternity – 1998-2000
- Hired to analyze and impact catalog sales of the $30 million maternity area. Forecasted unit purchases to the buying team; tracked sales and ensured stock levels would meet needs.

Althuser	Dallas, TX	1997

Ladies Sportswear Design Intern
- Hired initially to assist in pattern design layout and sample cutting for contractor production. Designed apparel for retail consideration, dyed fabric, sewed muslins for model fittings and served additionally as a fit model.

EDUCATION

Texas Woman's University	Denton, TX	1997
BA in Fashion Design		

Figure 8.8 Dana Smith's targeted resume with capabilities and accomplishments sections for a product development manager position.

JUDY ANNE BURNS

5716 Preston Road, Dallas, TX 75024
817-XXX-XXXX · candidatename@yahoo.com

JOB TARGET: SENIOR ASSISTANT BUYER

CAPABILITIES

Ability to develop balanced assortment plans by selecting trend-right key items that fit sales plans, volume groups and space and place, including contingency and exit strategies.

Analysis of trends and competitor market patterns to identify key opportunities.

Expertise working with Product Development Teams on all aspects of private brand merchandise   development of product, costing, quality, life cycle, and construction.

Demonstrated success in appropriately allocating merchandise to support marketing events and advertising, as well as monitoring inventory, managing overstocks and making appropriate merchandise allocations to stores based on current sales trend information.

ACCOMPLISHMENTS

Assisted buying unit in achieving a 15% increase in sales and a 30% increase in gross profit.

Helped develop effective business strategy in conjunction with planning team for a $110 million buying area by establishing financial and merchandise objectives and specifying actions needed to achieve them.

Assisted the buying unit in achieving an 18% increase in sales and a 10% increase in gross profit by managing individual stores inventory levels.

Applied knowledge of allocation software and supporting systems, metrics, and allocation methods to make allocation decisions that maximize sales and profit and minimize risk for a $92 million buying area.

WORK HISTORY

J.C. Penney Corporation	Plano TX	2003-present

Assistant Buyer for Girls 7-16 Dresses and Girls Plus—2005-present
Serve on corporate Assortment Planning Tool Committee as Children's Division Subject Matter Expert

Allocator for Girls 7-16 Dresses and Girls Plus—2004

Merchandise Analyst Trainee—2003-2004
Completed four-phase program for planning, buying, allocating, and in-store experience that incorporated hands-on training, roundtable discussions, and competitive shopping project.

Dallas Stars	Irving, TX	2003

Community Relations Intern—10 week internship

Limited Too	Fort Worth, Texas	2002-2003

Seasonal Sales Associate

Cheerleading Company	Dallas, Texas	2002

Production Intern—10 week internship

Casual Corner	Fort Worth, TX	2001-2002

Sales Associate and Cashier

Paul Harris	Fort Worth, TX	2000-2001

Sales Associate and Cashier

Victoria's Secret	Fort Worth, TX	1999-2000

Key Holder

EDUCATION

Texas Christian University, Fort Worth, TX	2003

Bachelor of Science—Magna Cum Laude
Double Major: Fashion Promotion; Advertising/Public Relations; General Business minor

Figure 8.9 Judy Anne Burns's targeted resume with capabilities and accomplishments sections for a senior assistant buyer position.

Chapter 9

The Interview and the Cover Letter

You can create the most amazing merchandising portfolio, but if you don't know how to use it when you apply and interview for positions, you may as well not have one. This chapter provides guidance in how to effectively market yourself by using your portfolio and accompanying application materials when applying and interviewing for positions in the fashion merchandising industry.

When conducting a job search, it is important that you focus on the type of position you are seeking. In some cases there may be a few related positions for which you apply (e.g., buying, planning, allocation). Geographic location is another consideration when starting a job search. Relocation may provide greater opportunities depending on where you live and the type of position you desire.

Job postings can be found in trade publications, newspaper classifieds, online job sites, official company Web sites, through headhunters, recruiters, and career placement services, and through informational interviews and networking. One of the most vital aspects of a job search is researching the companies in which you are interested. Research is essential but is often left to the last minute. Conducting research can give you information about the company, contact information for correspondence, corporate culture, history, products and services, whether the company is privately owned versus

publicly held, earnings information (publicly held only), number of employees, work environment, job or internship/co-op opportunities, how to apply, and more. You can get this information through individual company Web sites, recent annual or quarterly reports, and employer profiles on Internet resources such as www.vault.com, www.stylecareers.com, www.monster.com, and www.thealexanderreport.com. Vault.com not only has job listings but also offers employer profiles for fashion companies that include brief company history, employee surveys, message boards, and financial information. This site is great for obtaining corporate office addresses and phone numbers, company Web sites, and general career advice. Stylecareers.com is a fashion-only job listing site that provides a multitude of position postings. Monster.com is a general job search site that offers career advice and some company profiles. Thealexanderreport.com is a rich storehouse of information for business resources and services that is purely focused on the apparel industry. If you are looking for companies in specific areas in the fashion industry, this is a great place to start. Trade publications, newspapers, and newswire services are additional resources that can provide pertinent information regarding recent company-related news such as achievements, acquisitions, restructuring, or launch of a new product line. You can search www.google.com to find recent press coverage on the company—even research the people who will be interviewing you. When applying for a position it is important to familiarize yourself with the company at which you are seeking employment. This knowledge will provide facts about the company that you can use when you prepare cover letters, pertinent information for initiating contact with the employer, and valuable information that can be discussed during an interview to demonstrate your knowledge of the company. This research also provides direction for targeting your portfolio to the corporate culture, needs, and philosophy of the company. Also research the career path for the type of position in which you are interested. Look at company hierarchies and see where your position lies on the food chain. Speak to people just above your position and ask them how they got where they are today. A mentor in your field of interest can be an inspiration and an invaluable resource. Research national and regional salary ranges for the positions in which you're interested, so that you have realistic expectations and negotiating power when the job offer comes.

Networking is one of the strongest methods you can use to find out about positions that will be available or are currently open. The U.S. Department of Labor conducted many research studies during the past 20 years to find data about the methods people use to find employment. Use of networking and directly contacting employers proved to be the method used to obtain more than 80

percent of all jobs acquired (Career Momentum, Inc. 2006; CSix Connect 2003). Gilbert Career Resumes (2006), the leading fashion resume expert in the United States, stated, "Recent studies have shown that at least 50 to 60 percent of all jobs are obtained through networking." Networks may consist of colleagues, members of professional or social organizations and advisory boards, alumni, professors, mentors, friends, and family. Building a strong network of contacts can prove helpful when seeking job opportunities. Don't underestimate the power of networking; many job openings are filled by word-of-mouth through individuals who already know someone. Informational interviews allow you to learn firsthand about a job from an industry professional. These interviews are used for gathering information, not applying for a job. You might think they are a waste of time but these types of interviews allow you to build contacts within companies that may later lead to a job. Most successful people are flattered by the opportunity to mentor and advise someone who aspires to the same career path.

Networking is a key aspect in the development and maintenance of your career, whether you're seeking freelance work or a senior vice president position. Tap the available resources and motivate yourself to meet people and be successful. Donald Blair, a former student of the authors who went on to become national marketing and retail coordinator for Ittierre, was a master of networking who always capitalized on opportunities to grow personally and professionally. He summarized

this sentiment when he said, "Do not wait for things to happen to you . . . make things happen to you. You are responsible for the majority of your overall happiness: your successes, your accomplishments, your life. Take control while you have the time, the resources, and the energy."

Cover Letters

When conducting a job search, it is essential that you prepare a cover letter to accompany every resume and portfolio that you send out. Merely submitting a cover letter and resume to a potential employer will not necessarily get you an interview. Take charge of the process and make contact with the employer(s) for whom you wish to work. The most effective use of a cover letter is in response to a phone conversation or other means of contact with the employer. Use this tool to follow up after making initial contact. Do keep in mind that many places will specifically state: "No phone calls, please." It is very important that you respect this request. Including an individual marketing piece with the resume and cover letter can capture attention and strengthen your marketability as a potential contender for the desired position. The IMP can provide visual enticement of the capabilities you possess. Furthermore, the combination of the resume, cover letter, and IMP will assist in establishing your brand identity in the mind of a prospective employer.

Online applications typically give you opportunities to explain why you should be considered for a position. Your responses should contain information that you would traditionally incorporate into a cover letter—

pick three of the skills stated in the job description and match them to skills you possess. Use action verbs. If possible, tell about a notable achievement of yours and mention if you're already in touch with someone who works at the company. Say why this position is the next logical step in your career.

Do not cut corners when preparing cover letters. Beware of the generic cover letter templates that allow you to simply fill in the blanks with your information. Remember, some companies receive thousands of documents from potential candidates each week with cover letters that essentially state the same thing. Write the letter to capture the reader's attention and engage them so they want to read it entirely. Draft a personalized cover letter for each company to which you apply. Be passionate when you discuss why you'd like to work for this company. Convince the employer that you are the best candidate for the position by emphasizing how the skills you possess will benefit or assist the company in achieving its goals. Address the job posting, where you saw it, and why it appeals to you. See Figures 9.1 and 9.2 for cover letter examples.

Formatting the Cover Letter

Format the cover letter by adjusting the page margins, font style, and size to be consistent with the elements you used on your resume and portfolio. The document should be single-spaced. Personal contact information (name, address, phone numbers with area codes, and e-mail addresses) should appear at the top of the page using the same placement and format you did on the

Cover Letter Do's and Don'ts

Do

- Carefully proofread for grammar errors, including spelling and punctuation, as well as formatting errors.
- Address the letter by name to the person who is interviewing and hiring for the position.
- Keep the letter to one page.
- Create interest and desire to read the entire letter.
- Customize the letter by talking about the company.
- Be specific about what you want.
- Focus on the value you bring to the position and to the company.
- Vary sentence structure.
- Write clearly and concisely.
- Be yourself, sincere, professional, and confident.
- Use declarative statements.
- Print cover letters using a laser printer.
- Use a laser printer to print envelopes or labels for application materials that include your brand elements.
- Ask for a meeting or an interview.
- Have a well-respected professor or professional proofread the cover letter and give you feedback.
- Use proper capitalization for cover letters that you send via e-mail.

Don't

- Write a generic cover letter.
- Start every sentence with I.
- Write a lengthy letter. (An employer's time is valuable and you want them to read it.)
- Focus on what you will gain.
- Use dependent clauses.
- Be dishonest or deceitful.
- Use contractions.
- Be arrogant, obnoxious, or pushy.
- Use clichés.
- Close a letter with "Love."
- Use words that you would not use in conversation.
- Use all lowercase or all uppercase letters when e-mailing a cover letter.
- E-mail, fax, or mail a cover letter and resume from work unless applying internally.

resume. If you incorporated a logo or image into this area on the resume, you should incorporate it in the same place on the cover letter (i.e., use this as letterhead to provide continuity and a continued reminder of your brand identity). The overall look and style of the cover letter should match that of the portfolio, resume, and IMP. The graphic icons you choose are an expression of your mission—someone interested in apparel might design an icon of hangers in disarray to show their interest in that segment of the industry. Consistency and attention to detail will strengthen and reinforce your brand identity and overall candidacy for the position. Write out the date (month, day, year) below the personal contact information, and follow it with the employer's contact information (name, position title, company name, address). Leave one or two line spaces between personal information, date, and employer contact information.

Greetings and Salutations

The next cover letter element is the greeting. Always address the letter to the recipient's name followed by a colon. For instance, if you know the person is a male, then it is acceptable to use a greeting that states "Dear Mr. [last name]" and use the last name only. It is always safe to state the person's first and last name, rather than making a gender assumption. Avoid using "To whom it may concern" or "Dear Sir or Madam," which are quite impersonal. If you are unable to obtain the name of the person hiring for the position, it is acceptable to use the person's title, for example, "Dear Director of Sourcing" or "Dear Human Resources Personnel." By all means, make every attempt to obtain the person's name when possible. Personalizing the letter will increase the probability of the document being read or reviewed. Leave one line space below the greeting.

Body of the Letter

Align all of the text flush with the left margin. Do not indent the first line of each paragraph. Use one line space to separate each paragraph and the closing. When developing the body of the letter, make sure to write clearly and concisely. Sentences need to be brief and to the point to assist in ease of reading and maintain interest. The tone of the letter should be professional and reflect your personality and conversational style. Convey sincerity and enthusiasm about the company and the position you are seeking.

Cover letters typically consist of three main paragraphs—the opening, the **rationale**, and the closing and **plan of action**. Cover letters sent via e-mail contain the same content but are typically more concise. The body content should tell the employer what you have to offer. Match your skills to the job requirements and discuss accomplishments that support your claims. This area of the cover letter also allows you to state specific personality traits that enhance your ability to do the job.

Opening In the first paragraph, identify who you are and your purpose for writing. It is important to capture the reader's attention immediately. Make the first sentence engaging and to the point. Make use of the name of the contact who informed you of the position (providing you have approval) to gain the reader's attention. If you personally made contact with the employer, then state that you are following up on the phone conversation. You can make a statement about the company based on personal experience or conduct research to justify your interest in the company.

Rationale The second paragraph, the rationale, demonstrates why you should be hired for the position. Match your qualifications and accomplishments to what the employer is seeking. Discuss how your experience and expertise will benefit the company. Highlight key skills and accomplishments and skills that are relevant to the position and how these will be an asset to the company. Comment on recent company news or events to demonstrate your knowledge of the company. Current events that are impacting the industry may also provide a means for highlighting how the company can benefit from your expertise. Write about how you can assist in the efforts to reach established goals (bring fresh perspective, reduce costs, increase sales). This is not the time to concentrate on what you will gain from the position if given the opportunity. Stay focused on the value you can provide to the company based on what was stated in the job description. Making this direct correlation between the employer's needs and the skills you possess will strengthen your position as a candidate for the job. Those who have a long work history may include more than one paragraph to build their case and convey experience and value.

Closing and Plan of Action The last paragraph communicates apprecia-

Amanda Bockwoldt

29 Rebecca Dr., Dallas, TX 76248
studentname@hotmail.com
817-XXX-XXXX

Date

Ms. Kate Smith
Senior Director, College Recruiting
Gap, Inc.
Two Folsom St.
San Francisco, CA 94105

Dear Ms. Smith:

"Gap Inc. is committed to hiring individuals from around the world who are smart, passionate and fit with our diverse, fast-paced culture that thrives on creativity." In reading your quote in a recent press release on the company website, I immediately identified with your sentiments. As an Assistant Manager in a Banana Republic store, and a junior fashion merchandising major at Texas Christian University, I am excited to apply for your undergraduate summer internship program in merchandising.

In referring to my resume you will notice that my loyalty to Banana Republic is evident. I am passionate about my emerging career and have worked my way up at the store level. During my tenure in college I have obtained valuable skills in product design and development, marketing promotion, and planning that will allow me to contribute as an intern to special projects that are results driven. Working full-time and being a full-time student has allowed me to sharpen my time management skills. I am a driven, detail-oriented individual who performs well under pressure, with the ability to seamlessly multi-task throughout the day. As a current employee of this company, I truly understand the needs of our customers, as well as the business strategy that allows Gap Inc. stores to maintain market leadership.

Enclosed is my resume for your consideration. I will be in contact with you during the next week to discuss this internship opportunity. Should you want to reach me before then, contact me at (817) XXX-XXXX. If I am not available, please leave a message with my voicemail and I will be happy to return your call. Thank you very much for your time. I look forward to talking with you.

Sincerely,

Amanda Bockwoldt

enclosure: Resume and Individual Marketing Piece (IMP)

Figure 9.1 Amanda Bockwoldt's cover letter for an internship position.

Jennifer F. Green

2122 Wyndham Dr. ▪ Arlington, TX 76063 ▪ 682-XXX-XXXX ▪ candidatename@yahoo.com

Ms. Jane Smith
Human Resources Director
Tiffany & Co
727 Fifth Avenue
New York, NY 10022

Date

Dear Ms. Smith:

Since 2002, I have had the privilege of working in the jewelry industry for both Neiman Marcus and Zale Corporation. Through my training and hands-on work experience, I gained a great deal of knowledge about precious jewelry. From my familiarity with the industry, I learned that Tiffany & Co., with its reputation as one of the world's premier jewelers, would be an appealing place to work.

Through my training and experience at Neiman Marcus and Zale Corporation, I have established a reputation among my coworkers and my supervisors for effective leadership, teamwork and communication skills, a proactive nature and a willingness to give 110% in every project I am given. According to your website, Tiffany's provides "extraordinary training and support in an environment that emphasizes challenge through team-driven initiatives and focuses on critical thinking and open communication." I believe my personal attributes and experience and Tiffany's stated qualifications are mutually consistent.

My qualifications, detailed on my resume, coupled with my desire to enhance my merchandising and product development skills and continue to learn more about the complexities of the jewelry industry, make a buying position at Tiffany & Co an exciting prospect. As an associate buyer for semiprecious color, gold and silver at Bailey, Banks and Biddle, I developed the ability to negotiate terms with vendors and work with a team to develop and expand an exclusive silver line for all 73 of the Bailey, Banks and Biddle stores. Moreover, I researched sales history, trends and best sellers by collection, to introduce two new gold collections for the Fall of 2006. In addition to acquiring product development, merchandising and negotiation skills during my experience at Bailey, Banks & Biddle, I have also taken a personal interest in the jewelry itself. Through GIA distance education, I have been able to learn more about diamonds and colored stones through the completion of the Diamond Course and the Colored Stone Grading Course. I believe that I could apply these skills and knowledge effectively as a buyer and am confident that, given the opportunity, I would prove myself an asset to your company.

I realize that in retail, this time of year is one of the busiest. I would appreciate the opportunity to talk with you. If you would like to get in touch with me, please feel free to call me at (682) XXX-XXXX. If I am not available, please leave a message with my voicemail and I will be happy to return your call.

Thank you very much for your consideration. I look forward to talking with you.
Sincerely,

Jennifer F. Green

Figure 9.2 Jennifer Green's cover letter for an industry position.

tion for time and interest, requests an interview or meeting, and states your follow-up plan of action. Be specific and state how you will be contacting them and when. Although your phone number and e-mail address are in the personal contact information listed at the top, it is appropriate to reiterate the information. This information is typically included in a statement concerning how you can be contacted in the interim. Consider including a statement that will help the employer associate you with your brand identity or make a promise. Make sure you mention the availability of a portfolio for review. You might write, "If you are seeking an innovator with proven reliability to produce cutting-edge designs, please call me at (212) 555-5555," or state, "In an interview, I will show you my portfolio containing work that documents and demonstrates my accomplishments and suitability for this position." Plan to follow up within five to seven business days after sending your application materials (resume, cover letter, IMP). When an employer requests that you e-mail your resume and cover letter, it is appropriate to follow up within three to five business days due to the immediacy of delivery. Should you need to follow up a second time, wait approximately 7 to 10 business days before making contact, unless otherwise instructed by the employer.

Complementary Closing You can close a letter in many ways. Some suggestions include sincerely, sincerely yours, regards, best regards, with regards, best wishes, thank you, cordially, cordially yours, respectfully, and respectfully yours. Leave three or four line spaces for your signature, then type your name as it appears in the personal contact information at the top of the cover letter. On the last line of the page, type "enclosure:" using a colon and list all documents or items you are sending. For example, "enclosure: Resume and Individual Marketing Piece (IMP)."

When formatting a cover letter for e-mail, make it look as much like a business letter as you can: include the date, followed by a line space, followed by the recipient's information, leave a space, and introduce your greeting. Use a colon after Dear [Name]: . Leave two line spaces between the body of your letter and your "signature" or name.

For cover letters that you send via e-mail, the enclosure is the attachment. Also mention what the attachment documents are (e.g., resume and e-portfolio) in the closing and plan of action section. Below the **complementary closing** you will leave one line space and then type your full name with contact phone number (including area code) on the next line.

Preparing for the Interview

There are two main types of interviews—informational and job interviews. **Informational interviews** are another means of exploring career opportunities within a company. This type of interview is typically conducted when the company does not have current employment opportunities in your area of interest. However, informational interviews allow you to meet the employer, discuss future needs they may have, discuss your skills and experience, and express interest in the company. This type of conversation is an

Interview Do's and Don'ts

Do
- Be prepared to discuss how your qualifications are evidenced in your portfolio work.
- Be honest and be yourself.
- Show confidence in your qualifications, knowledge, and skills.
- Clearly communicate your qualifications, knowledge, and skills through use of the portfolio.
- Use the portfolio in conversation to provide visual evidence to reinforce a point you are trying to make.

Don't
- Dominate the conversation by asking too many questions.
- Be arrogant.
- Apologize for work in the portfolio. If you feel the need to apologize for the work, it should not be included.
- Bring a portfolio to an interview and not use it.
- Be late.

example of proactive networking. If you impress the employer, they will keep you in mind when positions become available or they may know another executive who needs a person with your skills and level of experience to fill a position.

In some cases you might be interviewed over the phone as an initial screening for qualifications and suitability for the position. If the phone interviewer believes you possess the knowledge, skills, and experience for which they are looking, a personal interview is typically scheduled. Mention in a **phone interview** that a glimpse of your portfolio will give the employer insight into who you are and what you are capable of accomplishing. Be prepared to meet with one or more people during the personal interview process. Personal interviews may range from a brief 30-minute meeting to several days of scheduled interviews and information sessions about the company. In addition, you may receive a short assignment or test that asks you to demonstrate skills or knowledge.

Once you are selected to interview, you need to prepare by making a list of key skills you possess for the job (see Worksheets 2.1 through 2.3) and reviewing your portfolio to make sure it will best serve you in your interview. You may need to create new work to highlight knowledge and skills within a particular area or to reflect the focus and style of the company at which you are interviewing.

Reviewing Portfolio Contents and Organization

As discussed in Chapter 3, general portfolios provide a sampling of skills for a variety of positions. This type of portfolio is often used by individuals seeking internship or co-op experiences and by recent graduates seeking their first job after college. Focused portfolios are specific to an industry segment or job target. Gather work that reinforces and illustrates your ability to perform the tasks specified in the job description and emphasized in the cover letter and resume. It is important to review the materials in your portfolio to determine if you need to make changes in organization, content, or format. Refer back to Chapters 4 and 5 to assist you in organization, layout, and presentation of evidence of skills and industry knowledge.

Preparing for Interview Questions and Discussions

To prepare for an interview, begin by performing an Internet search (using www.google.com or www.ask.com) to find recent articles on the company at which you are interviewing. Also search for information on the CEO and other important people within the organization. Libraries and career centers can also be helpful for researching company information. This knowledge will allow you to speak intelligently when answering questions about the company and why you want to work there. Research the career path for the position you are seeking. This information is readily available on many company Web sites. Once research has been conducted, you will need to prepare for questions the interviewer may ask you. See Box 9.1 for common questions interviewers have asked students and professionals in the fashion industry.

In addition to preparing for potential interview questions and scenarios, it is imperative that you compile a list of job-related questions to ask the employer during the interview process. Ask "how" and "why" questions that require a substantive explanation, rather than yes or no answers. Avoid asking questions concerning salary and benefits until an offer is made. Listen carefully to what the interviewer is asking and make sure you answer questions competently. Stay focused on each question as you formulate and offer a response. Provide specific examples when possible to support the point that you are trying to convey.

Using the Portfolio During an Interview

The portfolio is an important tool used to communicate and provide evidence of abilities that supports the resume and cover letter; it proves you can actually do what you say you can. Learning how to comfortably incorporate the portfolio into interview discussions is key. Commentary can be used in three ways—to discuss the portfolio as an interviewer reviews it, to use the elements within the portfolio to emphasize a point you are making and show work that you have done, and to transmit your brand identity.

How to Effectively Utilize the Portfolio in Conversation

As you prepare for the interview and formulate responses to possible questions an employer may ask, consider ways to introduce portfolio work into the conversation. Do not rely on the interviewer to ask to view your portfolio. Take the initiative to show

Box 9.1 Questions Asked During Interviews

What kind of manager/supervisor are you looking to work for?

What are you passionate about?

Who is your favorite designer? Name three traits about this person's designs that draw you to him or her.

What are the first three elements that come to mind when creating a visual display?

Who is our target customer?

What book are you reading right now? Tell me about it.

What magazines do you use for inspiration?

Describe a project that you did that was successful.

Describe a project that was unsuccessful and why.

What is your biggest strength that you would bring to this position?

What is your biggest weakness that you would bring to this position? How will you overcome this?

Why do you want to work for this company?

Tell me what you know about our company.

What aspect of this position do you find least appealing?

How would your previous boss describe you?

Tell me how you manage your time and prioritize multiple tasks.

Is there anything else you would like me to know about you?

What do you have to offer our company?

Why should I hire you?

Tell me what you learned from your internship/co-op experience listed on your resume.

How do you organize inspirational clips?

What type of approach do you think should be used for assortment planning?

What are you looking for in your next job?

Are you a team player? Tell me about a difficult situation you have encountered in working on a team and how you handled it.

For what reasons are you leaving your current or previous position?

the work you have already created to demonstrate your knowledge through visual evidence of skills. When there is a particular example in the portfolio that helps illustrate the point you are trying to make, use this opportunity to show the portfolio to the employer. Provide examples of your work that address and substantiate the qualifications you are trying to convey. Presenting work will demonstrate your specific understanding and competency within key areas. As a result, the visual images that are integrated into the discussion can reinforce your qualifications and act as a reminder of your brand identity. The introduction of the portfolio into the conversation should feel natural. Practicing using your portfolio during **mock interviews** will help you develop seamless transitions between verbal and visual communication. The integration of the portfolio into conversation will become second nature. Smile. Take pride in your work. Have in mind those adjectives that best describe you: efficient, creative, cooperative, innovative.

Commentary During Portfolio Review

Although your portfolio should not rely on you giving explanations of its content, you should be ready to talk about your work. Be prepared to discuss projects and individual pieces from initial concept through completion. You should clearly explain your role in team-based projects. The interviewer may ask questions concerning some of the work or may not ask anything at all. Watch the interviewer and use your intuition to determine when further explanation is welcome (e.g., a long pause when viewing pages). Discussion of work can also be used to reinforce your answers to interview questions. Be enthusiastic and confident. Remember, this is your work and you know it best; relax and sell your skills.

At the close of the interview, express your gratitude and interest in the position and in the company. Make sure to obtain information regarding how the interviewer will proceed in the hiring process. A thank-you note should be sent as a follow-up after the interview. Be prepared to send the thank-you note within 48 hours of the interview. Highlight the most memorable moment of the interview, and refer to the future potential you can bring to the position if hired. Provide your contact information again as a convenience for the employer.

Checklist for Evaluating the Use of a Portfolio During an Interview

○ Yes ○ No   Did the interviewee use the portfolio during the interview?

○ Yes ○ No   Was the interviewee comfortable and confident when introducing the portfolio into the conversation?

○ Yes ○ No   Did the interviewee effectively communicate the skills he or she possesses for the position by using examples from the portfolio?

○ Yes ○ No   Did the interviewee do an effective job in selecting work that showcased the skills, knowledge, and qualifications he or she was trying to communicate?

○ Yes ○ No   Were the contents of the portfolio relevant to the position?

○ Yes ○ No   Did the layout and organization of the portfolio communicate the candidate's broad knowledge of the industry (for general portfolios) or his or her specific area of expertise (for focused portfolios)?

○ Yes ○ No   Did the presentation or integration of the portfolio seem awkward or confusing?

○ Yes ○ No   Was the interviewee able to clearly explain project work when asked?

○ Yes ○ No   Was the portfolio commentary relevant to the position?

○ Yes ○ No   Was the portfolio appropriate for the position and company?

○ Yes ○ No   Did the resume, cover letter, and portfolio communicate a consistent image and brand identity?

○ Yes ○ No   Would you hire this candidate based on his or her ability to effectively verbally and visually communicate qualifications for the position?

After each presentation, review your performance and list the ways it could be improved.

Activities

1. Prepare for three mock/practice interviews to be conducted. Find three position postings for jobs (with different companies) for which you would be qualified and interested in applying. Research the companies, positions and career paths, and current events impacting the industry. Prepare a cover letter, a resume, an IMP, and a portfolio for each mock/practice interview.

2. Schedule the mock/practice interviewers. Interviewers might consist of classmates, professors, career center staff, industry professionals, mentors, friends, or family. The interviewer will need to review the application materials prior to the interview and develop questions. Or you can furnish them with challenging questions to ask you.

3. Conduct the interviews. Use the portfolio to provide the interviewer with evidence of your skills, competencies, personality traits, and characteristics. Videotaping or digitally recording each interview is helpful to demonstrate how you perform in an interview situation. It will help you recognize and overcome negative mannerisms, hesitations, and postures. Have the interviewer discuss ways to improve your interview skills and complete the Checklist for Evaluating the Use of a Portfolio During an Interview.

Chapter 10

Maintaining and Updating the Portfolio

In a creative business environment, a resume and a portfolio are essential components of any job application. A resume changes with every position and accomplishment and needs to be updated in a timely manner. This is also true of the portfolio. Portfolio development is an ongoing process. The fashion industry is fast paced and necessitates constant change. New plans are laid out for each season, new products are introduced, and new promotional campaigns are developed and tracked. All of these changes offer new material that complement and enhance a portfolio. It is also necessary to generate new work for a portfolio because many times you cannot show work that you did for a specific company since that work is the company's property. Once the work is in the public domain, however, you may capture and integrate it into your portfolio. While it is often tempting to consider portfolio development complete after you get a job, it is really just the beginning of the process. The original portfolio is a wonderful template with which to start, but all portfolios need to remain current with new work. Times change and companies often reorganize or downsize and you can find yourself looking for a new job. Individuals change jobs and career paths, sometimes frequently, so it is necessary that you keep the tools to help find that new position.

Portfolio revision might include a new layout, focus, job target, and/or additional options, such as a digital portfolio or a mail-away IMP. It is essential to keep your portfolio fresh and updated. You should keep all potential portfolio work, both hard copy files and digital files, for easy access. The digital files are the easiest to change, manipulate, and update.

Portfolio Review

A quick review of your existing portfolio is necessary to assess areas that might need updating or revision. It may have been many years since you interviewed for a new position or a promotion so you must review the entire portfolio for potential update. Elements of portfolio update would include the current encasement, introduction and divider pages, job target and subsequent skill set, and format and layout of the evidence pages.

The Portfolio Encasement

The most important feature of a portfolio is the cohesive brand image it projects. Since the portfolio's encasement is the first impression a potential employer gets, you need to assess it if the portfolio's branding image changes. If a leather or vinyl presentation case was initially your encasement choice and the portfolio was general in focus, you may need to change it if the new portfolio is targeted. An upgraded case or a customized encasement may be advisable to denote the change. You are now a successful merchandiser; you will want to show this to potential companies. Now is the time in your career when it is extremely important to brand your identity and if you strive for precision and quality in your work, your portfolio will reflect this. The portfolio of a professional in the industry should appear significantly different from a student or entry-level candidate looking for a first job. Your brand identity has evolved and all aspects of the portfolio should reflect this. A customized portfolio encasement could be an untraditional size and offer a unique element that a potential employer would notice and remember. The encasement might also change if you adopted a more focused portfolio targeted toward specific industries. In this case, a professionally designed cover would convey the brand image of the portfolio. The exterior and the interior of the hard cover portfolio need to reflect any change in your brand image. This image needs to be reinforced in all aspects of the portfolio, from the encasement to the resume.

The Introduction and Divider Pages

The introduction and divider pages are key elements in establishing a unique identity for the updated portfolio. Changing these pages alone gives any portfolio a new fresh look. You should develop these pages for the new branded image, which might include a new color, branding element, graphics, and font. A new introduction page might feature recent work that reflects your identity. Fashion companies pride themselves in always being ahead of the current

trends and this must be reflected in a professional's portfolio as well. This would include color, graphics, text, and visual images. The brand image should also showcase the experience gained in the workplace.

The Job Target and Skill Set

An updated job target should be carefully developed for the updated portfolio. Maybe you have multiple job targets you are considering. For example, if your first industry position was as an assistant store manager, you might be considering applying for a corporate buying position or you might wish to remain in management and seek a store manager's position. If this is the case, you need to develop two different target portfolios, which might contain some of the same or similar projects or be totally different. Sometimes multiple options for job targets might occur if the positions are similar yet require different skill sets. A new job target might be a buying position for a fashion retail company. There are multiple retail store chains and online companies in the industry that are searching for buyers. The job target is the same for these positions, but the skill set is different. A job target might also be marketplace specific and directed toward women's, men's, accessories, or home goods. This also makes a difference in skill set and competencies. See Figures 10.1 and 10.2 to view how these two might differ on a job target and skill set page in two different portfolios. The skill set that is necessary for the new job target is the essential outline for the work that you must present. In both figures, the skill set requires proficiency in retail math, evidence of profit generation,

Figure 10.1 A job target and skill set for an updated portfolio with a defined skill set.

evidence of assortment planning skills, and target marketing skills. This list of skill sets is an excellent resource in updating portfolio format and layout. It is essential that you show evidence of these skills through new work in the portfolio.

Portfolio Format

First portfolios often follow a general format because people who are starting their professional careers usually have a diverse body of work. A person who is starting out may not be familiar with the range of industry positions or may feel inclined to cast a wide net and apply to many opportunities to secure that first position. An updated portfolio, alternatively,

Job Target:

Buyer

Job Skill Set to Be Presented in This Portfolio:

Proficiency in retail math and evidence of profit generation, evidence of merchandise assortment planning skills, target market analysis, and marketing strategies

Figure 10.2 Another job target and skill set utilizing the same skill set but a different job target.

follows a focused format. After you work in the industry for a while, you become much more familiar with industry positions and the skills necessary for them.

If you decide to change your portfolio's format, you must take care to determine its focus. The portfolio layout plan will change depending on how detailed the work needs to be to demonstrate that you have valuable technical and organizational experience. A general portfolio might showcase work that involves all aspects of merchandising and product development. A focused portfolio will choose one or more steps in the process. It's always important to include process work when you update your port-

folio. How do you creatively solve a problem? No matter the segment of the industry you are targeting, employers look for creative problem-solvers and adaptable team players who can perform with grace under pressure. You get the chance to discuss these attributes in the interview, and your portfolio speaks for your technical abilities.

For example, developing a seasonal buying plan would involve sales analysis, socioeconomic and styling trend information for the upcoming season, and financial profit analysis. Product development process work could include market research, apparel line designs, and merchandising proposals. Individual page layouts showcase skills and should show a marked improvement from previous work.

Layout of the Portfolio Evidence Pages

The layout of the new portfolio pages may be identical to the existing portfolio, drastically different, or anywhere in between. The layout is dictated by the flow of the evidence needed to exhibit skills and capabilities denoted by the job target. A job description posted online or in the paper can guide the inclusion of skills in your portfolio. If the job description lists visual communication skills, you need to lay out pages that speak visually, with minimal text. If the position requires an understanding and command of retail profit analyses, show that you understand the relationship of stock to sales, turnover, and product planning. You could include both existing and new work that provides this evidence, if the pages are numbers-driven. If the pages are data-driven, they need to

be current. Layout should show a complete understanding of what a position requires, and some of the work should show your aspirations within the company. If you aspire to be a store manager, include a self-directed, long-range sales forecast developed from sales and socio-economic trends you've analyzed. If you are applying for an assistant brand manager position, develop a project to show how you might conceptualize a brand strategy for an apparel company. Show that you understand the skills and capabilities of the position.

A career change means an immediate job change and the possibility for career advancement along a unique course. The layout of portfolio pages should reflect all you have to offer a potential employer.

Updating the Portfolio

There are three strategies for updating your existing portfolio. The first is to replace existing work with new portfolio pages while following the original portfolio layout plan. Obviously, you would actually eliminate previous work from the portfolio and replace it with new pieces that you recently developed. Of course, you should archive all original creations and not throw anything away. Your cumulative body of experience is what makes you a valuable employee. You never know when you might wish to refer to a piece you created during an earlier phase of your career. In fact, it can be quite rewarding to revisit old pieces and observe your own growth, much like keeping a journal provides valuable opportunities to reflect. These artifacts increase in value over time.

The second strategy is to develop an entirely new portfolio layout with both existing and new work. This is recommended when changing from a general format to a more focused portfolio. It also includes changing the format from traditional to custom and to digital formats.

The third strategy is to create a second portfolio (and not alter your original one) that features targeted work for a specific position. You could use all new work or a combination of existing and updated work. You may also consider just creating a digital portfolio that complements your existing portfolio. You might also simply add an IMP, if you hadn't yet prepared one already. The more narrow and focused the job search, the more important the IMP.

Importance of Current Work

The fashion industry is constantly changing, so current work is always going to be the most important. An interesting layout or format can look dated if the product included or the setting in which the product appears is not timely. In the field of visual merchandising, photographs or sketches of store displays show both the display and the featured merchandise. While the display might be excellent to show mastery of props and styling, the apparel might be from a few seasons past and alter the impact. You therefore need to feature new ideas and concepts to maintain a current image. In the design field, employers often ask interviewees to design a line for a future season and submit it when they interview with the company. If you rise to the challenge, it will

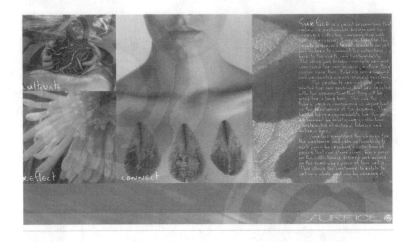

Figure 10.3 These portfolio page images show an entire project built from prints using CAD. The project shows the inspiration for the prints, garment sketches created to show how these prints might be used in fabrics and garments, and a marketing idea for the product line. This project shows skills, competencies, and knowledge of process.

make you a stronger candidate for an available position.

Integrating New Work into the Original Layout

You should upgrade your portfolio on a continual basis, preferably every year, although it is certainly beneficial to include a project as soon as it is ready. If your work is confidential and you cannot show it in your port-

folio, develop a project of your own based on similar criteria. A digital portfolio is very easy to update, since most work is developed on the computer or captured in a digital image. This would only require moving work you no longer want to show into an archive, and replacing this work with new images. Always take care to save the past work in case you need it in the future. If the

Source: Courtesy of Maria Pucpulo

plished at a co-op or an internship or perhaps for a senior thesis project, you can still incorporate it. An updated portfolio that reflects more current work and work from the industry is less likely to show process, since few professionals take a product from conceptual beginning through to consumer delivery. Careers become more specialized. If a student project that showcases the entire process remains strong, this might be important to leave in. If you feel proud of it and can discuss it articulately at an interview, by all means, be ready to stand behind all the work in your portfolio.

Another option for showcasing project work is to develop new pieces that represent additional parts of the process. For example, if a CAD designer only developed the fabric prints for a line of shirts in a company, but wanted to show an understanding of the broader apparel market, he or she might design a new "concept project" to showcase the prints and propose merchandising plans that launch the product line into successful sales. A color and trend conceptual board might be designed that includes the prints but also shows line direction. A group of garment flats might also be added to the presentation and the CAD designer could fill the flats with appropriate prints to showcase merchandising. See Figure 10.3 and 10.4 as examples. It is very important to show an understanding of the process if interviewing for a position with a different skill set from previously showcased ones. If interviewing for a director or manager position, it is imperative to show a total understanding of the process.

portfolio is set up in a PowerPoint presentation, adding new slides of work can be quite simple.

The ease with which you integrate new work into a traditional paper portfolio depends on the type of portfolio. Traditional portfolios where you simply slide work into existing pages are easy to update since they don't compromise or change the flow of the original layout. Custom portfolios may be a little more difficult to update depending upon how they were bound. If the pages were spiral bound, you can easily replace an old page with a new one by rotating the pages in the spirals. If the

portfolio was bound by glue or stitching, you will need to reassemble and bind the new one.

If the layout of the original portfolio was done well and this layout is still appropriate, then simply replace dated work with newer examples of the work. This is certainly the case when the first portfolio contained student work and the current work is professional and coming from the fashion merchandising industries. It is still advisable to begin with the strongest piece of work and end with the second strongest. The third could be in the middle, and if there is a strong student project or one accom-

Source: Courtesy of Maria Puopulo

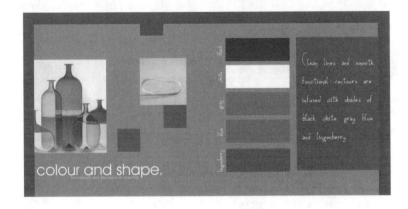

Figure 10.4 Process pages show color schemes, trend forecasts, and creative inspiration in addition to fabric development and styling.

pages that have been reworked to show buying competencies, a marketing focus, and trend analysis skills. Notice that some work transferred well and other pieces were replaced with work that demonstrates the skills necessary in the new job search. It is important to remember that if the job target has changed, the layout of the portfolio may need to change as well. Some changes may be minor, others extensive, but in both cases, previous work might still fit just fine in the new layout, enhanced by the integration of new work.

Adding an Additional Portfolio Format

Professionals who seek a new job within the same industry may find it advantageous to add an additional format to either their original portfolios or updated ones. This additional form might be a smaller, more focused custom portfolio, an e-portfolio, a Web page, or a Web site. These formats are appropriate for

Developing a New Layout and Integrating New Work

Revamping a general portfolio into a focused one always requires a layout change. If the portfolio is being focused because of a job target change, the skills needed for that job will dictate how you will lay out the portfolio. Figure 10.5 shows the layout of a senior-level capstone project shown in a general portfolio developed for an entry-level position search. Figure 10.6 shows the same work focused into two new layout

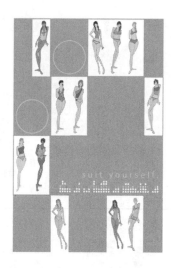

Figure 10.5 Elizabeth Post's senior thesis project investigates the swimwear market and styles developed for specific body types.

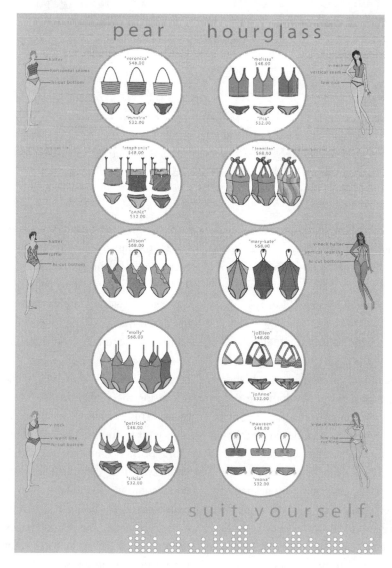

clearly targeting a company or niche market. The best of the portfolio work can be formatted for a digital portfolio or pulled together to make small, targeted portfolios that address narrow audiences. Figure 10.7 shows an example of a process book for developing a line for a brand. The brand is fictitious but the process is real and clearly shows skill, conceptual development, and a knowledge and grasp of the process. Additional projects involve a more focused portfolio and that works for multiple job searches. Portfolio work can be used multiple times, yet reconfigured to target a specific part of the industry.

Eliminating/Repurposing/ Replacing Work

It is always difficult to eliminate work, particularly work that you have proudly shown before. You must critically evaluate every portfolio piece and decide if it is time to eliminate or replace it. Sometimes it is necessary to ask someone who is objective to give you necessary feedback. Asking a mentor or another professional in the industry to evaluate and rate portfolio work will be infinitely helpful in editing current work. Often the template of the work can remain, though the details need to be updated.

The fashion industry has many overlapping positions within companies. As you search for a new

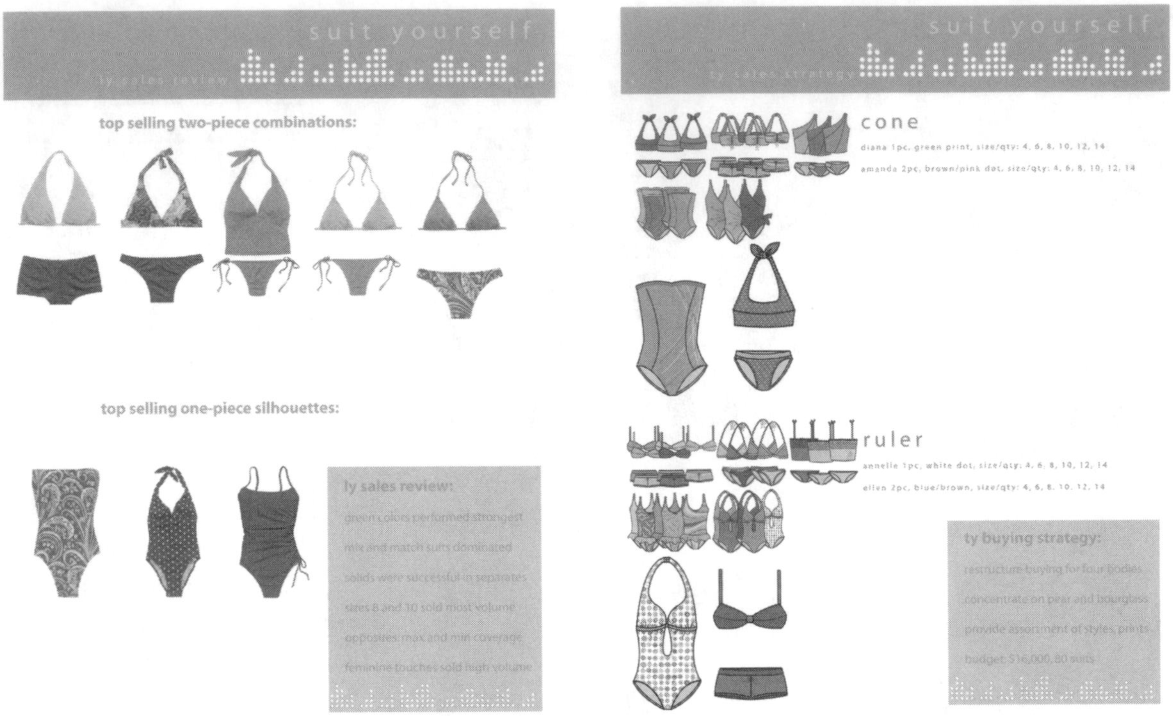

Figure 10.6 Elements from Elizabeth Post's collection, as adapted by Meredith Smith for a buying portfolio. These elements showcase her skills in choosing swimwear for her "buy" from Elizabeth's line. A buying strategy page for the line shows how you might reformat the same project to showcase different skills.

position, you might find that some of the skills and competencies that you express on pages in your current portfolio can be adapted slightly to a new position. You might just shift the purpose of the page slightly to emphasize another part of the document or image, for example, if you had work that showed your skill in the visual merchandising of a retail store. This might be a digital image or a sketched image of a window or in-store display. This image got you the job as a visual merchandiser but now you want to be regional visual merchandise manager and have to show some new work. A solution might be to show a group of images that manifest diversification of style,

diversification of product, or diversification of format. Every display image you have can be cropped, edited, or recolored to show how it might be integrated into a new display.

Changing the Brand Image of the Portfolio

The fashion industry is very brand cognizant. Brand development is extremely important when a company wants to be a destination brand or store for a target customer. It is just as important that each portfolio convey a sense of who that merchandiser is. This image changes over time and needs to be updated in the resume, portfolio, and IMP. Coach is a very well-respected brand in the

fashion accessory business. Of late, Coach has taken on a trendier look with some of their product lines. Their new signature logo bags and colorful lines show another side to the brand that has been known for consistency in quality and design. Coach has repositioned its brand to target new buyers of the line, while not losing the quality image of the brand. This is what has to happen with your portfolio. The brand image of the portfolio must evolve with your brand image, and the longer your tenure in the industry, the more experienced you become. The introductory, divider, and resume pages are perfect places to reinforce what the portfolio represents, yet subtle

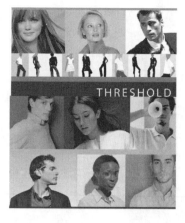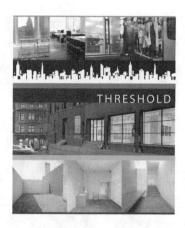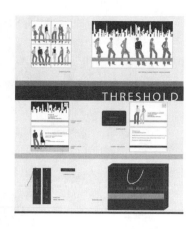

Figure 10.7 John Kelly developed this senior thesis project to show his total understanding of the brand essence of his self-directed line, Threshold.

brand changes allow the portfolio to focus a spotlight on newer work. A change in the grid layout for pages will also change the brand image. If the grid layout is simple and consistent throughout the portfolio, then it evokes a calming and classic feeling. If the grid changes up on some pages and develops a quicker rhythm, it takes on a fast and forward-moving image. The use of color can be extremely important, from the background of the pages to images, to text. Color can be utilized in blocks that lead the reader's eye through the page itself and through the portfolio. The original branding element in the portfolio may still be applicable in a new portfolio but may need strengthening. If you hadn't yet included a branding element, then it is crucial that you establish one based on your career goal now. A branding element is the opportunity for you to promote yourself as an ideal candidate for a specific position.

When you prepare a new portfolio for a specific job within a specific company, your personal branding element should complement the company's branding. The brand, however, needs to be uniquely original and not borrowed from any other person or company.

Integrating the Company Image and Philosophy into the Design and Layout

Understanding the branding equity of a company is essential in today's marketplace. A corporate image is how the company is perceived by the public. If executed successfully, this image and philosophy should permeate through a company and be evidenced in the work produced, the employees hired, and all company policies. The image and philosophy helps to tie the public to the company and reinforce brand loyalty. Before preparing a portfolio for a company, research the company's philosophy carefully. Read the company mission statement and search for tangible and intangible evidence of compliance with the mission statement. How does the public feel about the company, its products, and its services? Who are its customers? Is the marketing of the brand consistent throughout all aspects of the business? How might you develop a line for the company if you were hired for product development? Figure 10.7 shows a self-directed branded product development project executed to show image and brand essence. The designer has outfitted his client with a complete wardrobe for the niche upscale urban market. From conceptual image to line design to marketing, the essence of the brand remains consistent. This project can be presented to any retail company to show an understanding of line development.

Figure 10.8 shows a company analysis developed by a student for an interview with JCPenney. Notice how both projects incorporate a logo and interpret the company's brand image into all of their process work. The projects were successful and both students were hired by these respective companies.

Women's Career Wear

Autumn 2006

JCPenney

Macy's

Ann Taylor

Ann Taylor

Competitive Info.

Macy's

-Designing for most TM.

-Large career category with some designer brands.

-Top of the trend curve.

-Prices are much higher.

Ann Taylor Loft

-Comparable price points.

-Comparable customer & style.

-Image is slightly above due to parent store.

-Sale events are comparable.

Forecast

-Few steps away from Macy's styling, still large gap in price points. Rise price points?

-Watch Ann Taylor higher end stores for trends. Follow.

-Beat Loft w/ lower price points.

Target Market

JC Penny's Customer

-38 to 40 year-old female.

-Working mother of two.

-Balances work and home life.

Apparel Wants & Needs

-Career pieces that can transfer to after work wear that are trend right.

-Mix/match items.

-Comfortable yet fashionable.

-Pieces that can work into her already established wardrobe.

-Easy to care for/durable (yet comfortable) fabrics.

the suit is back

WORTHINGTON

Trend Research

Silhouettes have a strong female sensibility. Focus is on proportions, feminine shapes and discreet decoration. Continuing exploration of looser/voluminous shapes.

-Quiet, harmonious print combinations work in tonal colors.

-Exaggerated jackets and voluminous collared blouses, w/added belt.

-Layered dark colors.

-Everyday easy pieces, working together.

-Feminine texture gives surface and silhouette definition.

-Pattern or solid knits in deep rich colors.

Source: Courtesy of Melissa Ballmer

Figure 10.8 Melissa Ballmer developed this project for JCPenney prior to her interview with the company for a full-time position. She showcases research skills and familiarity with the competition, as well as the brand equity of JCPenney's brands, in a clean, precise presentation.

Using the Portfolio for Job Reviews and Promotions

The fashion industry employs many professionals on a freelance basis. These freelance professionals compete for jobs within one company or within many companies. Portfolio work is often necessary to prove you are the perfect candidate for a job. Often reviews are based on job performance, and it is significant if the professional can pull together proof in a portfolio of a job well done. Written text that supports profit and/or sales increases at a store help make the case for a raise or promotion.

Professionals must be able to work in teams. It takes many talents to develop, promote, and sell quality merchandise to the public. Evidence of team building is becoming an essential prerequisite for any promotion. The portfolio is a way of showing teamwork and team building in a visual manner. If you show a team project in your portfolio, be careful to indicate the portion of the project that is yours and the portion that was completed by others on the team. Discussion of various projects in a job review or promotion meeting is greatly enhanced when you show examples.

It is important to keep your portfolio current and generate new work on a regular basis because it benefits your continued professional development and may give you an opportunity to develop creative projects that you don't have an opportunity to create in your current position. Enjoy maintaining and updating your portfolio, and it will be your strongest tool for career advancement.

Portfolio Update Do's and Don'ts

Do

- Carefully review all work currently in your portfolio.
- Determine the portfolio type that is best for your career at this stage.
- Determine if multiple portfolio types (traditional, custom, digital) are preferable for your career at this point.
- Carefully consider how pages should be designed and laid out.
- Utilize design elements and principles to complement your work and showcase strengths.
- Determine alternative layout plans for your portfolio flow.
- Proofread all text for grammar errors, including spelling and punctuation.
- Pay attention to details.
- Update the page grid, if necessary, to develop new page design and layout.
- Update the brand identity of the portfolio to best reflect current career choices.

Don't

- Insert new work into an old format just for convenience.
- Add new work to a new portfolio type but not to your primary portfolio.
- Show professional work that is the property of a company without permission.
- Misrepresent yourself or your work.
- Present teamwork as your own individual work.
- Include work about which you are unsure. It is better to omit it or create a new replacement piece.
- Forgo grid design for page layout to save time. Images and text placed crooked or haphazardly on the page will negatively impact the professionalism of the overall portfolio and make you look sloppy.
- Display a brand identity visually similar to any company logo.
- Use music in a virtual presentation without obtaining written permission.

Activities

1. Determine the skills and competencies essential for your updated job target. Develop a skills inventory (utilizing Worksheet 2.1) for your new target.

2. Develop a new portfolio layout plan utilizing Worksheet 5.2. Lay out what you believe an ideal portfolio should contain for your new job target. If it is necessary to create new page layouts, refer to Worksheet 5.1 for suggested layout templates.

3. Create a new, updated image for the portfolio and your IMP. The image needs to convey the branded image of who you are today and the career path you envision for yourself. Incorporate this branded image throughout your portfolio.

Appendix

Worksheets

Skills Inventory Worksheets

Worksheet 2.1
Skills You Possess

Complete the worksheet to help you compile the skills you currently possess. Your list should be a comprehensive one that you narrow down further depending on specific job targets and objectives in Worksheet 2.2.

Begin by reading all of the skill categories listed below and write down the skills you possess in each section. If a skill falls in two or more categories, list it only once in the group that best represents how you would use the skill in the desired position. Indicate your level of proficiency with each skill.

Levels of Proficiency

Understand—You have an awareness of the skill(s) needed to complete a task and may have applied it one or more times.

Working Knowledge—You possess the skill(s) needed to perform a task but may need minor instruction to complete it.

Proficient—You possess the skill(s) needed to effortlessly complete a task with accuracy and proficiency.

Skill Categories

Write your skills on the lines provided, and indicate your level of proficiency.

Creative

	Level of Proficiency	
Understand	Working Knowledge	Proficient
○	○	○
○	○	○
○	○	○
○	○	○
○	○	○

Analytical

	Level of Proficiency	
Understand	Working Knowledge	Proficient
○	○	○
○	○	○
○	○	○
○	○	○
○	○	○

Technology

	Level of Proficiency		
	Understand	Working Knowledge	Proficient
_____	○	○	○
_____	○	○	○
_____	○	○	○
_____	○	○	○
_____	○	○	○

Research

	Level of Proficiency		
	Understand	Working Knowledge	Proficient
_____	○	○	○
_____	○	○	○
_____	○	○	○
_____	○	○	○
_____	○	○	○

Communication/Language

	Level of Proficiency		
	Understand	Working Knowledge	Proficient
_____	○	○	○
_____	○	○	○
_____	○	○	○
_____	○	○	○
_____	○	○	○

Other (Specify)

	Level of Proficiency		
	Understand	Working Knowledge	Proficient
_____	○	○	○
_____	○	○	○
_____	○	○	○
_____	○	○	○
_____	○	○	○

Worksheet 2.2
Skills Needed for a Specific Job Objective or Job Target

Research the job you would like to pursue, and document the skills required for the position below. If a skill falls in two or more categories, list it only once in the group that best classifies how you would use the skill on the job.

Job objective or job target

_____

_____

Skill Categories

Creative

_____

_____

_____

_____

Analytical

_____

_____

_____

_____

Technology

_____

_____

_____

_____

Research

_____

_____

_____

_____

Language

_____

_____

_____

_____

Other

_____

_____

_____

_____

Once you have compiled the list of skills for a specific position, compare the skills with those you currently possess, as documented on Worksheet 2.1. Place an asterisk (*) next to all of the skills that are listed on both Worksheet 2.1 and on Worksheet 2.2. This is an important step that will save you time as you complete Worksheet 2.3.

Worksheet 2.3
Matching Skills Possessed with Skills Needed for a Specific Position

This worksheet helps pair your skills with those an employer seeks for a specific job opening. Organize the skills that appear in both Worksheets 2.1 and 2.2 (those items with asterisks next to them) in order of importance as they relate to the job opening. As you list the skills, check the box next to each skill that best represents your level of proficiency.

Job target

_____

_____

Matched Skills List

	Level of Proficiency		
	Understand	Working Knowledge	Proficient
_____	○	○	○
_____	○	○	○
_____	○	○	○
_____	○	○	○
_____	○	○	○
_____	○	○	○
_____	○	○	○
_____	○	○	○
_____	○	○	○
_____	○	○	○
_____	○	○	○
_____	○	○	○
_____	○	○	○
_____	○	○	○

What skills do you lack for the position?

_____

_____

_____

_____

How will you obtain these skills?

_____

_____

_____

_____

_____

Once you have completed Worksheet 2.3, it will provide a clear picture of the skills you want to emphasize in the portfolio. If there are skills that you do not currently possess for a desired position, it is important that you work on acquiring those skills. You can do so by taking a class or completing a training program, or gaining experience through internships or co-op positions. If you are moving within a company, they may offer workshops or seminars that can provide you with the necessary skills.

Portfolio Concentration and Organization Worksheets

Worksheet 3.1
Determining the Type of Portfolio Concentration That Is Best for You

Use this worksheet to assist you in determining whether a general or focused portfolio best suits your current job search. Based on the material discussed in Chapter 3 and your evaluation of the various types of portfolios, answer each of the following questions by selecting either general or focused portfolio. Explain why your selections.

1. My job focus is in a specific segment of the industry.

   ○ **General Portfolio**   ○ **Focused Portfolio**

   Why? _____

   _____

   _____

   _____

2. My job objective involves a learning curve on the job.

   ○ **General Portfolio**   ○ **Focused Portfolio**

   Why? _____

   _____

   _____

   _____

3. I wish to work for a large company that offers a training program.

   ○ **General Portfolio**   ○ **Focused Portfolio**

   Why? _____

   _____

   _____

   _____

4. I wish to work for a small company that offers positions where I can multitask.

   ○ **General Portfolio**   ○ **Focused Portfolio**

   Why? _____

   _____

   _____

   _____

5. I have strong, targeted skills that I would like to showcase, but I am open to working in many facets of the industry.

    ○ **General Portfolio**   ○ **Focused Portfolio**

Why? _____

_____

_____

_____

6. I want to eventually progress into a management position.

    ○ **General Portfolio**   ○ **Focused Portfolio**

Why? _____

_____

_____

_____

7. I do not believe I have strong creative skills, yet I know my problem-solving skills are very creative.

    ○ **General Portfolio**   ○ **Focused Portfolio**

Why? _____

_____

_____

_____

8. I am concerned about making a professional impression with my portfolio's presentation.

    ○ **General Portfolio**   ○ **Focused Portfolio**

Why? _____

_____

_____

_____

9. I have prepared extensive research for many classes and projects or in current or past positions and would like to showcase this ability.

    ○ **General Portfolio**   ○ **Focused Portfolio**

Why? _____

_____

_____

_____

10. The majority of my work is analytical.

    ○ **General Portfolio**   ○ **Focused Portfolio**

Why? _____

_____

_____

11. I do not believe my GPA reflects what I have to offer a company.

    ○ **General Portfolio**   ○ **Focused Portfolio**

Why? _____

_____

_____

12. I have a significant body of visual work but it is in varied sizes, formats, and orientation.

    ○ **General Portfolio**   ○ **Focused Portfolio**

Why? _____

_____

_____

13. I need to do an extensive job search in a short period of time.

    ○ **General Portfolio**   ○ **Focused Portfolio**

Why? _____

_____

_____

14. I am open to relocating for my job and expect to pursue national and perhaps even international opportunities.

    ○ **General Portfolio**   ○ **Focused Portfolio**

Why? _____

_____

_____

15. I would like to show what I have learned while employed in either full-time or part-time jobs and/or internships or co-ops, but I cannot show any of the work due to the proprietary nature of the work.

    ○ **General Portfolio**   ○ **Focused Portfolio**

Why? _____

_____

_____

Worksheet 3.2
Organizing Portfolio Contents Based on Portfolio Concentration

Use this worksheet to assist you in gathering work samples and preliminary organization based on your portfolio's concentration (general or focused). The following list of sample qualifications were extracted from career Web sites of major department stores, specialty stores, and mass-market retailers. This is not an exclusive list, but rather an example for this activity. Prepare a list of work that you either have completed for the portfolio or plan on developing to include in the portfolio. Indicate work that you believe meets at least one of the qualifications for each industry segment. When you complete the list, determine if your contents plan indicates a general or focused portfolio.

Buying and Merchandising

- written and oral communication skills

- understanding of target market

- command of retail math concepts

- creative problem-solving/risk-taking skills

- understanding of merchandising trends

Portfolio Content Work

_____

_____

_____

_____

_____

Retail Sales Management

- leadership ability

- strong communication/interpersonal skills

- ability to prioritize, plan, delegate, and adapt

- command of retail math concepts

- organization and time-management skills

Portfolio Content Work

_____

_____

_____

_____

_____

Product Design/Development

- strong conceptual skills

- strong sense of style and color

- knowledge of silhouettes/fabrication/color/graphics

- creative problem-solving skills

- knowledge of clothing design/fit/construction

Portfolio Content Work

_____

_____

_____

_____

_____

Fashion Marketing

- detail-oriented, organized, and flexible

- strong marketing research skills

- knowledge in target market analysis

- strong visual/oral/written communication

- creative thinking skills and craft

Portfolio Content Work

_____

_____

_____

_____

Portfolio Type/Concentration Suggestions

1. Does the work you possess fit into only one or two of the industry segments listed above?

   ○ **Yes – Focused**   ○ **No – General**

2. Does the work you possess fit into three to four of the industry segments listed above?

   ○ **Yes – Focused**   ○ **No – General**

Note: When you possess work that fits into three closely related industry segments, you can use a focused concentration.

Portfolio Development Worksheets

Worksheet 4.1
Selecting Portfolio Work to Match Job Target/Objective Skill Set

Use the following worksheet to evaluate existing portfolio work in relation to your skill set for a determined job target or objective. Assemble the checklists completed for all potential portfolio pieces to assist you in completing this worksheet. Assign each portfolio piece a name as a description (target market, market buy, specs, hat project, and so on). If you have multiple job targets/objectives, complete multiple worksheets.

Job target/objective

_____

_____

_____

Skill Set	_Portfolio Piece Applicable_
_____	_____
_____	_____
_____	_____
_____	_____
_____	_____
_____	_____
_____	_____
_____	_____
_____	_____

Worksheet 4.2
The Portfolio Plan

Use the following worksheet to develop a layout plan for your portfolio and detail the work that you will include in it. List each skill set and assign the corresponding portfolio piece name(s) and number(s). You may document multiple portfolio pieces under one skill set. The number indicates the order of each piece and assists in the physical assembly of your portfolio. You can revise the order at any point in the process. Remember to select a strong first and last piece and build process skills with multiple portfolio pieces.

Piece #	Skill Set to Document	Portfolio Piece Name
1		
2		
3		
4		
5		
6		
7		
8		
9		
10		
11		
12		
13		
14		
15		

Portfolio Layout Worksheets

Worksheet 5.1
Page Layout and Development

Format 1

Text	Image	Heading
		Brand

Format 2

Brand	Heading
Image	Text

Format 3

Heading
Image

| Brand | Text |

Format 4

Text	Image	Brand
Text	Image	

Format 5

Image	Brand
Text	Heading

Format 6

Heading	Brand	Image
	Text	
Image		Image

Format 7

Image		Heading
Image	Text	Image
Image		Brand

Format 8

Brand	
	Heading	Image
Image	Text	

Format 1

Format 2

Format 3

Format 4

Format 5

Format 6

Format 7

Format 8

Worksheet 5.2
Organization of Content and Portfolio Layout

1. Cover

2. Introduction pages

3. _____

4. _____

5. _____

6. _____

7. _____

8. _____

9. _____

10. _____

11. _____

12. _____

13. _____

14. _____

15. Resume

Layout #_____

Brand Development Worksheet

Worksheet 7.1
Developing Your Brand

Make a list of words that describe you and record them below under the section entitled "Your Perception." Once you complete this list, ask friends and family members to describe you and record their responses under "Their Perception." Once each list is complete, review the words used by others to describe you. Is your perception the same as their perception? Evaluate how they differ. Remember, your brand is perceived in the minds of others. Use this information to determine the most important aspects you want to reinforce through your brand identity and to guide the development of your brand logo.

Your Perception

Their Perception

_____ _____
_____ _____
_____ _____
_____ _____
_____ _____
_____ _____
_____ _____
_____ _____
_____ _____
_____ _____
_____ _____
_____ _____

Resume Development Worksheets

Worksheet 8.1
Documenting General Resume Information and Experience

This worksheet helps you to document your education, work experience, skills, honors/awards, professional affiliations, and activities.

Personal Information

Name_____

Address _____

City_____, State_____Zip_____

Temporary address (if applicable)_____

City_____, State_____Zip_____

Phone (_____) _____ _____

E-mail address_____ _____

Personal portfolio Web page link (if applicable) _____

Education

Name of college/university_____

City_____, State_____Zip_____

Starting month and year_____

Graduation month and year_____

Degree sought/degree(s) earned_____

Major_____

Minor/concentration_____

Cumulative grade point average _____ GPA within major_____

Honors (President's or Dean's list recognition—list number of semesters/quarters, graduation honors such as cum laude, magna cum laude, summa cum laude, and so on)

_____

_____

Study abroad experience(s)—Who sponsored the trip, length of the trip, destination; list courses taken

_____

_____

_____

Name of college/university_____

City_____, State_____Zip_____

Starting month and year_____

Graduation month and year_____

Degree sought/degree(s) earned_____

Major_____

Minor/concentration_____

Cumulative grade point average _____ GPA within major_____

Honors (President's or Dean's list recognition—list number of semesters/quarters, graduation honors such as cum laude, magna cum laude, summa cum laude, and so on)

_____

_____

Study abroad experience(s)—Who sponsored the trip, length of the trip, destination; list courses taken

_____

_____

_____

_____

Name of college/university_____

City_____, State_____Zip_____

Starting month and year_____

Graduation month and year_____

Degree sought/degree(s) earned_____

Major_____

Minor/concentration_____

Cumulative grade point average _____ GPA within major_____

Honors (President's or Dean's list recognition—list number of semesters/quarters, graduation honors such as cum laude, magna cum laude, summa cum laude, and so on)

_____

_____

Study abroad experience(s)—Who sponsored the trip, length of the trip, destination; list courses taken

_____

_____

_____

Certifications/Training/Workshops

Name of certifying/sponsoring organization_____

City_____, State_____Zip_____

Date certification was granted

Month_____Day_____Year_____

Dates of recertification

Month_____Day_____Year_____

Month_____Day_____Year_____

Dates of continued education

Month_____Day(s)_____Year_____

Month_____Day(s)_____Year_____

Month_____Day(s)_____Year_____

Name of certifying/sponsoring organization_____

City_____, State_____Zip_____

Date certification was granted

Month_____Day_____Year_____

Dates of recertification_____

Month_____Day_____Year_____

Month_____Day_____Year_____

Dates of continued education

Month_____Day(s)_____Year_____

Month_____Day(s)_____Year_____

Month_____Day(s)_____Year_____

Computer Training

List software programs in which you are proficient and your application/use.

_____

_____

_____

_____

_____

_____

_____

Work Experience

Internship and co-op experiences should be listed in this section (make distinction next to job title).

Name of company_____

City_____, State_____Zip_____

Dates of employment

Beginning

Month_____Day_____Year_____

Ending

Month_____Day_____Year_____

Job title_____

Description of duties, capabilities, and accomplishments/results

_____

_____

_____

_____

_____

Awards/recognition

_____

_____

_____

Name of company_____

City_____, State_____Zip_____

Dates of employment

Beginning

Month_____Day_____Year_____

Ending

Month_____Day_____Year_____

Job title_____

Description of duties, capabilities, and accomplishments/results

_____

_____

_____

_____

_____

Awards/recognition

_____

_____

_____

Name of company_____

City_____, State_____Zip_____

Dates of employment

Beginning

Month_____Day_____Year_____

Ending

Month_____Day_____Year_____

Job title_____

Description of duties, capabilities, and accomplishments/results

_____

_____

_____

_____

_____

_____

Awards/recognition

_____

_____

Name of company_____

City_____, State_____Zip_____

Dates of employment

Beginning

Month_____Day_____Year_____

Ending

Month_____Day_____Year_____

Job title_____

Description of duties, capabilities, and accomplishments/results

_____

_____

_____

Awards/recognition

_____

_____

Name of company_____

City_____, State_____Zip_____

Dates of employment

Beginning

Month_____Day_____Year_____

Ending

Month_____Day_____Year_____

Job title_____

Description of duties, capabilities, and accomplishments/results

_____

_____

_____

_____

_____

Awards/recognition

_____

_____

Name of company_____

City_____, State_____Zip_____

Dates of employment

Beginning

Month_____Day_____Year_____

Ending

Month_____Day_____Year_____

Job title_____

Description of duties, capabilities, and accomplishments/results

_____

_____

_____

_____

Awards/recognition

_____

_____

Name of company_____

City_____, State_____Zip_____

Dates of employment

Beginning
Month_____Day_____Year_____

Ending
Month_____Day_____Year_____

Job title_____

Description of duties, capabilities, and accomplishments/results

_____

_____

_____

_____

_____

Awards/recognition

_____

_____

Name of company_____

City_____, State_____Zip_____

Dates of employment

Beginning
Month_____Day_____Year_____

Ending
Month_____Day_____Year_____

Job title_____

Description of duties, capabilities, and accomplishments/results

_____

_____

_____

_____

Awards/recognition

_____

_____

Name of company_____

City_____, State_____Zip_____

Dates of employment

Beginning

Month_____Day_____Year_____

Ending

Month_____Day_____Year_____

Job title_____

Description of duties, capabilities, and accomplishments/results

_____

_____

_____

_____

_____

Awards/recognition

_____

_____

Honors/Awards

Name of award/honor_____

Reason for award/honor_____

Date award/honor was received

Month_____Day_____Year_____

Significance of the award/honor_____

Name of award/honor_____

Reason for award/honor_____

Date award/honor was received

Month_____Day_____Year_____

Significance of the award/honor_____

Name of award/honor_____

Reason for award/honor_____

Date award/honor was received

Month_____Day_____Year_____

Significance of the award/honor_____

Professional Affiliations/Memberships

Name of organization_____

City_____, State_____Zip_____

Dates of involvement
Month, year began to present or ending date of membership

Beginning month_____ Day_____ Year_____

Ending month_____ Day_____ Year_____

Offices held (elected or appointed)_____

Committee membership_____

Description of committee duties_____

_____

_____

Name of organization_____

City_____, State_____Zip_____

Dates of involvement
Month, year began to present or ending date of membership

Beginning month_____ Day_____ Year_____

Ending month_____ Day_____ Year_____

Offices held (elected or appointed)_____

Committee membership_____

Description of committee duties_____

_____

_____

Collegiate Affiliations/Memberships/Organizations

Name of organization_____

City_____, State_____Zip_____

Dates of involvement
Month, year began to present or ending date of membership

Beginning month_____ Day_____ Year_____

Ending month_____ Day_____ Year_____

Offices held (elected or appointed)_____

Committee membership_____

Description of committee duties_____

_____

_____

Name of organization_____

City_____, State_____Zip_____

Dates of involvement
Month, year began to present or ending date of membership

Beginning month_____ Day_____ Year_____

Ending month_____ Day_____ Year_____

Offices held (elected or appointed)_____

Committee membership_____

Description of committee duties_____

_____

_____

Name of organization_____

City_____, State_____Zip_____

Dates of involvement
Month, year began to present or ending date of membership

Beginning month_____ Day_____ Year_____

Ending month_____ Day_____ Year_____

Offices held (elected or appointed)_____

Committee membership_____

Description of committee duties_____

_____

_____

Name of organization_____

City_____, State_____Zip_____

Dates of involvement
Month, year began to present or ending date of membership

Beginning month_____ Day_____ Year_____

Ending month_____ Day_____ Year_____

Offices held (elected or appointed)_____

Committee membership_____

Description of committee duties_____

_____

_____

Community Service/Volunteer Activities

Name of organization_____

City_____, State_____Zip_____

Dates of involvement
Month, year began to present or ending date of membership

Beginning month_____ Day_____ Year_____

Ending month_____ Day_____ Year_____

Position title_____

Description of service and contributions made_____

_____

_____

_____

Name of organization_____

City_____, State_____Zip_____

Dates of involvement
Month, year began to present or ending date of membership

Beginning month_____ Day_____ Year_____

Ending month_____ Day_____ Year_____

Position title_____

Description of service and contributions made_____

_____

_____

_____

Name of organization_____

City_____, State_____Zip_____

Dates of involvement
Month, year began to present or ending date of membership

Beginning month_____ Day_____ Year_____

Ending month_____ Day_____ Year_____

Position title_____

Description of service and contributions made_____

_____

_____

_____

Worksheet 8.2
Job Targets and Drafting Job Objective Statements

Use the following worksheet to list job targets and position descriptions within specific companies for which you would like to work.

Job Target
State the job target exactly as it appears in the position posting. Example: Account executive, specialty stores

_____

Company Contact Information

Company name_____

Contact name and title_____

Address_____   _____

City_____, State_____   _____Zip_____

Phone (_____) _____ Fax (_____) _____

E-mail_____ Web address_____

Job Description
State the job description exactly as it appears in the position posting.

_____

_____

_____

_____

List the functions, responsibilities, and opportunities this position offers below
Job functions/activities
Example: Service current accounts and drive new business.

_____

_____

_____

Job responsibilities/duties
Example: Building and maintaining relationships with key clients to grow sales in highly competitive fast-paced environment.

_____

_____

Job opportunities

Example: Travel and grow sales to expand new private label business.

_____

_____

_____

List the activities you would prefer the job to have below

Activities

Example: Develop new business by cold calling, corresponding with potential clients, presentations, travel, and conscientious follow-up on all customer leads.

_____

_____

_____

Job Objective Statement

Use the information from the above lists (job functions, responsibilities, opportunities, and activities), and job description to draft a job objective statement. Job objective statements should be written in a clear, concise manner using the present tense. Be sure to use an enthusiastic but professional tone. Objective statements can range from 15 to 50 words.

Example: Develop and maintain specialty store accounts for a high-end private brand with the opportunity to travel and build new business in a dynamic fast-paced environment.

_____

_____

_____

_____

Worksheet 8.3
Drafting Qualifications Statements

Use the following worksheet to develop qualifications statements for use on a targeted resume.

Job Target
State the job target exactly as it appears in the position posting.

_____

Job Description
State the job description exactly as it appears in the position posting.

_____

_____

_____

_____

_____

_____

_____

_____

_____

_____

List experience and/or training you possess that qualify you for the above-listed position.
Use quantifiable statements to highlight what you have accomplished by stating specific numbers, percentages, time frames, and results.

_____

_____

_____

_____

_____

_____

_____

_____

_____

_____

_____

Briefly summarize the above-listed experience into 3 to 8 bulleted statements.
Remember to use nouns and adjectives to describe experience (See Box 8.2).

- _____
- _____
- _____
- _____
- _____
- _____
- _____
- _____

Worksheet 8.4
Drafting Capabilities and Accomplishments Statements

Use the following worksheet to develop capabilities and accomplishments statements for use on targeted or capabilities resumes.

Job Target

State the job target exactly as it appears in the position posting.

_____

Job Description

State the job description exactly as it appears in the position posting.

_____
_____
_____
_____
_____
_____
_____
_____
_____
_____
_____

List capabilities, competencies, and abilities you possess that qualify you for the above-listed position.

_____
_____
_____
_____
_____
_____
_____
_____
_____
_____
_____
_____

Briefly summarize the above-listed capabilities into 4 to 8 bulleted statements.

Remember to use action verbs to describe experience (See Box 8.2).

- _____
- _____
- _____
- _____
- _____
- _____
- _____
- _____

List specific accomplishments you have achieved that support/validate the capabilities listed above.

Use quantifiable statements to highlight what you have achieved by stating specific numbers, percentages, time frames, and results.

_____

_____

_____

_____

_____

_____

_____

_____

_____

_____

_____

_____

Briefly summarize the above-listed accomplishments into 3 to 5 bulleted statements.

Remember to use action verbs to describe experience (See Box 8.2).

- _____
- _____
- _____
- _____
- _____

Glossary

accomplishments Activities and endeavors undertaken by an individual that demonstrate skill level and capabilities as well as communicating results achieved that validate/substantiate the capabilities

alternating rhythm Controls the pace of visual awareness/eye movement through the use of many visual elements to alternate and vary the pattern

analogous colors Colors positioned next to one another on the color wheel (red, red-orange, orange)

artifact A tangible finished product

asymmetrical balance Informal balance; uneven placement of items on the page

balance The arrangement of one or more elements in a design or on a page that visually provides a sense of stability and equilibrium; the distribution of visual interest on a page

brainstorming The sharing of research, discussion of the findings, and free exchange of ideas and implications without regard to eventual solution

brand The perception others have of you; an identifiable image that reflects your personality, work ethic, level of professionalism, creativity, individuality, quality of work you produce, and how you carry yourself

brand benefits The skills and capabilities you bring to a potential job position

brand essence The benefits a brand has to offer, such as the brand's position in the marketplace, and a visual image that represents and communicates who you are

brand identity An image created through the use of color, logo, graphic elements, text, and layout to connect an individual to his or her work and make a memorable impression on an employer

brand position The segment of the industry where you wish to work

branding elements Visual cues that help establish the overall brand identity of the portfolio and supporting materials

capabilities Skills an individual possesses in relation to the level of proficiency and ability to perform particular tasks

capabilities section A summation of selective work experience, qualifications, competencies, and accomplishments specific to one company; used by those seeking to acquire another internal position

CFDA Council of Fashion Designers of America

chronological resume Resume in which information is organized in sequential order of employment beginning with the most recent position; used by individuals who do not have large gaps in their employment history and want to emphasize a pattern of work history that relates directly to a desired job target/position

clip art Images that are part of the public domain and can be used to enhance a presentation

cognitive skills Ability to assimilate information

color Hue that is created from light rays reflecting off the surface of an object

companion format A digital portfolio presentation that is used to accompany a printed portfolio

competencies Abilities possessed by an individual that allow him or her to perform job-related functions and tasks

complementary closing Indicates the end of the letter such as sincerely, sincerely yours, regards, best regards, with regards, thank you, cordially, cordially yours, respectfully, and respectfully yours

content A collection of visual material that represents an individual's qualifications and presents his or her capabilities, knowledge, and skills

cool colors Green, blue, and violet hues

cover letter A letter that communicates your interest in a position and convinces an employer why you are the best candidate for a position by emphasizing your skills and experience

creative resume A nontraditional resume, developed to gain an employer's attention through the appearance and presentation of information; these resumes may utilize a chronological, functional/skills, or targeted format

custom portfolio An individualized presentation of contents created and bound into a book format or arranged in a custom-designed case and manufactured for the individual

deliverables Tangible results of work

design principles Balance and symmetry, proportion and scale, and context and placement

digital portfolio A virtual presentation of work on CD, as an e-portfolio, as a personal Web site, or as a posting on a career site

divider pages Pages that organize and define sections of work/skills within the portfolio

dpi/dpu Dots per inch/unit

elements of design The component parts that combine to make up the whole, known as design; point, line, shape, color, and texture

employability The capacity of an individual to add value to a company through his or her ability to achieve and facilitate results in a given job

encasement The aesthetically pleasing outer case or container used to hold portfolio work for professional presentation

e-portfolio A portfolio sent via e-mail containing a PDF file of content images that can be set up to open as individual images or viewed as a continuous group

fashion design portfolio Primarily visually driven, this portfolio contains original designs of apparel or other product lines and/or fabric designs that can be communicated through fashion illustrations, technical drawings, sketches, and CAD-generated pieces

focused portfolio Showcases a targeted body of work that is narrow in scope

format The style, size, and shape of an artifact

functional/skills resume Highlights abilities of an individual that directly relate to the desired position; related skills are the focal point and are divided into groups and listed in order of importance to the job target; used by individuals who lack or have limited practical work experience related to the jobs they seek

general portfolio Showcases a wide spectrum of skills in an organized and logical format

Gestalt When two or more lines form a connection or grouping

GIF A digital compressed file format for drawings and Internet images that allows images to cross formats and be viewed; Graphics Interchange Format

grid A page layout system that utilizes a series of horizontal and vertical lines to align design elements; used for aligning and layout of all elements on the page, including images, text, and white or negative space

ideations Multiple solutions for opportunity development resulting from brainstorming

individual marketing piece (IMP) An individualized, condensed introduction to you as a brand; a smaller, powerful, promotional extension of the portfolio that can be used as a mail-away or leave-behind piece; a compact brand identity presentation

innovative media Customization of technology or resources used in the development of portfolios

interview A formal or informal conversation or meeting conducted by an employer to evaluate an individual's qualifications

informational interview A formal or informal conversation or meeting requested by an individual as a means of exploring a company and potential career opportunities; typically conducted when the company does not have current employment opportunities available

introduction page The first page of a portfolio; establishes your name and brand and makes a connection to the type of work showcased in the portfolio

job objective A statement listing the functions and responsibilities of the job you ultimately want and the opportunities and activities you would like the job to have

job search Conducting research to provide information about current job opportunities, company information such as contact(s) for correspondence, corporate culture, history, products and services, whether the company is private or publicly held, number of employees, work environment, how to apply, and so on

job target A job/position title

JPEG Digital format for compressing color image files for ease of transport; Joint Photographic Experts Group

landscape orientation Horizontal page orientation

line Created by connecting a series of points; creates a visual path where the eye moves from one point on a page to another

manual skills Ability to physically perform tasks

merchandising The process of planning, developing, selecting, marketing, and presenting cohesive consumer targeted goods for profit in a competitive market with regard to timing, assortment, styling trends, and price point

merchandising portfolio Primarily text-driven with a balance of visual images and elements that create excitement and interest in the presentation. Contents can include text-driven computer-generated pieces, such as market analyses, product specification and costing sheets, merchandising and allocation plans, and promotion materials. Visually driven contents can include original designs of apparel or other product lines, and/or fabric designs, space planning and store layouts that can be communicated through illustrations, technical drawings, and CAD-generated pieces, and photographs of visual merchandising displays.

mock interview An exercise in practicing interview skills to prepare for interviews with industry professionals for the purposes of obtaining a job, an internship/co-op opportunity, or information

monochromatic One color in different values, tints, and shades (turquoise, blue, navy)

negative space *See white space*

networking Building a group of personal and professional contacts

neutrals White, beige, brown, gray, black

page design The organization of visual and written material and white or negative space

page layout The manner in which objects and text are arranged on the page; a grid is used for placement

PDF A portable document file that is viewed universally on Adobe Reader

PDM Product data management software created by Gerber

phone interview An initial screening process used by employers to evaluate candidates' qualifications and fitness for the position

plan of action Follow-up strategy indicates when and how you will contact the prospective employer after he or she receives and reviews your cover letter, resume, and related materials

PLM Product line management software created by Lectra

point A simple mark on a blank page that begins a design

portable format *See companion format*

portfolio A compilation of work that visually documents skills and what you can offer a company presented in a logical, professional manner

portfolio piece An individual and personally developed example of professional work that communicates evidence of skill level, results, and accomplishments in a high-quality presentation format that is current and timely

portfolio plan A map of how the portfolio will be laid out, organized, and assembled

portrait orientation Vertical page orientation

positive space The text and/or graphics in a page layout composition

proficient Possession of skill(s) needed to effortlessly complete a task with accuracy and expertise

product development The process of bringing a consumer-desired product from concept to the marketplace; process includes consumer, market and product research, design, merchandising, production, and marketing

process work The developmental work that begins when an opportunity is determined in the marketplace and ends when a final line has been developed

progressive rhythm Controls the pace of visual awareness/eye movement through building or decreasing the size, shape, color, or intensity of graphic or text elements

proportion The balanced relationship of visual parts to the whole; relationships among size, shape, space, quantity, and color

objective *See job objective*

qualifications Knowledge and expertise of an individual based on experience

qualifications section Brief one- to two-line statements on a resume conveying capabilities and accomplishments that specifically address the credentials sought by an employer

raster Computer-generated images made up of a series of pixels (tiny squares); software programs include Adobe Photoshop and Lectra's U4ia.

rationale Discussion of how an individual's expertise and experience will benefit a company by matching qualifications and accomplishments to those the employer seeks; justification as to why one individual is more qualified and a better fit for a company to hire.

regular rhythm Controls the pace of visual awareness/eye movement through repetition and creates a predictable pattern

resolution The quality of an image in relation to the number of dots per inch or per unit (DPI/DPU)

results Evidence of successful application of skills demonstrating competence; can indicate growth potential of an individual

resume A written document that summarizes education, work experience, capabilities, accomplishments, and results, as well as featuring additional information regarding volunteerism, language proficiency, or any additional information to support an applicant's fitness for a particular position

resume format The organization of information that best markets an individual's experience and qualifications for a position; formats include chronological, functional/skills, targeted, creative, and capabilities

rhythm Controls and sets the pace of visual awareness and alerts the viewer when key elements demand additional examination; planned eye movement across the page; types of rhythm include regular, alternating, and progressive

rule of thirds One third of the page is written matter or text, one third of the page is visual or graphic content, and one third of the page is dedicated to white or negative space

salutation The greeting used in a cover letter

sans serif typeface Letter strokes that do not contain cross strokes or accents; fonts include Arial, Century Gothic, and Gill Sans

scale The size of an object

self-directed work Created under the direction of the individual to showcase skills that are not demonstrated already in the portfolio; allows an individual to target the work they are developing for a specific firm or specialization

self-generated work *See self-directed work*

serif typeface Letter strokes that end in cross strokes or accents; fonts include Times New Roman, Courier, or Garamond

shape An element defined by its outline; the result of closed lines

skill Knowledge learned through hands-on experience, which provides an individual with competency or expertise in a given area

skills page Communicates abilities and proficiencies possessed by an individual that are emphasized and evidenced in the portfolio

skill set The knowledge and abilities an individual possesses to perform the necessary tasks to be successful at a job/position

skills resume *See functional/skills resume*

space Used to separate images and text on a page while providing the eye with a place to rest

statement of interest A concise summation of the desired position detailing why a person is qualified, specific abilities, and experience

style Your unique brand identity

symmetrical balance Formal balance; mirror image of objects placed on the page

targeted resume Purely focused on work experience, competencies, and results related to a specific job position/target; created exclusively to address the qualifications and individual requirements of a particular company. Used by individuals who have established a strong record of employment and possess expertise and proficiency in a particular area of the industry.

texture The surface quality of an object that provides dimension and authenticity

TIFF Digital file format for compressing solid color graphics; Tagged Image File Format

triadic harmony Three colors spread equally apart around the color wheel (red, blue, yellow)

understand When an individual is aware of the skill(s) needed to complete a task and has used this know-how one or more times

unity When all visual elements contribute to an aesthetically pleasing whole

virtual presentation The communication of portfolio material through a digital venue such as a Web site or Web page

vector Computer-generated images made up of points that create line segments; software programs include Adobe Illustrator and Lectra's Kaledo Style

visual cues Elements that represent and connect your brand to your work and help establish a memorable impression; elements include color, logo, graphics, text, and layout

visual rhythm *See rhythm*

warm colors Yellow, orange, and red hues

Web-based portfolio A digital portfolio contained in a designated Web site

Web portfolio *See Web-based portfolio*

white space The space on a page that does not contain text, graphics, or images, also known as negative space

working knowledge When an individual possesses the skill(s) needed to perform a task but may need/require minor instruction to complete the job

References

Bureau of Labor Statistics, U.S. Department of Labor (2006–2007). Textile, apparel, and furnishings occupations. *Occupational Outlook Handbook* (2006–2007 ed). Retrieved March 25, 2006 from http://bls.gov/oco/ocos233.htm

Career Momentum, Inc. (2006). Networking. Retrieved May 8, 2006 from www.madison.com/jobs/viewstory.php?storyID=1007&type=jobs

CSix Connect (2003). Welcome. Retrieved May 8, 2006 from http://csix.org/

Cibulka, Barbara. Interview with Phyllis Borcherding. December 27, 2005.

D'Alessandro, D. & Owens, M. (2005). *Career Warfare: 10 rules for building a successful personal brand and fighting to keep it.* New York: McGraw-Hill.

Dickerson, K. (2003). *Inside the Fashion Business* (7th ed.). Prentice Hall: New Jersey.

Garment Industry Development Corporation (2001). *The Fashion Industry and New York City.* Retrieved February 20, 2006, from www.gidc.org/industry.html

Gilbert Career Resumes (2006). The Integrated Job Search. Retrieved May 8, 2006 from http:www.fashionresumes.com/resources.html

International Labour Organization (ILO) (2000, October 18). *Global employment levels in textile, clothing and footwear industries holding stable as industries relocate.* Retrieved February 25, 2006, from www.ilo.org/public/english/bureau/inf/pr/2000/38.htm

International Labour Organization (ILO) (2005, October 27). *Global textile and clothing industry urges new role for ILO on post-MFA jobs impact.* Retrieved March 25, 2006, from www.ilo.org/public/english/bureau/inf/pr/2005/42.htm

McAtee, Ann. Interview with Phyllis Borcherding, May 22, 2006.

Neumeier, M. (2003). *The Brand Gap: How to bridge the distance between business strategy and design.* California: New Riders Publishing.

Radwick, D. (2006, February 21). *NPD reports U.S. apparel industry posts growth second year in a row.* Retrieved March 25, 2006, from www.npd.com/dynamic/releases/press_060221.html

Sterling, M. (2006). Do you make your first impression your best impression? Retrieved March 12, 2006 from http://entrepreneurs.about.com/cs/marketing/a/uc051603a_p.htm

Warren, C. (2004, August 1). You're branded (like it or not). *American Way Magazine*, 55–57.

Index